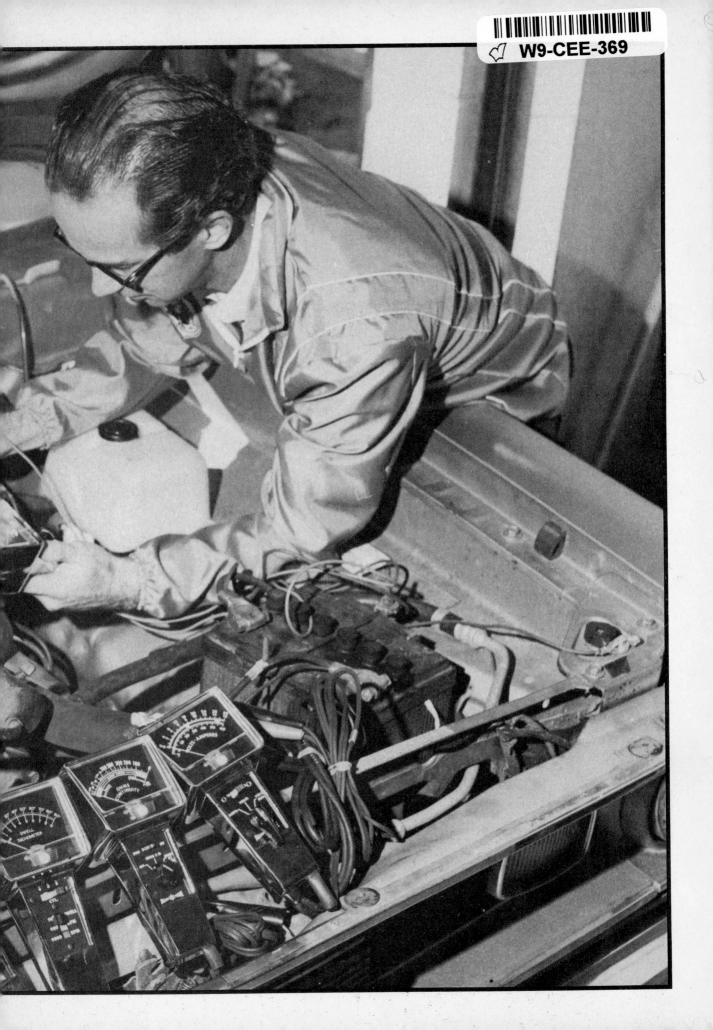

INTRODUCTION

Petersen's BASIC AUTOMOTIVE TROUBLESHOOTING is a new approach to troubleshooting manuals. It is intended to provide the reader with basic procedures for locating a wide variety of problems, from an engine that will not start to electrical problems in lighting circuits. Of course, books on automotive troubleshooting are not new. The first ones had to be written to provide information about their newfangled mechanical gadgets for the first automobile owners.

What is different in this Petersen book is the way the information is presented. Most books of this type are written for mechanics. They assume a certain level of technical knowledge and access to a complete line of special tools. This book, one of a series, is for the beginner, for the man or woman who simply wants to be able to locate troubles with the tools at hand. It is useful for students in auto shop classes as well, a handy guide for quickly isolating trouble before breaking out the manufacturer's shop repair manual for precise instructions on how to repair a certain problem.

A simple, clear text, combined with easy-to-understand illustrations which eliminate unnecessary details, is the key to this approach. Thoroughly explained, step-by-step troubleshooting methods are presented in a manner that allows a person with a limited background in automotive mechanics to do many jobs that would previously have required a trip to the local garage.

Anybody who owns an automobile will find this book a valuable reference guide to keep in the glove compartment or tool kit in their car. With only the few simple tools described here and by following the instructions, a frustrating breakdown along the highway may be reduced to only a minor delay. This book can save you both time and money, and that's no small reward for the person who needs his car for business or pleasure.

It would be an impossible job to write a book covering *all* makes and models of engines, cars and trucks. This book was designed to *briefly* cover all auto systems in sufficient depth to solve most automotive problems.

We do not go into actual maintenance or repairs, but tell you what to look for and what should be done about it. We often refer you to a shop manual, which can be purchased at a new car dealership upon request, or to other Petersen automotive books (see list on page 5).

BASIC AUTOMOTIVE TROUBLESHOOTING

ISBN 0-8227-5012-0

Library of Congress Catalog Card No. 74-76521

PETERSEN AUTOMOTIVE BOOKS

LEE KELLEY/Editorial Director
BRUCE CALDWELL/Editor
JACKIE ANDERSEN/Managing Editor
SPENCE MURRAY/Automotive Editor
SUSIE VOLKMANN/Art Director
LINNEA HUNT-STEWART/Copy Editor
LINDA SARGENT/Copy Editor
ANNE SLATER/Copy Editor
FERN CASON/Editorial Coordinator

PETERSEN PUBLISHING COMPANY

R.E. PETERSEN/Chairman of the Board; **F.R. WAINGROW**/President; **ROBERT E. BROWN**/Sr. Vice President, Publisher; **DICK DAY**/Sr. Vice President; **JIM P. WALSH**/Sr. Vice President, National Advertising Director; **ROBERT MacLEOD**/Vice President, Publisher; **THOMAS J. SIATOS**/Vice President, Group Publisher; **PHILIP E. TRIMBACH**/Vice President, Financial Administration; **WILLIAM PORTER**/Vice President, Circulation Director; **JAMES J. KRENEK**/Vice President, Manufacturing; **LEO D. LaREW**/Treasurer; **DICK WATSON**/Controller; **LOU ABBOTT**/Director, Production; **JOHN CARRINGTON**/Director, Book Sales and Marketing; **MARIA COX**/Director, Data Processing; **BOB D'OLIVO**/Director, Photography; **NIGEL HEATON**/Director, Circulation Marketing and Administration; **AL ISAACS**/Director, Corporate Art; **CAROL JOHNSON**/Director, Advertising Administration; **DON McGLATHERY**/Director, Advertising Research; **JACK THOMPSON**/Assistant Director, Circulation; **VERN BALL**/Director, Fulfillment Services

CONTENTS

CONTENTS

HOW AN ENGINE WORKS

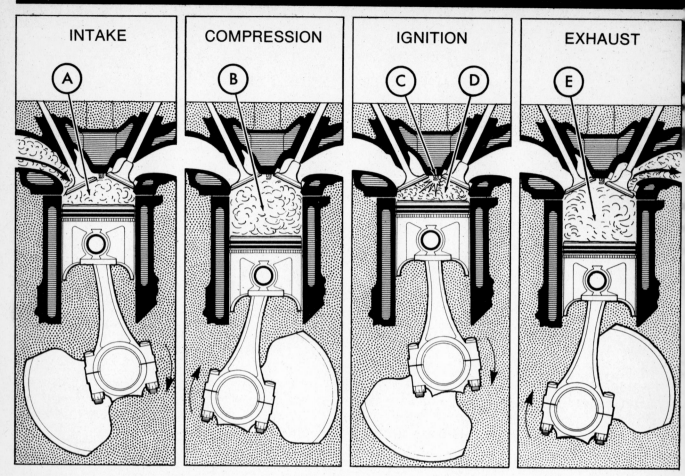

| INTAKE | COMPRESSION | IGNITION | EXHAUST |
| A | B | C   D | E |

The four-stroke engine requires two complete revolutions of the crankshaft to complete one full cycle of operation. During these two revolutions the piston will make two upward movements and two downward movements. This is where the four-stroke engine gets its name—a total of four piston movements are necessary to complete one full cycle of operation.

The drawing above represents a simplified four-stroke engine and can be used to trace the four stages of a complete cycle of operation. The illustration shows only a single cylinder for clarity. Let's follow our simple four-stroke engine through one complete cycle of operation and learn how it works.

The four-stroke cycle of operation begins with the piston near TDC (Top Dead Center—its highest point of travel in the cylinder) and moving downward. The intake valve is open, allowing a fresh air/fuel mixture to enter the combustion chamber. As the piston moves downward, it creates suction, which pulls the air/fuel mix inside the cylinder (A). When the piston reaches the bottom of its travel, the intake valve closes, trapping the air/fuel mixture inside the cylinder. This is the first of the four separate operations (strokes) in the four-stroke engine, and it is known as the *intake stroke.*

On the second stroke, the piston moves upward again, compressing the mixture in the cylinder (B). When the piston reaches the top of the cylinder (this movement is known as the *compression stroke),* the spark plug (C) fires, igniting the air/fuel mixture. The mixture burns rapidly, creating a powerful pressure which forces the piston down in the cylinder. This downward movement is the third stroke and is known as the *power stroke.* This is the only time the engine is actually producing power (D). During the time interval of this power stroke, the pressure of the expanding gases inside the cylinder dissipates itself.

The final stroke of the piston in the cylinder is the *exhaust stroke* (E). As the piston reaches the bottom of its travel in the cylinder, known as BDC (Bottom Dead Center), the exhaust valve opens. When the piston begins moving upward on the exhaust stroke, the burned gases are forced out of the cylinder through the open exhaust valve and into the exhaust pipe. When the piston reaches the point of TDC (Top Dead Center) once more, the exhaust valve closes and the intake valve opens. With one full cycle of operation completed, the engine is ready to start over with the entry of more of the air/fuel mixture.

HOW TO TROUBLESHOOT

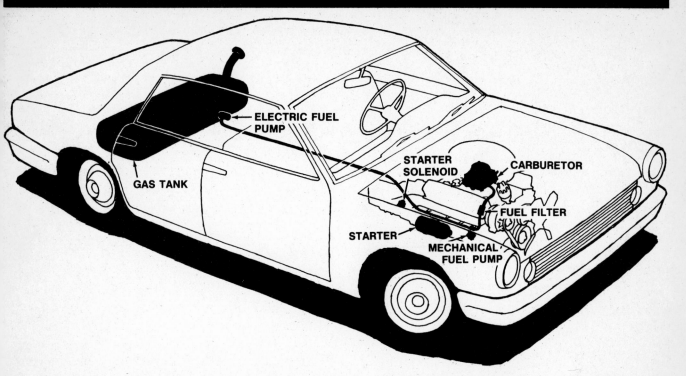

Automotive troubleshooting, which is finding a problem and reducing it to a single easily replaced or repaired part, isn't a mysterious art, though it may seem that way to someone watching an experienced mechanic work on his car. What looks like magic is really just using some common sense (and a reference book like this one).

To troubleshoot is to use a process of elimination. By a series of simple GO/NO GO checks, any automotive mechanical problem can be solved. The best way to become an expert troubleshooter is not to run out and buy hundreds of dollars worth of tools and take night classes on automotive engineering. Just learn how to use a few simple hand tools and how to work methodically, dividing the parts of a problem until you have reduced it to a single, isolated area. If there is one rule to follow when trying to find out what is wrong with a car, it's *don't jump to conclusions.* Many different problems may have nearly identical symptoms.

The most basic rule, one that you will see repeated frequently in this book, is *don't overlook the obvious.* More mechanical problems are discovered and remedied by a careful visual examination of the problem area than you might suspect. For example, in troubleshooting electrical system problems (an area in which even experienced mechanics seem to have trouble), the actual cause of a failure can often be found simply by looking closely at suspected problem areas. Such things as loose connections, broken wiring, corrosion, etc., are easy to see if the troubleshooter will just take a few seconds to check things out.

Once you have established a system for checking things, stick to it. This book is designed to help the beginning troubleshooter approach each separate problem with an easy-to-follow method of determining just where the problem lies. Following our system of fault detection is not only a good way of being able to find and fix problems right from the start, but it is also a good way to learn about the various parts of the automobile.

Rather than jumping in feet first when you're looking for the source of a problem in a car, relax. Take a few minutes to go over in your mind what the possible solutions are, and read completely through the section of the book on how to troubleshoot what you think is your problem. Make sure that you have the necessary tools on hand. It's asking for trouble to have to stop and go looking for something several times while you are checking out a system.

If the suspected bad part is easily replaced, substitution is often a good way to check out an idea. For instance, if you suspect you have a bad spark plug wire, exchanging it for one of the others on the engine that it will reach should cause the problem to move if the wire is indeed bad. Substitution is not always possible with expensive parts that would have to be purchased before a swap could be made, but keep it in the back of your mind. Even with low-cost parts, refer to the detailed troubleshooting portions of the book for a final examination to assure yourself that the bad part has actually been located before changing it.

If the car you are working on is difficult to start or will not start at all, the problem can be reduced to one of three main systems. These are the starting system, the ignition system and the fuel system. In this chapter, these have been organized into three separate categories with guidelines to make it easier to find and fix any problem. To determine which of the three sections you need to use to troubleshoot a problem, follow the preliminary steps listed below in order to be sure of satisfying all conditions for starting the car's engine.

PRELIMINARY CHECKLIST

Before trying to troubleshoot the different parts of any of the three systems which make the engine start and run, you should first eliminate obvious problems which may be preventing the engine from working.

IS THERE GAS IN THE GAS TANK?

This can be checked by removing the filler cap and either rocking the car and listening for the sound of fuel sloshing in the tank or using a light to see down into the tank (if the filler pipe is not curved). Another method which can be used on cars which have a straight filler pipe is to put a ruler or stick down into the tank and then check it to see if it is wet with gas. NOTE: Many gas tanks will not empty completely even when the car is "out of gas." Unless gas is several inches deep inside the tank, the fuel pickup may not be supplying gas to the engine.

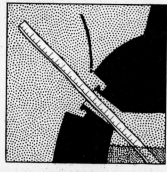

WARNING: DO NOT USE ANY FLAMING OBJECT, SUCH AS A MATCH OR CIGARETTE LIGHTER, TO LOOK INSIDE A FUEL TANK!

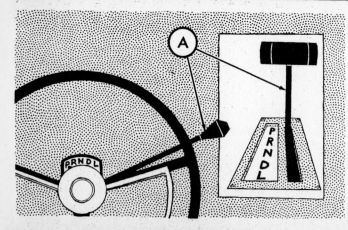

IS THE AUTOMATIC TRANSMISSION IN "P" or "N"?

Cars equipped with automatic transmissions will not start unless the transmission shift selector lever (A) has been placed in the PARK (P) or NEUTRAL (N) position. There is a switch called the neutral safety switch that is part of the starting circuit. This switch prevents the starter from working unless the shift lever is in one of these two positions. This is a safety feature, designed to keep the car from jumping forward (if left in gear) when the starter is used.

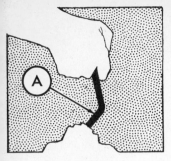
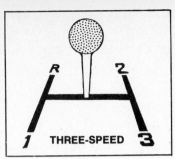
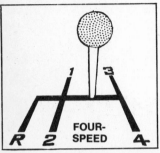
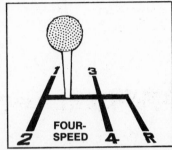

IS THE STANDARD SHIFT TRANSMISSION IN NEUTRAL?

Cars and trucks equipped with a standard (manual) shift transmission should have the shift lever (A) placed in the neutral position before attempting to start the engine. Placing the transmission in neutral will prevent forward motion of the car when the starter is operated.

On standard transmission cars manufactured after 1970, the clutch pedal must be depressed before the starter will function. There is a switch much like the neutral safety switch on automatic transmission-equipped cars to prevent the starter from working unless the engine is separated from the driveline by depressing the clutch pedal.

CAUTION: ALWAYS ENGAGE THE EMERGENCY BRAKE BEFORE STARTING THE ENGINE. THIS PREVENTS THE CAR FROM ROLLING WHEN THE TRANSMISSION IS IN NEUTRAL.

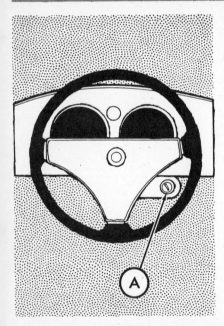
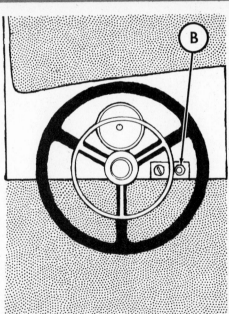

IS THE IGNITION ON?

While most modern automobiles are equipped with a key-lock type of ignition switch (A), some older cars and many light trucks have a separate starter switch (B, C). This is usually located on the floorboard near the gas pedal or on the dashboard. With a modern key-lock ignition switch, the starter is engaged by turning the key to the START position. When the engine has started, the spring-loaded switch returns to the ON position.

With older cars that have the separate starter switch, the ignition key is turned to the ON position and the starter switch is depressed until the engine has started. Then the switch is released.

After all four of the preliminary questions have been answered to your satisfaction, you can go on to the basic starting checklist. Using the four quick checks below, the possible location of any engine problem related to starting can be reduced to a single system. This system can then be examined and fixed, using the detailed checks in later chapters of the book to find and correct the actual problem.

BASIC STARTING CHECKLIST

STARTING SYSTEM CHECK

● Test engine cranking system by turning ignition key to the START position. (On cars equipped with separate starter switches, turn key to ON and depress the starter.)

● Listen for the sound of the starter engaging and cranking the engine over.

● If nothing happens or the only sound you hear is a rapid clicking, yet the engine will not turn over, your next step is to troubleshoot the starting system.

● If the starter is cranking the engine over in a normal manner but the engine will not start, continue to the ignition check below.

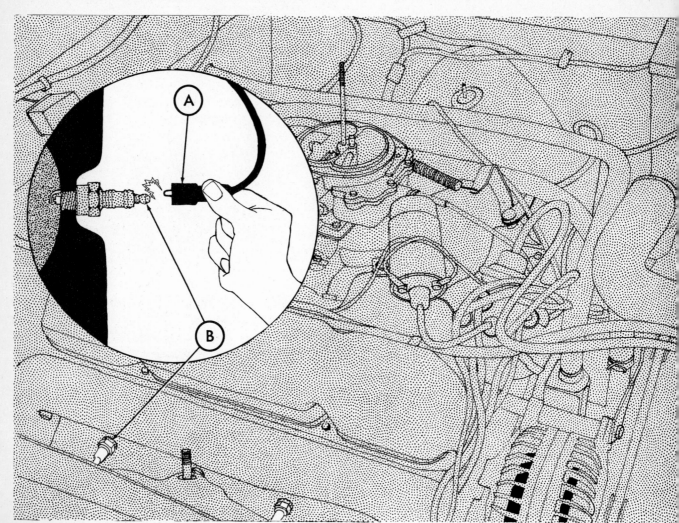

IGNITION SYSTEM CHECK

● To test the ignition system for operation, open the hood of the car and remove one of the spark plug wires (A) from a spark plug (B). Hold the spark plug lead approximately ¼-inch from the tip of the spark plug and crank the engine over. This usually requires two people, one to hold the spark plug lead, another to operate the starter. (Use a paper clip for this check.)

WARNING: BE SURE TO HOLD THE SPARK PLUG BY THE INSULATED COVERING. HOLDING THE SPARK PLUG LEAD BY THE METAL TIP CAN GIVE YOU AN ELECTRIC SHOCK.

● If there is no spark or only a very weak spark when the engine is cranked over, you can only proceed by troubleshooting the engine's ignition system.

● If there is a strong spark when the starter is operated but the engine will not fire, proceed to the fuel system check on the next page.

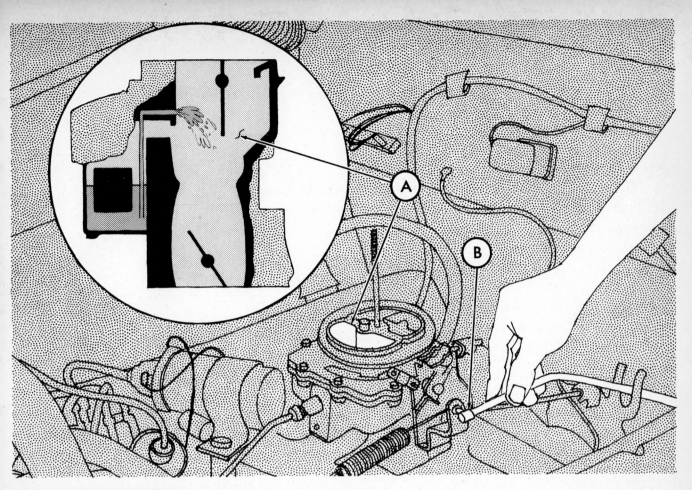

FUEL SYSTEM CHECK

● Remove the air cleaner or air cleaner cover to gain access to the top of the carburetor.

● Grasp the throttle linkage (B) and open and close the throttle several times while watching for a small stream of fuel in the bore (A) (opening) of the carburetor. Opening the throttle means pulling or pushing the linkage so that it operates in the same way it would if the gas pedal were being pushed.

● If you cannot see any fuel squirting into the bore of the carburetor, your next step is to troubleshoot the car's fuel system.

● If fuel can be seen squirting into the carburetor but the engine will not start, go to the engine compression check below.

ENGINE COMPRESSION CHECK

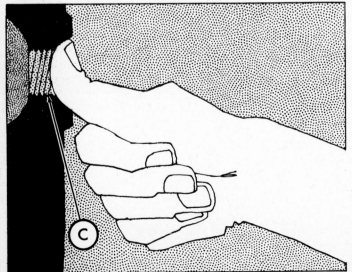

● Compression is the pressure built up inside the cylinder when the piston moves up on the compression stroke. To check this quickly, remove one of the spark plugs, place your finger over the spark plug hole (C) and crank the engine over with the starter. Note: This also usually requires two people, one to operate the starter, the other to check compression.

● If the compression is good, the rising pressure in the cylinder will force your finger off the hole. If you have gotten this far without finding any problems in other systems, check all cylinders for lack of compression.

● If there is a lack of compression in any or all cylinders, it indicates a serious internal problem. Proceed to the ENGINE COMPRESSION CHECKS on page 131.

TROUBLESHOOTING THE STARTING SYSTEM

In this chapter we will go into more detailed checks of the starting system of the automobile. Some of the checks described in this chapter will require simple test equipment, but the use of such equipment will be held to a minimum for the benefit of the home troubleshooter who may not have such specialized tools at his disposal. Checks requiring very specialized testing tools will be mentioned, but only to inform the reader of what can be done to confirm or deny specific problems. This information will enable the reader to take suspected bad parts to a shop for a check-out and to understand what tests and repairs may be required at the shop.

THE BATTERY

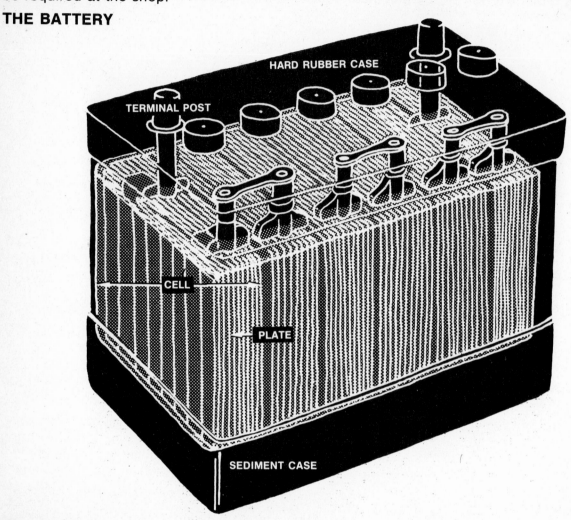

The battery used in automobiles is known as a storage battery. This is not entirely correct. The battery produces its electrical energy by electrochemical action without an external source of electrical energy. The battery does not "store" electrical energy; rather it is simply ready to produce electricity from this chemical source instantly.

Automobile batteries are of the lead-acid type. In them, electricity is produced by a chemical reaction between two types of material suspended in an acid solution.

The battery is an acid-proof container filled with this acid. The two materials which produce the electrochemical reaction are in plates hung in the acid solution. When these two dissimilar materials are acted upon by the acid, a chemical reaction takes place. One set of plates acts as a positive terminal for electricity; the other acts as a negative terminal. A flow of electricity takes place inside the battery.

As this current is used in the electrical system of the automobile, the plates are slowly altered by the repeated chemical reaction. This chemical reaction continues to manufacture more electricity, but unless something is done to replenish the battery, it will finally discharge all the available electrical potential. This is called discharging the battery.

Once the available supply of electricity falls below a certain point, the battery can no longer supply the force necessary to operate the different parts of the electrical system.

(Information on how the battery is recharged while in use will be found in the chapter on charging systems.) The process of recharging does not add electrical energy to the battery (remember, the battery does not "store" electricity); recharging only reverses the effect of the chemical process by reversing the current flow and building up the plates so that the battery can again provide a full flow of electrical current.

In actual practice, the automobile battery is made up of a number of smaller batteries called cells. These cells are encased in the acid-proof outer container and are connected in series to provide the correct electrical potential. Each has its own supply of acid, and each cell is actually a complete battery by itself.

While the battery is the most important part of the ignition and charging systems as well as supplying electricity for all the electrical accessories, it is also the most important part of the starting system.

TROUBLESHOOTING THE BATTERY

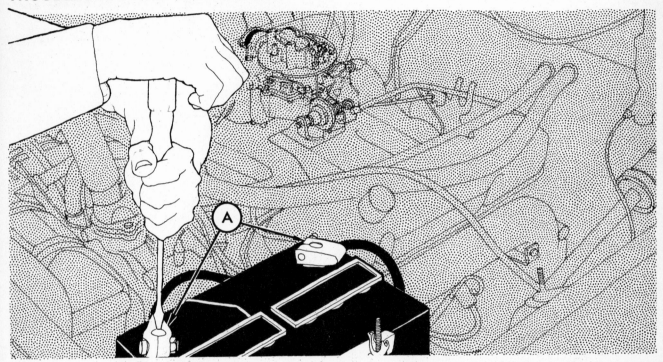

If the battery is to operate correctly, it must be in good internal condition (not discharged or damaged). Also, the connections (A) which feed current from the battery to the other parts of the electrical system and back again must be in good condition. The electrolyte (battery fluid) should be up to the full marks on the inside of the filler holes.

WARNING: THE WHITE MATERIAL ON A CORRODED BATTERY POST OR CONNECTOR IS ACID. DO NOT GET IT ON YOUR SKIN OR IN YOUR EYES. IT CAN ALSO DAMAGE CLOTHING. IF YOU ACCIDENTALLY GET ACID ON YOUR SKIN OR IN YOUR EYES, WASH IMMEDIATELY WITH CLEAR WATER. SEE A DOCTOR IF BURNING SENSATION PERSISTS.

One quick method of checking electrical connections on the battery for a good connection is to force something between the metal of the post and the metal of the connector. (Some batteries don't have the posts on the top; they are located on the side and use a screw type of connector.) The metal used for battery connections is mostly lead and is quite soft. A screwdriver jammed into the area between the battery post and the connection often creates a good connection if corrosion or dirt is the cause of the problem.

If, after this is done, the battery seems to provide more starting force (that is, if the starter cranks better or the headlights are brighter), the problem is most likely in the connections. Loosen the connections with a wrench and examine them carefully for signs of corrosion. This is usually a whitish buildup of material around the battery post and connector. It can also be just a fine film that is not easy to see, but if corrosion is present, the surface of the post and the inside of the connector will be dull instead of shiny.

NEUTRALIZING ACID

CAUTION: DO NOT LET ANY OF THE BAKING SODA GET INTO THE BATTERY. IT CAN NEUTRALIZE THE ACID IN THE BATTERY AND RUIN IT.

The acid buildup on battery posts and connectors can be neutralized with a solution of baking soda and water. Sprinkle dry baking soda on the top of the battery and connections, making sure that the filler caps for the acid are on securely. Add a small amount of water to the baking soda. If it starts to bubble and you can hear a fizzing sound, there is battery acid present on the surface of the battery. The baking soda will help to neutralize it, and it can be removed with a stiff-bristle brush. Several applications of baking soda and water may be necessary to completely remove all corrosion buildup from the surface of the battery.

REMOVING TERMINALS

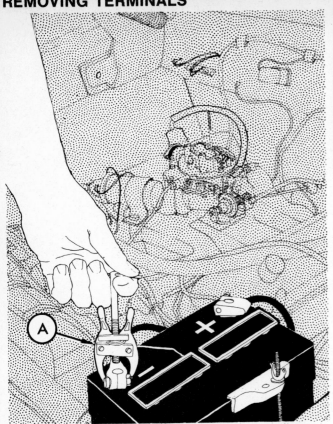

Post-type terminals should never be forced off the post. Use a twisting action to loosen the connector. If it is too tight to remove in this manner, use a battery cable puller (A). Too much force applied to the post can damage the post or loosen it in the battery case material.

When replacing the connector on the post after cleaning, it helps to use a socket to drive the terminal firmly onto the post before tightening the nut with a wrench. Be sure the socket is larger in diameter than the post and apply force only to the connector. Striking the top of the post may drive it down into the soft battery case and damage it.

CLEANING TERMINALS

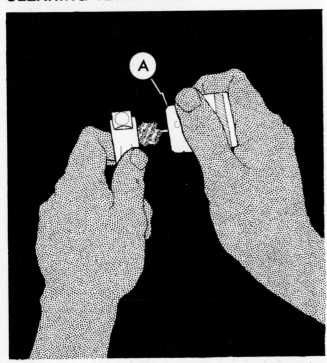

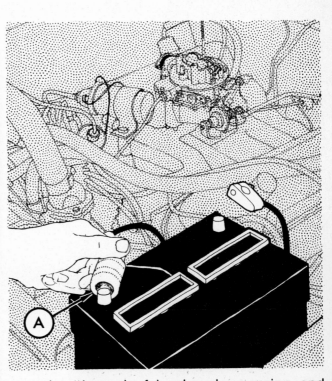

The battery posts or terminals themselves can be cleaned of hardened corrosion and restored to their normal condition by the use of a wire brush and post cleaner (A). If a post cleaner and wire brush are not available, sandpaper, steel wool or even a knife blade can be used to clean the post and inside the connector. All residue or corrosion should be cleaned from the inside of the connector where it contacts the post. The post itself should be cleaned in the same mernner. Properly cleaned, the post and connector will have good electrical conducting properties. A light film of grease or paint over the connection after it is tightened in place will help prevent the buildup of new corrosion.

VISUAL BATTERY CHECK

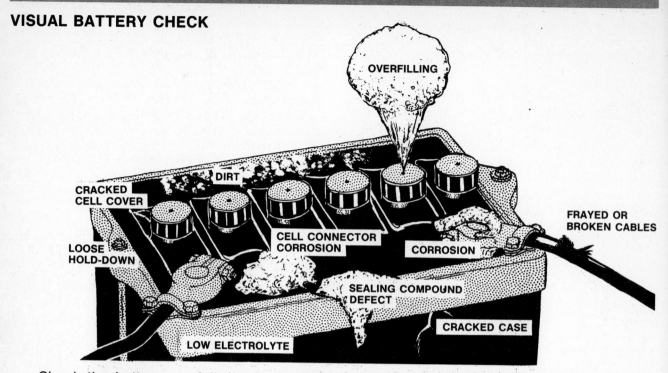

Check the battery carefully for visual signs of battery problems. If the battery still shows no signs of life after the cables and posts have been examined and cleaned (if necessary), remove the battery and have it tested by a mechanic with the proper test equipment

The mechanic will test the battery in two ways. First he will make a test to determine the battery's state of charge (how much electricity it has left) by using a battery tester. The tester measures the voltage of the battery. He will then test the battery acid with a hydrometer. This tester measures the acid content of the fluid in the battery and gives the mechanic much valuable information about the battery's condition. If you wish to purchase these troubleshooting tools, you can get information on using them from Petersen's BASIC AUTO REPAIR MANUAL and BASIC IGNITION AND ELECTRICAL SYSTEMS.

USING THE VOLT-OHM METER

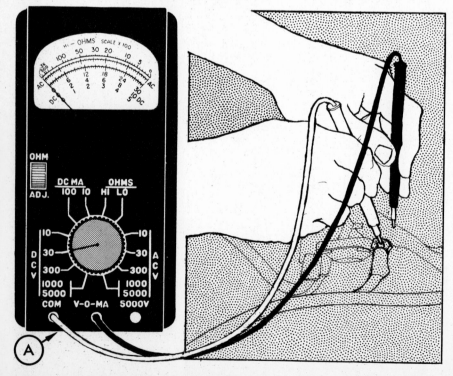

One item of electrical test equipment that should be available to the troubleshooter is the volt-ohm meter or multimeter (A). This inexpensive device combines the functions of a voltmeter (voltage checker), ammeter (current checker) and ohmmeter (resistance checker) in one unit. The multimeter shown here and elsewhere in this book is designed to represent a multiple-function volt/amp/ohm/meter. There are several types of such multimeters available through auto parts stores and tune-up equipment sales outlets.

With this meter, you can perform a further check of battery condition with the battery still in the car.

HIGH RATE DISCHARGE TEST

If after inspecting the battery and cables the battery appears good but will not crank the engine over enough for satisfactory starting, you can check it by performing a high-rate discharge test if you have access to a multimeter.

There are two types of batteries used in automobiles. One is rated at six volts capacity, the other at 12 volts capacity. Both should crank the starter for a certain length of time before their capacity drops below a certain level. First check the voltage of the battery before the starter is engaged. Connect the multimeter to the battery posts in the manner shown (multimeter plus [+] lead to battery plus lead and multimeter negative [-] lead to battery negative lead). Set the meter selector switch to read voltage. A good six-volt battery should show a reading of 5.5 volts or better. The 12-volt battery should show 11.5 volts or better.

Remove the ignition lead (high-tension lead; that is, the lead from the coil to the center post of the distributor cap) to prevent the engine from firing. Then crank the starter while watching the meter. After 15 seconds of continuous cranking, the voltage should not have dropped below 4.8 volts for a six-volt battery and 9.6 volts for a 12-volt battery. If after this test or any of the other tests the battery appears to be at fault, remove it and have it recharged or replace it with a new battery. This will correct many problems, as the battery is often at fault.

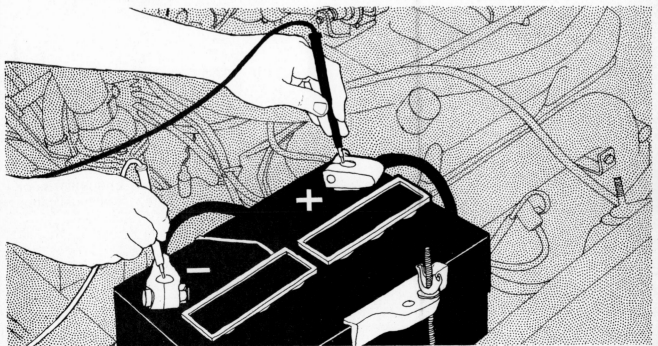

NOTE: WHEN A BATTERY FAILS BEFORE IT REACHES THE END OF ITS NORMAL SERVICE LIFE, INSPECT THE REST OF THE SYSTEM TO SEE IF SOMETHING ELSE CAUSED THE PROBLEM.

TROUBLESHOOTING STARTER SOLENOIDS

The starter is an electric motor which requires a large amount of current to make it work correctly. Since it would be impractical to run the heavy wires from the battery to the starter through the ignition switch in the driver's compartment, some form of remote switching is required. This remote switch is the starter relay or solenoid. Operated by a smaller voltage from the ignition switch or starter button, it switches the heavy current on and off to operate the starter.

Some starter solenoids are separate parts of the system, located on the firewall or inner fenderwells (B), while other solenoids are actually part of the starter unit (A). In some cases, the solenoid mounted directly on the starter housing also operates the starter drive, to engage and disengage the starter motor from the flywheel.

In the starter system checkout section, we showed how to determine if the solenoid was at fault by using a jumper wire to bypass it. In that section we said that if bypassing the solenoid made the starter work, the solenoid was faulty and should be replaced. This is not always necessary. Replacement will get the car fixed and back in service, but some kinds of solenoids can be repaired.

The remote solenoids are in most cases sealed relay units which must be replaced, but the solenoids which are part of the starter can sometimes be repaired. The shop manual should be consulted for information on locating and removing the starter and solenoid.

> **NOTE:** MOST STARTERS ARE VERY DIFFICULT TO REMOVE BECAUSE OF THEIR LOCATION AND SURROUNDING EQUIPMENT.

TROUBLESHOOTING STARTER SOLENOID

CLEANING SOLENOID PLUNGER

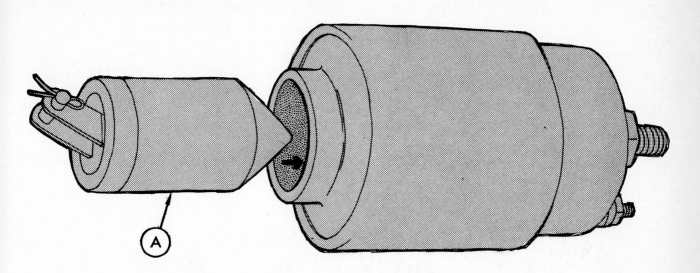

One possible problem in the solenoid is grease or dirt, which may be keeping the solenoid plunger from moving far enough to work properly. Check the shop manual for instructions on disassembling the solenoid and how to clean it. Do not grease the plunger (A) or its housing before putting it back together.

CHECKING SOLENOID CONTACTS

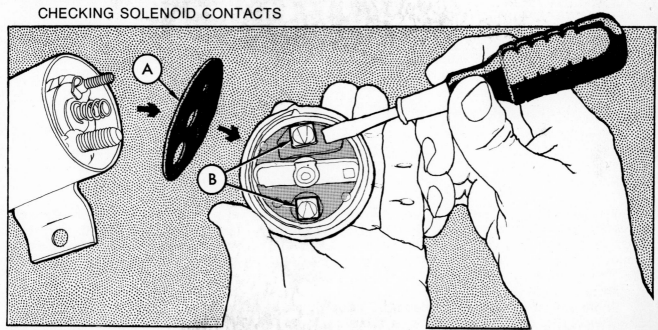

Whenever the solenoid operates, the contacts of the switch portion create a small electrical arc as they open and close. This will in time burn the contacts until they do not make a good connection. In most solenoids, the movable contact is a ring or plate (A), which can be turned over to utilize the unused side. The fixed contacts (B) can be cleaned and smoothed with a fine file or emery paper. On some models, the fixed contact on the hot (battery) contact can be rotated to provide a good contact surface. While the solenoid is disassembled, a careful check should be made of all wiring and electrical connections inside the dust cover on the end of the solenoid. Often troubles consist of nothing more than a broken wire or a corroded connection. Specific instructions for repairing solenoids can be found in the manufacturer's shop manual for the type of car you are working on.

TROUBLESHOOTING SWITCHES

If the starter system check showed that one of the controlling switches was suspect, they can be tested in one of several ways.

TROUBLESHOOTING THE STARTING SYSTEM

CHECK THE OBVIOUS FIRST

If the battery and solenoid are good but one of the switches (starter or neutral safety switch) proves bad when bypassed (that is, the starter works when the switch is bypassed), you know the starter is good and that something is wrong with the switch or the surrounding wiring. Make a careful visual check of the switch and the wiring connected to it. It may be necessary to remove the switch from its location to really look at it closely. This can be quite a problem, since most ignition and neutral safety switches are concealed inside the steering column. See the shop manual for information on how to remove the switch.

If you bypassed the switch at the relay or solenoid instead of at the back of the switch itself, the wiring leading from the relay to the switch may be bad. This wiring usually goes through a plug in the firewall. Trace the wiring by hand as far as you can go.

NOTE: MOST WIRING IS COLOR-CODED TO MAKE IT EASY TO FOLLOW. A WIRING DIAGRAM IN THE SHOP MANUAL WILL OFTEN GIVE THE COLORS OF THE WIRES.

SUBSTITUTE SWITCHES

If the switch is readily available from a parts supplier, you can simply purchase a new switch and substitute it to confirm whether or not the old switch is bad.

NOTE: ELECTRICAL ITEMS PURCHASED NEW CANNOT BE RETURNED FOR REIMBURSEMENT. BE FAIRLY CERTAIN THAT THE SWITCH IS YOUR PROBLEM *BEFORE* YOU BUY.

This technique saves time on small parts which are not expensive. With some models of key-operated switches, it is not necessary to buy the entire switch assembly. Only the actual switch section need be replaced.

CHECK THE SWITCH WITH A METER

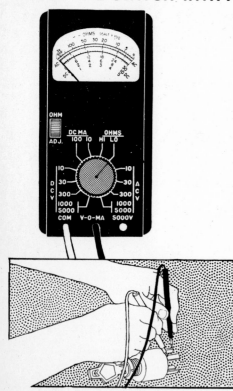

If you have a multimeter available, you can troubleshoot a switch either in or out of the circuit. Checking the switch in the circuit (all wires attached and battery connected) is somewhat more difficult than checking the switch after it has been removed.

To check the switch after removal from the wiring, use the resistance-measuring feature of the meter—the ohmmeter function. A good switch will have infinite (so great it cannot be measured) resistance when it is off and zero resistance when it is switched on.

Suppose you want to test a key-operated ignition switch with a meter. After removing the switch from the wiring, set the meter to the ohm function. Connect one side of the meter to the hot (battery) contact on the switch. Connect the other side of the meter to the "start" contact on the switch. Insert the key into the switch and turn it to start. With the switch in any position other than start, there should be no meter needle movement (infinite resistance). As soon as the switch is placed in the start position, the needle should swing to the other end of the scale, indicating a complete lack of (zero) resistance between the contacts of the switch. If the reading is not close to zero or the reading is intermittent (does not repeat the same reading each time), the switch is bad and should be replaced.

NOTE: MOST SWITCHES ARE NOT DESIGNED TO BE REPAIRED.

TROUBLESHOOTING THE STARTER

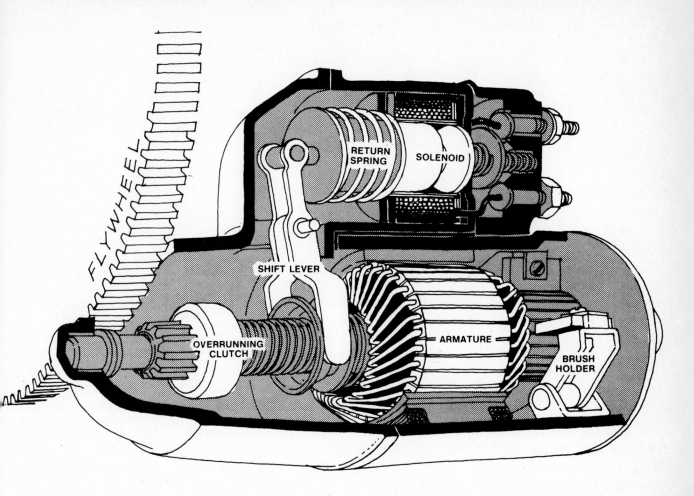

If the battery, solenoid and all controlling switches check out okay, there is very little left in the starting system except the starter itself that can cause a no-start problem. If you have not removed the starter to check the solenoid, begin testing the starter by first carefully examining the wiring and connections around it.

> **NOTE:** THE STARTER IS SUBJECT TO MUCH EXPOSURE TO DIRT AND OTHER DEBRIS BECAUSE OF ITS LOCATION NEAR THE BOTTOM OF THE ENGINE. IT MAY BE NECESSARY TO CLEAN THE STARTER BEFORE EXAMINING IT. CLEANING MAY TEMPORARILY CURE A FAULTY CONNECTION PROBLEM, BUT IT WILL SOON RETURN UNLESS A COMPLETE CHECK AND REPAIRS ARE MADE.

The following is a list of the things that could be wrong with the starter:

BAD CONNECTIONS

This means dirty or broken connections or wiring. Replace or repair wiring. Corrosion or oil buildup on the outside of the starter case can cause the starter to malfunction.

BAD GROUND CONNECTIONS

The electrical system of the starter is "grounded" to the engine. Check to make sure that all bolts holding the starter to the engine are tight. Loose bolts can also cause binding of the starter drive.

INTERNAL WIRING PROBLEMS

The internal wiring of the starter is quite complicated and should be left to a professional mechanic to check, as it requires several types of special tools. You can disassemble the starter using the shop manual and inspect it for obvious signs of damage, but it usually requires a trip to the shop for repair.

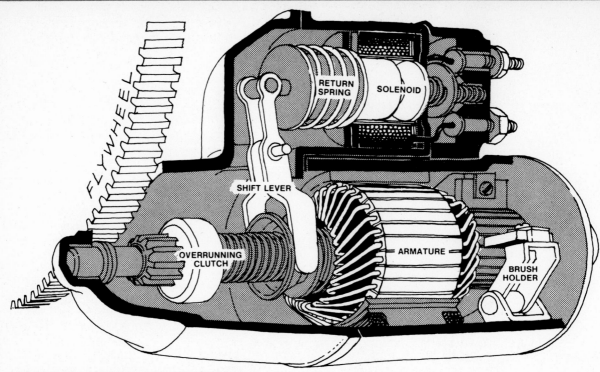

STARTER DRIVE MALFUNCTION

The starter drive couples the motor portion of the starter to the ring gear on the flywheel to make the engine crank over. This drive can be the source of the problem, especially if the starter spins but will not crank the engine when the ignition switch is turned to start. If you have removed the starter, try to turn the starter by hand. If it is binding, chances are that either the drive or a bearing is bad. You must replace the entire drive assembly.

HYDRAULIC LOCK

Not really a starter malfunction, this occurs when large amounts of some fluid (gasoline, oil or water) get into the cylinders of the engine and prevent movement of the engine. These liquids are not compressible, so if they get into the cylinders, the engine becomes "locked." If you suspect this, remove all the spark plugs and try to crank the engine over. If it now cranks easily and you can see any fluid coming from the spark plug holes, the problem is a hydraulic lock.

If the fluid is gasoline, it indicates a stuck float in the carburetor. If it is water, there could be a blown head gasket or cracked block or head. If it is oil, the oil could be too thin.

NOTE: THIS PROBLEM USUALLY OCCURS AFTER THE CAR HAS BEEN RUNNING HARD ON A WARM DAY.

COLD WEATHER INFORMATION

Starting system performance is greatly reduced in cold weather. To prevent problems, the battery should be kept fully charged. Because of the location of most starters, snow, ice and slush can become packed around the starter, and it may freeze. The salt used on roadways during bad weather can cause considerable corrosion if left on the underside of the car, and this can affect the starter. Keep the underside of the car as clean as possible.

HOT WEATHER INFORMATION

Some starting problems, such as slow starting, can be the result of a cooling system malfunction rather than a starter problem. High engine temperatures can increase internal friction in the engine, putting an extra load on the starter. If you experience continued hard starting problems (slow starting) during hot weather, check out the cooling system to make sure that it is functioning properly.

ARMATURE TESTING

If you suspect electrical trouble within the windings of the starter motor armature or the field coils, take them to a starter/generator repair shop. Such testing cannot usually be accomplished at home. The professional shop will have a device known as a "growler," which is used to test armatures for shorted windings. If a defect is found, replace the armature.

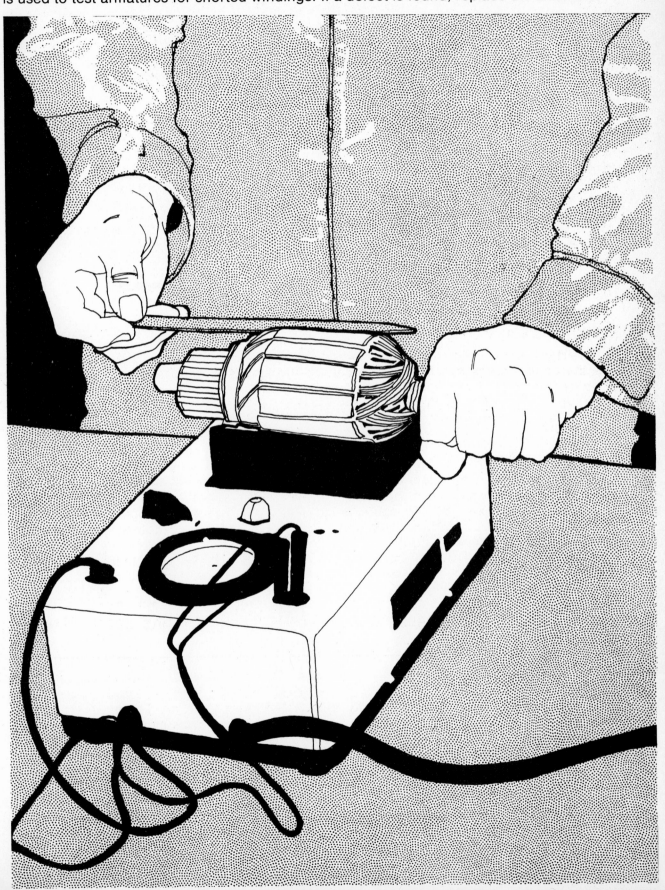

TROUBLESHOOTING THE IGNITION SYSTEM

This chapter deals with the ignition system. The operation of the ignition system is probably more critical to good engine operation than any other part of the engine. The strength of the spark needed to fire the air/fuel mixture compressed in the cylinders is approximately 20,000 volts. Just a small loss of spark strength will interfere with the normal operation of the ignition system and cause problems. The ignition system discussed in this chapter is the conventional battery/coil type which uses a set of breaker points in the distributor to control the timing of the spark. Transistorized and all-electronic ignition systems require several types of highly specialized test equipment to troubleshoot properly; therefore we will not go into them in great detail.

The ignition system performs two functions. First, it boosts the relatively low voltage of the battery to the very high voltage needed to fire the spark plugs. Second, it controls or "times" the exact moment of firing of each spark plug to coincide with piston movement in each of the cylinders.

This ignition system is broken down into two circuits. The primary circuit is the low-voltage side of the system and comprises the battery, the primary side of the ignition coil, the distributor points and condenser. The secondary circuit consists of the secondary side of the coil, the high-tension lead between coil and distributor, the distributor cap and rotor, the spark plug wires and the plugs themselves.

HOW THE IGNITION SYSTEM WORKS

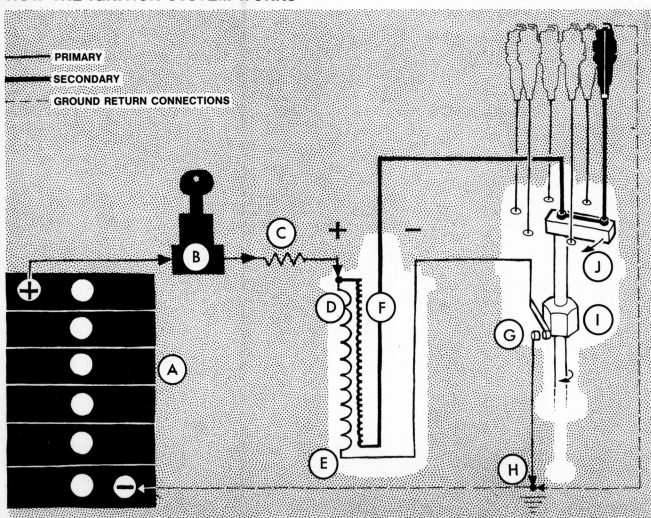

When the ignition switch (B) is turned on, the electrical current flows from the battery (A) through the switch to the primary winding (D) of the coil, through the winding and to the distributor points (G). As long as the distributor points are closed, there is a complete circuit (H), allowing current to flow in the primary winding.

This flow of current produces a strong magnetic field in the coil which stays there until something makes the current stop flowing. That "something" is the ignition points. The distributor, where the points are located, is gear-driven by the engine. There is a small cam (I) which opens and closes the points as the shaft in the distributor turns. Each time the cam opens the ignition points, the flow of current from the battery to the primary winding of the coil stops.

When the current flow stops, the collapse of the magnetic field around the primary winding induces a sharp pulse of high voltage in the secondary winding (F). This action is exactly like a power line transformer in reverse. The power transformer creates a low-voltage, high-current electricity for use in homes, and the ignition coil creates a high-voltage, low-current electricity to fire the spark plugs.

This brief pulse of high voltage is passed through the high-tension lead (the center lead in the distributor cap) of the coil to the distributor cap. Inside the distributor cap is a rotating contact (J—rotor) which transfers the pulse from the high-tension lead to one of the spark plug contacts inside the cap. Connected to the spark plug contacts are the spark plug wires and the spark plugs themselves.

Each time the distributor shaft rotates enough for the cam to open the points, the high-voltage pulse developed in the secondary of the coil is directed to the correct spark plug by the rotor and creates a strong spark across the tip of the spark plug to fire the air/fuel mixture inside the cylinder.

One important factor in the ignition is timing. Ignition timing means delivering the spark to the correct plug, and it must arrive at exactly the right moment for firing the compressed air/fuel mixture to produce the necessary power.

It takes a small but measurable amount of time for the ignited air/fuel mix to expand and create the pressure that pushes the piston down to make the engine run. This means that as engine speed (rpm) increases, the spark must come slightly earlier to allow time for burning to be well under way when the piston reaches top dead center (TDC).

There are several ways to accomplish this. All are known as ignition advance; that is, advancing the firing of the spark by a small fraction of a second. One such system is vacuum advance, which utilizes engine vacuum to make this change. The other system is mechanical advance, which uses a system of weights and springs in the distributor to advance the spark as the distributor shaft turns faster as engine speed increases. Most modern distributors use a combination of these two systems to create the correct advance for the engine.

TROUBLESHOOTING THE PRIMARY CIRCUIT

If there is a problem in the primary circuit, make a careful visual examination of all parts of the primary circuit: battery (A), coil (E), ballast resistor (C) if there is one, ignition switch (B), contact points (G) and all wiring.

The battery should be inspected for signs of corrosion around posts and connections. Battery cables should be looked at closely to make sure they are not corroded or broken. Insulation on all wires should be checked to see if there are any places where worn or frayed coverings might let wires short out against the engine or body. Heavy coatings of oil or grease can create a path for a shorted circuit. In some cars, a separate battery cable runs from the positive (+) post of the battery to provide current for the ignition system and other electrical parts. This will be a smaller cable alongside the heavy cable running to the starter. If this is broken or loose, the starter will crank, but no other systems will work. If no immediate problem can be seen, follow this list of individual troubleshooting steps for the primary circuit.

CHECKING THE IGNITION CIRCUIT

Unlike the starting system, the ignition switch supplies electricity to the primary circuit in two positions. In the "on" position, it supplies electricity through a ballast resistor or a resistance wire which lowers the voltage slightly to match the requirements of the coil. In the "start" position, when current is also being supplied to the starter to crank the engine, the ballast resistor or resistance wire is bypassed to increase the voltage on the coil and increase the strength of the spark. If the engine appears to start when the ignition switch is turned to start but dies as soon as the switch is released to the on position, there is something wrong with the ballast resistor or resistance wire circuit. Also check bulkhead or firewall plugs through which this wiring passes.

The quickest way to test the switch is with the multimeter. If the switch is hard to get at, you can make a quick check by making a couple of measurements on the coil.

TROUBLESHOOTING THE IGNITION SYSTEM

CHECKING BATTERY VOLTAGE AT COIL

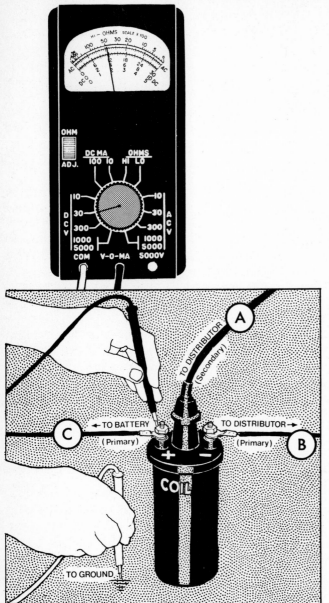

In addition to the high-tension lead (A) coming out of the coil, there are two smaller connections. One connects the primary (+) side of the coil to the battery (C). The other connects the primary (-) side to the contact points in the distributor (B).

> **NOTE:** ALL SETTINGS AND VOLTAGES USED IN THIS SERIES OF CHECKS ARE FOR 12-VOLT IGNITION SYSTEMS. FOR READINGS ON SIX-VOLT SYSTEMS, CHECK THE SHOP MANUAL.

Isolate the coil primary (-) from the ground (B) either by removing the wire running from the coil to the points or by removing the distributor cap and cranking the engine until the points are open.

Connect one lead of the multimeter between the BAT (+) side terminal and the other lead to a good ground. Set the multimeter selector switch to read DC volts (direct current) at a range higher than 12 volts.

Turn the ignition switch to on. The meter should indicate 12 volts at the BAT (+) side terminal of the coil. If the normal voltage is not present, then the switch, the coil or the wiring between the battery and switch is bad.

> **NOTE:** ALTHOUGH THIS READING IS TAKEN THROUGH THE PORTION OF THE WIRING THAT CONTAINS THE BALLAST RESISTOR OR RESISTANCE WIRING, IT DOES NOT MEASURE A CHANGE IN THE RESISTANCE OF THESE PARTS. TO COMPLETE A CHECK OF THIS CIRCUIT, PERFORM THE NEXT TEST.

RUNNING VOLTAGE CHECK

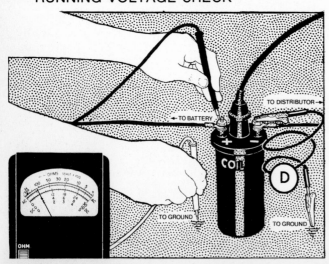

Connect a jumper cable (D) between the distributor primary (-) terminal and ground. Leave the meter connected as in the previous check.

Turn the ignition switch to on. The voltage should be between 5 and 7 volts. If the voltage is lower than 5 volts, the ballast resistor or resistance wire may be faulty or there may be a loose connection between the coil and ignition switch or between the ignition switch and the battery. If there are more than 7 volts present, check the wire between the coil and the contact points. If you suspect the ballast resistor or resistance wire (one or the other will be installed in the primary circuit), check the shop manual for replacement instructions.

CRANKING VOLTAGE CHECK

The multimeter shown here and elsewhere in this book is designed to represent a multiple-function volt/amp/ohm/meter. There are several types of such multimeters available through auto parts stores and tune-up equipment sales outlets.

This check sends current to the coil through the wire which does *not* contain the ballast resistor or resistance wire.

Leave the meter connected and the jumper wire installed in the same location as in the previous checks.

NOTE: THE HIGH-TENSION LEAD (A) SHOULD BE REMOVED FROM THE COIL TO PREVENT CYLINDER FIRING.

Turn the ignition switch to start.

The meter should indicate approximately 9 volts. (Ford automobiles will indicate approximately 7 volts.) The cranking voltage should always be greater than the running voltage reading in the previous test. If no voltage is present, check the ignition switch and the wiring in the cranking circuit.

If the voltage is low, nearly that of the running circuit, the starter may be drawing too much current or the battery may be weak.

NOTE: SEE THE HIGH-RATE DISCHARGE TEST IN THE SECTION ON STARTERS.

If all the primary circuit checks are good, it is safe to assume that the wiring between the battery, the ignition switch and the coil is good. The ignition switch is also good.

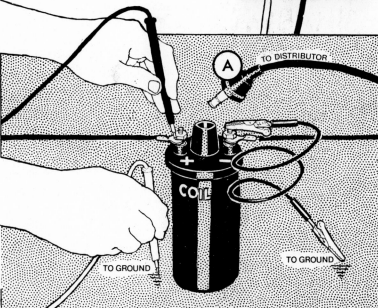

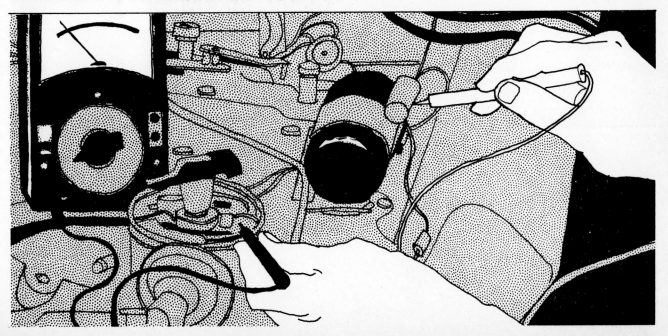

PRIMARY WINDING RESISTANCE CHECK

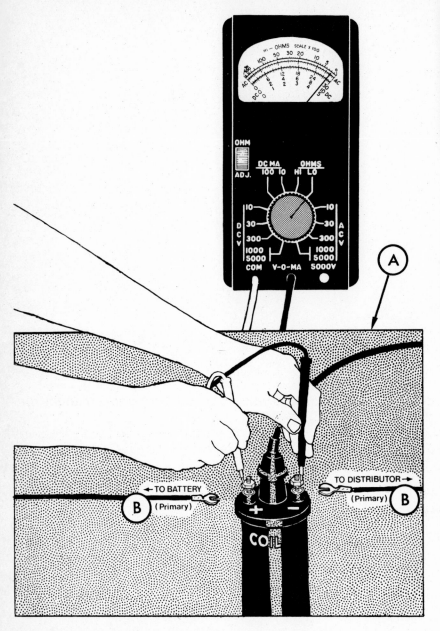

CAUTION: ALWAYS BE SURE THERE IS NO VOLTAGE IN THE CIRCUIT WHEN USING THE METER TO READ RESISTANCE. DISCONNECT THE BATTERY GROUND CABLE (-) TO AVOID DAMAGE TO THE METER

NOTE: INEXPENSIVE MULTIMETERS MAY NOT BE ACCURATE ENOUGH TO MEASURE THE VERY SLIGHT RESISTANCE OF A GOOD PRIMARY WINDING IN THE COIL. IF THE MEASUREMENT APPEARS TO BE ZERO OHMS, CHANCES ARE IT IS GOOD.

To check the internal resistance of the primary side of the coil, remove the wires (B) from the primary connections (+) (-) and connect the multimeter to the coil as shown in the drawing (A). With the meter selector switch set to read resistance (ohms), use the lowest range of ohms measurement. The reading should be approximately 1.5 ohms. If the reading exceeds 3.0 ohms, replace the coil.

PRIMARY LEAKAGE CHECK

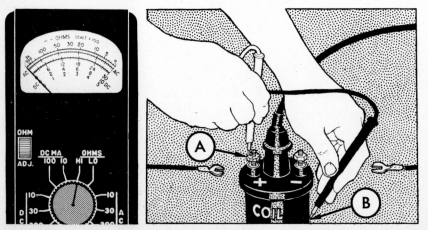

Use the same test hookup as for the previous check. Set the meter selector switch to read the highest resistance range. Touch one probe (A) of the test leads to one of the primary terminals (+) or (-). Touch the other lead (B) to the case of the coil. This checks for a breakdown of the insulating qualities of the coil case. If the needle moves at all to read any other resistance than infinity, replace the coil.

CONTACT POINTS CHECKS

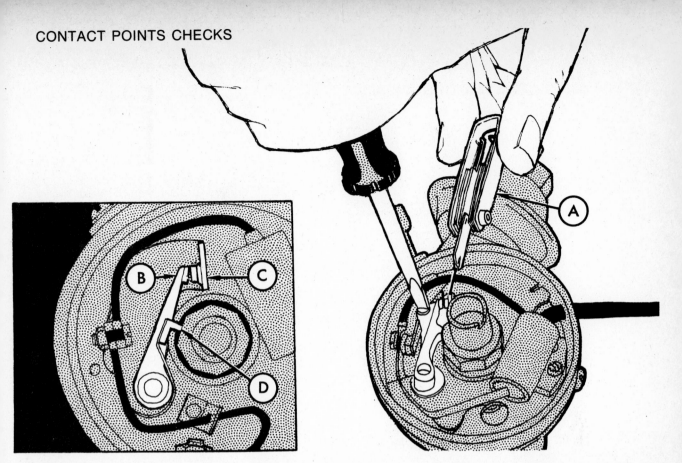

The contact points can be checked for operation by cranking the engine over with the distributor cap removed.

The point setting should be checked with a feeler gauge (A). See the shop manual for proper settings.

If points show only minor pitting or burning, they can be cleaned with a point file and re-gapped instead of being replaced. If pitting or burning is excessive, new points and condenser should be installed.

Point alignment should be checked on points which show mild pitting that is not centered on the point contact surface. Bad point alignment shortens point life considerably, and a poor spark will result until the problem is corrected.

NOTE: IF THE POINTS MUST BE ALIGNED BY BENDING, *NEVER* BEND THE MOVABLE ARM (B). ALWAYS BEND THE FIXED CONTACT (C). ALSO INSPECT THE RUBBING BLOCK (D) ON THE POINTS FOR WEAR AND LUBRICATE IF NECESSARY.

CHECKING THE CONDENSER

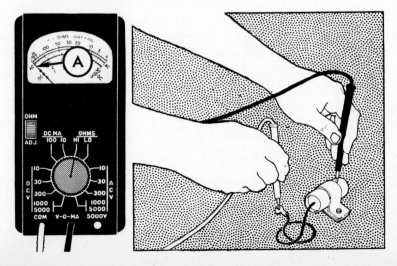

The condenser can be checked with the multimeter to determine its electrical condition, but the best course of action when a faulty condenser is suspected is to replace it. If you do wish to check it, remove the condenser from the distributor and connect the multimeter, one lead to one side of the condenser and the other lead to the other side. The meter selector switch should be set to read resistance (ohms) on the highest range. If the reading is below the infinity mark (A—it may drop and then rise to infinity when the meter is first connected), replace the condenser.

TROUBLESHOOTING THE SECONDARY CIRCUIT

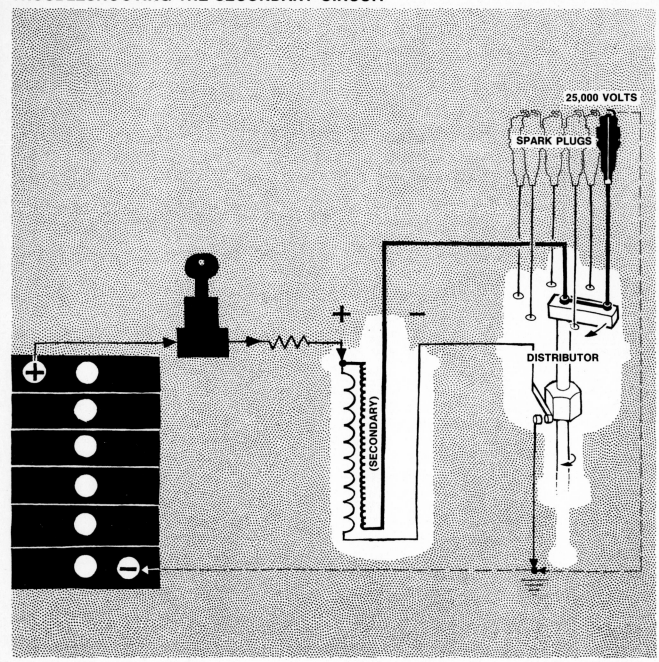

The secondary circuit is made up of the secondary winding (high voltage) of the coil, the distributor cap and rotor, the high-tension lead and spark plug leads and the spark plugs themselves. Careful inspection of all the wiring in the secondary circuit is mandatory. In the primary side of the ignition, the highest voltage was the battery voltage of six or 12 volts, depending on the car. In the secondary system, voltages may exceed 20,000 volts. This extremely high voltage needs only a small breakdown in the insulating qualities of wires or parts to short out. These breakdowns are not always readily visible to the naked eye. Accumulations of oil or grease on wiring can break down insulation. Carbon buildup on spark plugs and the inside of the distributor cap can cause arcing or shorting of the high voltage. Even moisture is a frequent cause of secondary system failure.

All elements of the ignition system should be kept clean and free of oil, dirt and water. Rubberized wiring should be inspected for signs of rotting or cracking. Where spark plug wires pass close to the exhaust manifolds or exhaust pipes, the wires should be inspected for signs of melted or burned insulation. Below is a series of checks on individual parts of the secondary side of the ignition system.

SECONDARY WINDING RESISTANCE CHECK

Set the multimeter selector switch to read resistance and connect it to the coil as shown in drawing (D).

NOTE: SEE PETERSEN'S AUTOMOTIVE TUNE-UP AND TEST EQUIPMENT BOOK FOR PROCEDURES ON VARIOUS ELECTRICAL TESTING UNITS.

Remove the high-tension lead (B) and insert one probe (A) into the coil tower. The other probe (C) should be in contact with one of the primary terminals (+) or (-).

The resistance reading should be compared against that listed in the shop manual for the type of automobile you are working on. If the reading is above or below the specification listed, replace the coil.

NOTE: THE VALUE OF RESISTANCE VARIES WITH EACH TYPE OF COIL.

This check of the coil with the multimeter is not perfect, as it cannot duplicate the effect of the 20,000 volts. If you desire, a coil can be checked by a shop with specialized test equipment that more closely simulates actual running conditions.

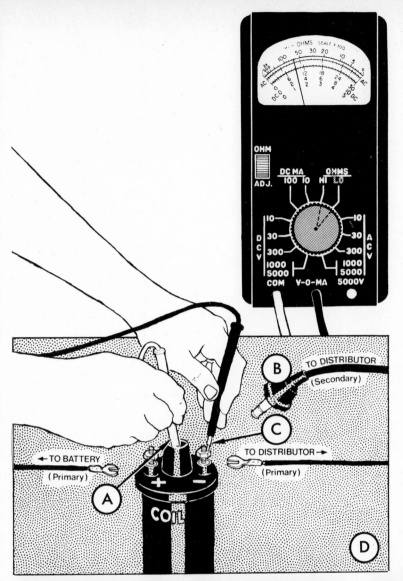

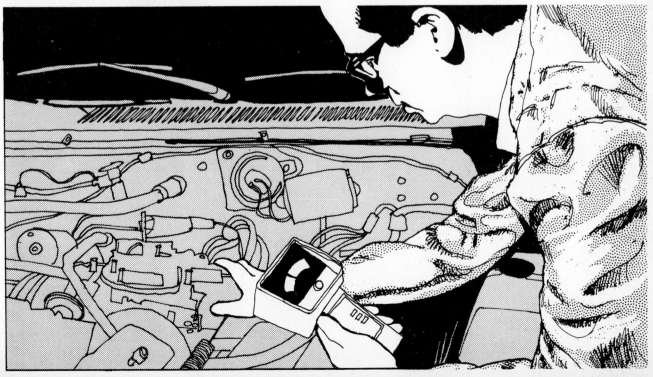

TROUBLESHOOTING THE IGNITION SYSTEM

CHECKING THE DISTRIBUTOR CAP

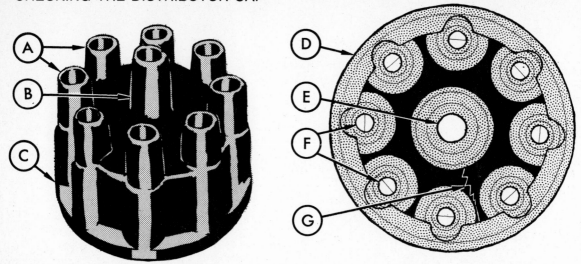

Checking the distributor cap is primarily a visual job. Clean the exterior of the cap (C) carefully and examine all the wire sockets (A) where the high-tension (B) and spark plug wires plug into the cap. If there is any dirt, corrosion or evidence of arcing, you may be able to clean it up with a small wire brush or some sandpaper, but if the problem is severe, replace the cap.

Inside the cap (D) are the contacts (F) for the rotor. There is a tiny gap between the metal tip of the rotor and the spark plug contacts. As the rotor whirls past each contact, the electrical pulse makes an arc between the rotor and contact. In time, this causes a buildup of burned metal particles on the contact or on the rotor tip. The buildup can be corrected with a small file or sandpaper unless the burning is bad. If it appears to be too bad to fix, replace the cap. The center contact (E) on the cap is in constant contact with the spring-tensioned contact on top of the rotor. The former will usually not show any pitting or burning but may be dirty or oily.

Carefully check inside and out for hairline cracks in the cap. These can cause a short circuit of the high-voltage pulse. On the inside of the cap, a crack (G) can sometimes be detected by a carbon buildup along the crack. This carbon track is a perfect short circuit for the high voltage and can cause failure of the ignition system.

CHECKING THE ROTOR

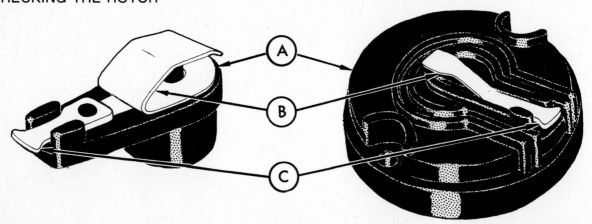

The rotor (A) can be checked by visual methods. Inspect it for carbon tracking which would indicate a crack and examine the metal contacts (C) for burning or pitting. The spring-loaded center contact (B) should be checked to make sure it has enough tension to keep it in firm touch with the center contact in the distributor cap. Small amounts of pitting can be corrected with a fine file. If the cap is too badly worn to repair by this method, replace it.

CHECKING SECONDARY WIRING

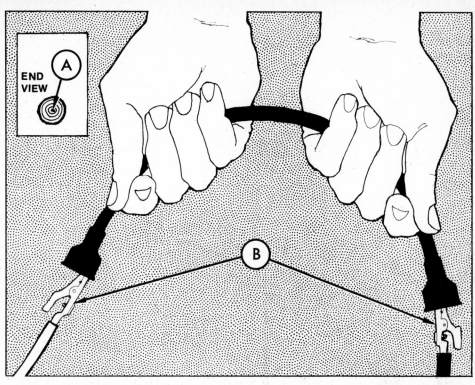

The high-tension and spark plug wires can be checked with the multimeter to make sure they provide a good path for electricity. There are two basic types of wiring used for spark plugs and high-tension leads. The first, which is not found on most modern automobiles as *factory* equipment, is metallic wire. This type has a solid or stranded copper wire center (A) conductor. The second kind of wiring is the resistance wiring used to eliminate electrical interference with radios and other electrical equipment. This second type, which is standard equipment on all modern automobiles, does not use a metallic center conductor. The conductor is a group of nylon or fiberglass fibers which are impregnated with carbon, an excellent conductor of electricity.

All secondary wiring should be free of dirt, oil and grime. The insulated covering should show no signs of burning or cracking. When checking the outside condition of wiring before it is removed from the engine, look closely at those areas where the wire is held in clamps or holders and where it passes close to hot exhaust manifolds or pipes.

The internal condition of the wiring can be checked with the multimeter. Set the multimeter to read resistance (ohms). Use a pair of alligator clips (B) on the test probes, which will leave your hands free to make movement tests.

NOTE: ALLIGATOR CLIPS ARE SMALL, SPRING-LOADED CLAMPS WHICH FASTEN TO THE PROBE TIPS.

Connect the meter probes to each end of the wire (spark plug or high-tension lead). On metallic wire, you should get a very low resistance reading, but on carbon resistance wiring, the reading may be as high as 40 K-ohms (40,000 ohms). If the steady reading is above 40 K-ohms, replace the wire.

In both cases, hold the wire in your hands. Wiggle it and watch the meter. Any fluctuation of the needle, especially if it goes to the high end of the scale (infinity), means that there is a broken or burned spot somewhere inside the wire. Replace such a wire.

CAUTION: WHEN REMOVING WIRES FROM THE DISTRIBUTOR CAP FOR TESTING, REMOVE ONLY ONE WIRE AT A TIME TO PREVENT A MIXUP OF THE FIRING ORDER WHEN RECONNECTING. CARBON RESISTANCE WIRE CAN BE BROKEN BY ROUGH HANDLING. WHEN REMOVING IT FROM SPARK PLUGS AND DISTRIBUTOR CAP, HOLD IT BY THE EXTREME END RATHER THAN PULLING ON THE WIRE.

TROUBLESHOOTING SPARK PLUGS

At the end of the ignition system line is the spark plug, screwed into a hole in the cylinder head. If this part malfunctions, the air/fuel mixture in the cylinder will not fire regardless of the condition of the rest of the ignition system.

Spark plugs are simple devices. They have no moving parts and only one adjustment. The simplest method of checking them for possible faults is to replace them. However, learning to "read" a spark plug can give the troubleshooter valuable information about the condition of not only the ignition system but other parts of the engine as well.

TYPICAL SPARK PLUG

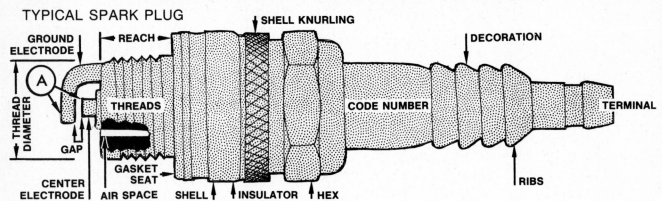

The spark plug does not create the spark. It simply gives the electrical pulse of the ignition secondary a place to make the spark. The two electrodes (A) at the bottom of the spark plug are inside the combustion chamber at the top of the cylinder. When the ignition points open, the high-voltage pulse of electricity flows through the high-tension lead to the distributor, then to the rotor, which sends the pulse to one of the contacts in the cap, then out of the cap and down the spark plug wire to the spark plug. When this high-voltage pulse reaches the center electrode of the spark plug, the tremendous difference between the center electrode and the side electrode, which is grounded, causes a sharp electric arc to jump from one electrode to the other. This arc is what fires the air/fuel mixture.

Each spark plug is designed to perform under certain conditions. When replacing spark plugs, always use the recommended plug, unless a competent mechanic advises a change in type for a specific reason. There are conversion charts for spark plugs which convert spark plug numbers of one manufacturer into the system used by another. As long as you follow the directions on these charts, you can use any listed plug.

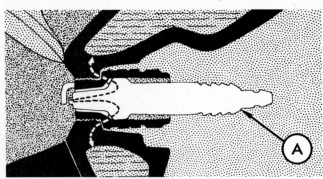

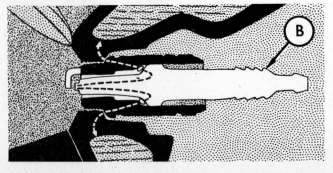

To suit different engines and varying kinds of driving, spark plugs are designed in different heat ranges. This heat range has nothing to do with the heat of the spark. The heat range refers to the plug's ability to transfer heat from the hot firing tip to where the metal body of the plug touches the cylinder head. The rate of heat transfer is controlled by the distance that heat has to travel. A spark plug with a short heat travel distance (A) is called a "cold" plug. A spark plug with an extra-long heat travel distance (B) is called a "hot" plug. Those with in-between heat conduction properties are known as normal-range plugs. Cold plugs are best used for high-speed operation. Racing cars often use cold plugs. Hot plugs are used for cars that do a lot of short-trip driving with lots of idling. Taxicabs are a good example. The normal plug is the type you are most likely to find in your car. They are used for average driving at both slow and fast speeds.

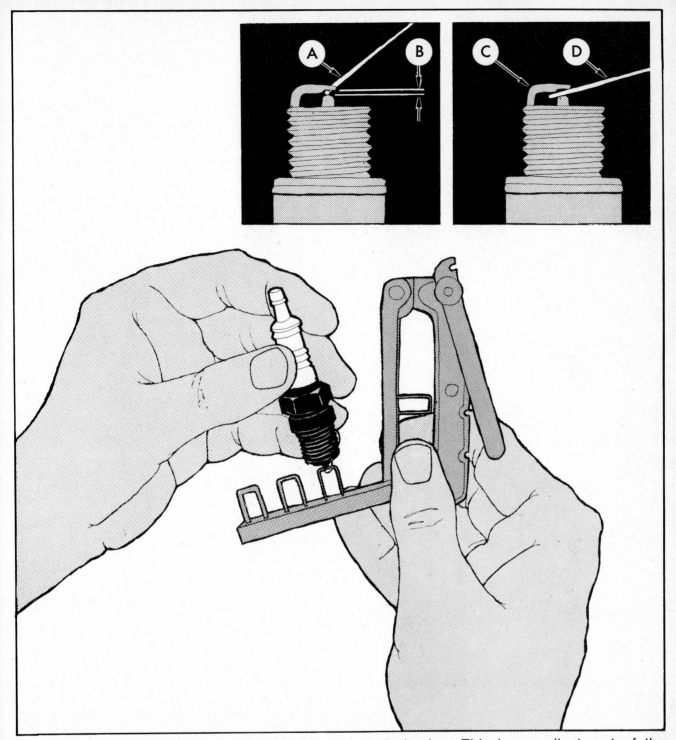

There is only one adjustment possible on a spark plug. This is an adjustment of the distance between the two electrodes (B). This distance, called ''gap,'' is important to the way the spark produced will fire the air/fuel mixture inside the chamber. If the gap is too narrow, the engine will idle roughly. If the gap is too wide, the spark may not be able to fire across the distance, and the engine will misfire.

A round wire gauge (A) is much better than a flat gauge (D) for gapping spark plugs. Never bend the round center electrode. You will break the insulation around the tip. Always bend the side (or ground) electrode (C). When bending the side electrode to gap the plug, don't pound on it with pliers or a screwdriver handle. Bend the electrode so that the gauge used just slides between the two electrodes with a slight feeling of resistance. A normal gap for most spark plugs used in today's engines is .025-inch to .035-inch. Even though plugs are pre-gapped to the correct range by the factory, you should always check and gap new plugs before installing them.

SPARK PLUG PROBLEMS

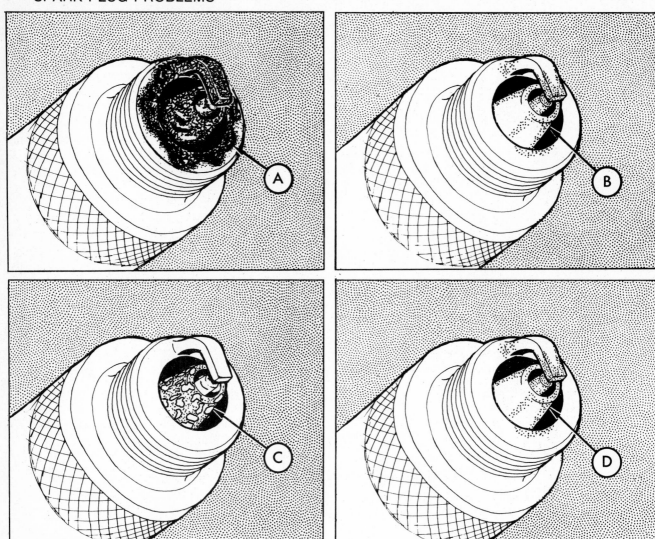

This drawing shows several typical problems that can develop with spark plugs. Many of these can be cured by hand or by cleaning them with a spark plug cleaner, a machine that uses a spray of fine sand driven by high air pressure to remove all deposits. Spark plugs that have suffered some sort of damage should always be replaced.

Some of the problems that spark plugs develop can be clues to other problems. A plug showing a wet, oily deposit (A) indicates crankcase oil is being passed into the cylinders through worn rings, worn valve guides or possibly a ruptured fuel pump diaphragm. A dry, fluffy black coating (B) on the plug tip indicates carbon fouling. This can be caused by a too-rich mixture (an imbalance of fuel to air), a choke malfunction, clogged air filter, most carburetor problems or a sticking exhaust manifold heat control valve. Carbon buildup can also be the result of a weak spark in the ignition system or low-speed driving with long periods of idling. If only one plug is carbon fouled, it's a good idea to check the compression in that cylinder. Also examine the spark plug lead and distributor cap to see if there is a problem associated with that plug.

If the insulated tip (C) of the spark plug is burned or blistered, it can mean serious cylinder overheating. This may be the result of using plugs with an improper heat range, ignition timing too far advanced or a lean mixture (an imbalance of air to fuel). Other problems could be a faulty cooling system or sticking valves.

Residues of the additives in gasoline (D) can build up on the surface of the plug tip after long use. Some of these are good conductors of electricity when hot. If the buildup is not too severe, the plug can be restored by cleaning and re-gapping. But if the coating is too thick, the plugs affected should be replaced.

TESTING IGNITION ADVANCE

Most distributors have a combination of centrifugal and vacuum advance. The centrifugal advance is a purely mechanical method of advancing the firing of the spark, using weights and springs (A) inside the distributor body. The vacuum advance uses engine manifold vacuum to operate a diaphragm (D) on the side of the distributor housing that advances the firing of the spark plug.

As explained earlier, as engine speed (rpm) increases, the spark for each cylinder must be triggered slightly sooner to allow time for full ignition of the air/fuel mixture before the piston reaches top dead center (TDC) and starts back down on the power stroke. This is accomplished by moving the breaker plate (C), which is the metal plate the points are located on, inside the distributor housing. Since firing time is controlled by the cam (B) on the distributor shaft as it opens and closes the points, moving the plate forward or backward changes the instant in time that the points open and close.

The following are only two rough checks of the advance operation. To completely check advance takes test equipment and knowledge beyond the scope of this book. But these tests will help you find out if your distributor needs to be checked by a mechanic.

> **NOTE:** BECAUSE OF EMISSION (SMOG) CONTROL REQUIREMENTS, THERE MAY BE SEVERAL ADDITIONAL ELECTRICAL CIRCUITS ASSOCIATED WITH THE IGNITION. CHECK THE SHOP MANUAL AND SEE PETERSEN'S BASIC IGNITION AND ELECTRICAL SYSTEMS.

CHECKING CENTRIFUGAL (MECHANICAL) ADVANCE

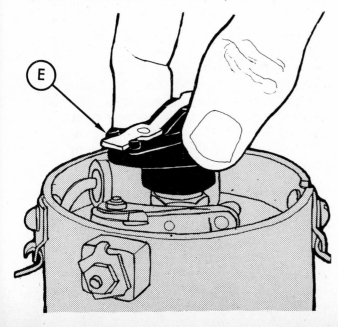

Remove the distributor cap. Grasp the rotor (E) and see if you can turn it in the same direction that the distributor shaft normally rotates. You will feel the pressure of the advance retaining springs trying to hold the movement back. Let go of the rotor. Check to see if it goes back to its original position easily, without sticking or hesitating. Grasp the rotor again and try turning it in the opposite direction. If you cannot turn it, the mechanical advance is probably good. Actual malfunctions of the centrifugal (mechanical) advance feature are rare.

CHECKING VACUUM ADVANCE

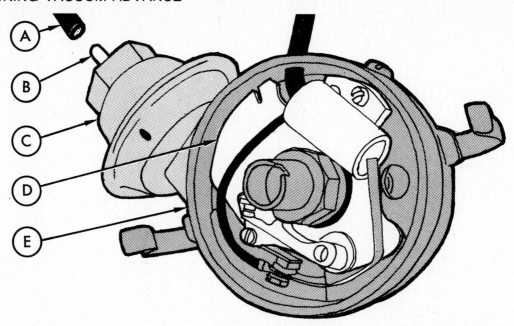

To check the vacuum advance, remove the distributor cap and rotor. Find the vacuum line (A) where it connects to the vacuum diaphragm (C) on the side of the distributor.

NOTE: IF THERE IS MORE THAN ONE LINE TO THE DIAPHRAGM, CONSULT THE SHOP MANUAL TO SEE WHICH ONE IS THE *PRIMARY* VACUUM LINE.

Disconnect the vacuum line and put it aside. Move either the breaker plate (D) or the distributor housing (E—check the shop manual to see which moves by vacuum) as far as you can in one direction. While holding the breaker plate advanced as far as possible, place your finger tightly over the vacuum inlet (B) at the diaphragm. Now let go of the breaker plate. There should be no movement of the breaker plate. Remove your finger from the vacuum inlet. The breaker plate should return smoothly and without binding to its original position.

If the breaker plate moves back while you are still holding your finger over the hole, there is a leak in the diaphragm and the unit should be removed and replaced as soon as possible.

THE TIMING LIGHT

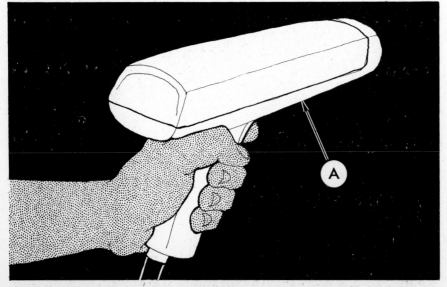

Ignition timing can be checked by the use of a test tool known as a timing light (A). This device is used to "freeze" a mark on some rotating portion of the engine (usually the large pulley on the crankshaft) to determine if the ignition is firing in correct relationship to the rotation of the engine. To time the engine, you will need a timing light, a wrench and the shop manual to tell you the exact correct reading that you will be checking for (see also Petersen's AUTOMOTIVE TUNE-UP & TEST EQUIPMENT).

TIMING MARKS

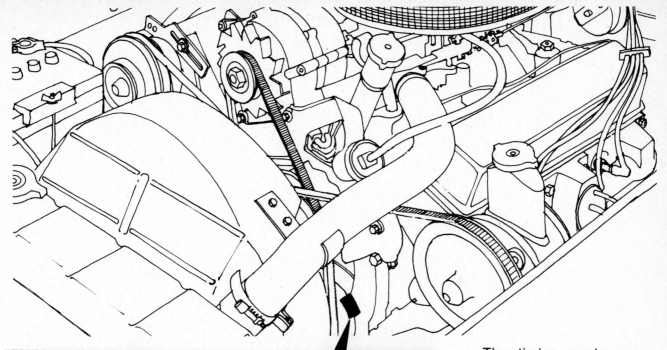

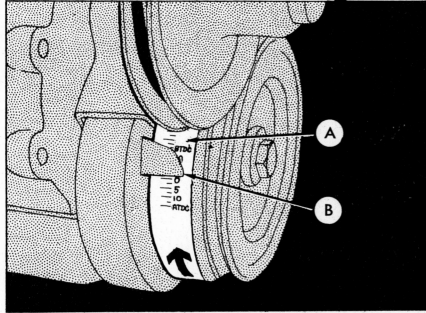

The timing marks are a series of lines (A) or degree marks with a fixed pointer (B) attached to the engine block or pulley. If the engine is in correct time, each time the number one cylinder fires, the pointer will be aligned with one of these degree marks. One of these marks, usually the center one, will be labeled 0, TDC or DC, to denote Top Dead Center. There will be marks on either side of the TDC mark showing a number of degrees both advanced and retarded from that point. Check the shop manual to find the exact degree timing mark for your car.

USING THE TIMING LIGHT

CAUTION: WHEN LEANING OVER A RUNNING ENGINE, DO NOT WEAR LOOSE CLOTHING OR JEWELRY THAT MIGHT BECOME TANGLED IN THE FAN BELT. AVOID PLACING HANDS OR TIMING LIGHT TOO CLOSE TO FAN BELT OR FAN BLADES.

NOTE: POINT GAP HAS AN EFFECT ON TIMING. BE SURE THAT POINTS ARE IN GOOD CONDITION AND CORRECTLY GAPPED BEFORE SETTING OR CHECKING THE TIMING.

Connect the timing light. When the trigger is squeezed, the pulse of the number one plug will trigger the light. It will flash, showing the relationship of the timing marks to the pointer. By pointing the light at the pointer, you can watch the mark appear to freeze in the flashing light. If the timing is not set according to the shop manual, follow the instructions in the shop manual and adjust it.

TROUBLESHOOTING ELECTRONIC IGNITIONS

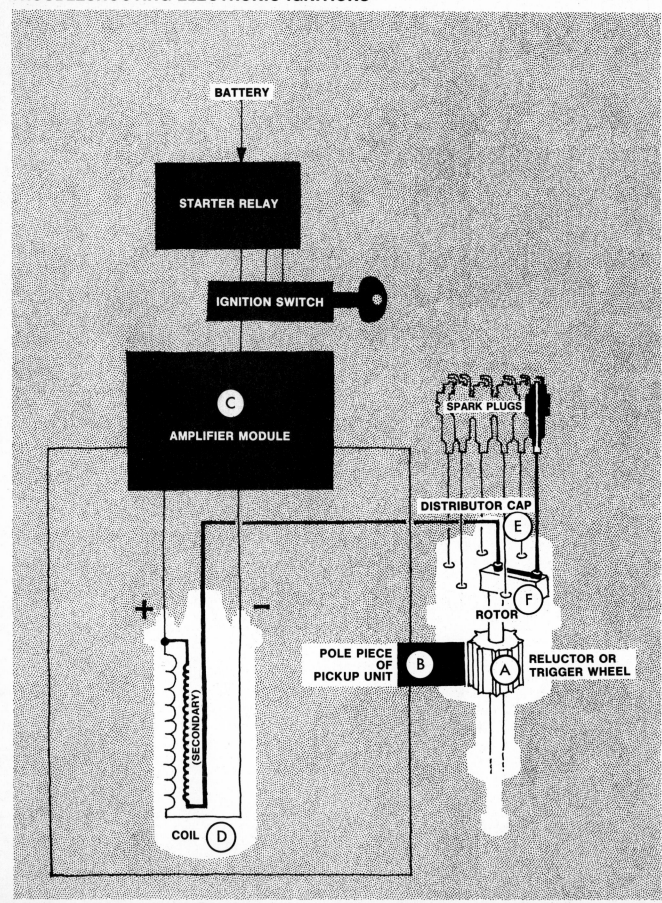

BATTERY

STARTER RELAY

IGNITION SWITCH

C
AMPLIFIER MODULE

SPARK PLUGS

DISTRIBUTOR CAP

E

F

ROTOR

+   −

POLE PIECE OF PICKUP UNIT   B   A   RELUCTOR OR TRIGGER WHEEL

(SECONDARY)

COIL   D

When stringent emissions laws forced Detroit to install electronic ignitions as standard equipment on all cars in 1975, motorists gained a lot more than clean air. Except for some reduction in the amount of invisible poisons leaving your tailpipe, most emission devices can't make the claim that they do anything *good* for the car or car owner. The electronic ignition system, though, with its high-voltage spark, no points or condenser and reduced maintenance both increases spark plug life and saves precious gasoline.

These virtues call for some explanation. Detroit's plan was to comply with government pressures that called for today's vehicles to maintain their low emissions levels for tens of thousands of miles with virtually no periodic maintenance. The weak points in this noble plan have always been those two basic parts of a conventional ignition system, the distributor's points and the spark plugs. Both are subject to continuous wear in normal operation. As these parts wear and their spark gaps grow gradually larger, the keen edge of a tune up dulls and emissions increase.

Unless we could all be convinced to give up current engines overnight, there was no feasible way to eliminate spark plugs, so the Detroit automakers set out to eliminate the conventional guts of the distributor. Chrysler was first on the market with their unit in 1973. Although several points-elimination systems have been used since then, all makes now use a magnetic pulse type of unit like those first Chrylser systems.

MAGNETIC-PULSE SYSTEM

Basically, an engine needs a way to trigger the flow of electricity from the coil to the spark plugs. The distributor then doles out the electricity to the four, six or eight cylinders. In a conventional system, the points open and close, thereby building and collapsing the magnetic field in the coil, every time the distributor cam pushes on the rubbing block. But the rubbing block wears down and the points deteriorate because the high voltage flows across their contacts.

With an electronic ignition, the distributor cam is replaced by a four, six or eight-bladed central piece called by various manufacturers a reluctor, an armature or a trigger wheel (A). Mounted where the point set would be is a magnetic pickup assembly. As the blades pass by, the pole of the pickup (B) senses the presence of the metal blade (even though there is no metal-to-metal contact) and sends a signal to the electronic control module or "black box" (C). The module then triggers the coil (D), sending the built-up secondary voltage to the distributor cap (E). There the rotor (F) sends it to the correct plug wire in the usual way.

No contact between parts means no wear and no gap setting. As a result, with no points to wear out, higher voltages can be used with electronic ignitions. In fact higher voltages were made necessary by today's lean mixtures. Larger plug gaps are required to fire these mixtures, and larger gaps require more juice. These higher voltages also require better spark plug wire insulation, which is why all our new cars have expensive, silicone-jacketed plug wires.

CAUTION: SILICONE SPARK PLUG WIRES ARE FRAGILE AND EASILY STRETCHED. SUCH STRETCHING BREAKS DOWN THE CARBON CORE. NEVER REMOVE A SILICONE WIRE BY PULLING ON THE WIRE ITSELF. USE PLASTIC OR FIBER PLIERS ON THE BOOT ONLY. WHENEVER A SILICONE WIRE IS REMOVED FOR A TEST, PUT SOME SILICONE SPRAY OR GREASE INSIDE THE BOOT BEFORE REINSTALLING IT ON THE SPARK PLUG OR DISTRIBUTOR CAP.

These new electronic ignition systems work so well most of the time that there isn't much to describe about troubleshooting them. When something does go wrong, it may be a complicated matter to electronically track it down and fix it. The factory shop manuals have page after page of detailed instructions on how to check electronic ignitions, using diagnostic tools you probably don't have. Also, none of the electronic parts of these systems are even repairable. They are just replaced when a test shows negative results. Many electronic ignition tests *can* be done at home, using a multimeter and the *shop manual* for your car. The specifications and procedures are different for General Motors, Ford, AMC and Chrysler Corp. cars.

CHECKING FOR SPARK AT THE PLUGS

What you can do when an engine tune-up problem crops up on your car is to troubleshoot it in a normal manner. Only if and when you've narrowed the problem down to the electronics do you need to turn the job over to your dealership mechanic.

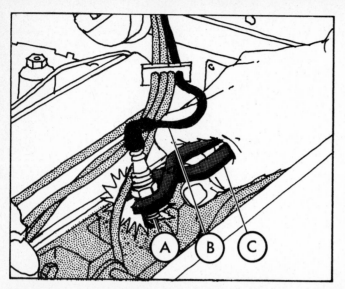

The simplest test you can make is to test for a good spark at the plugs. The new electronic ignitions are good enough so that if you get a spark at the plugs, you can assume that something else and not the ignition is responsible for the trouble.

Since the metal end of the plug wire is usually buried deep inside the boot, the easiest way to test for spark is with a spare plug. Stick the spare plug (A) in the boot (B). With insulated pliers (C), ground the side of the plug against the engine while cranking the engine. If a healthy spark appears with your test plug, the engine problem may be with your plugs. Check, clean and regap them or replace them. If there still isn't a good spark, there are some other basic checks you can make.

CAUTION: RUNNING AN ENGINE WITH A PLUG WIRE DISCONNECTED SENDS RAW FUEL THROUGH THE EXHAUST SYSTEM, WHICH IS DAMAGING TO THE CATALYTIC CONVERTER. LIMIT YOUR INDIVIDUAL TESTS TO 10–15 SECONDS ONLY. TOTAL TEST TIME SHOULD NOT EXCEED FIVE MINUTES.

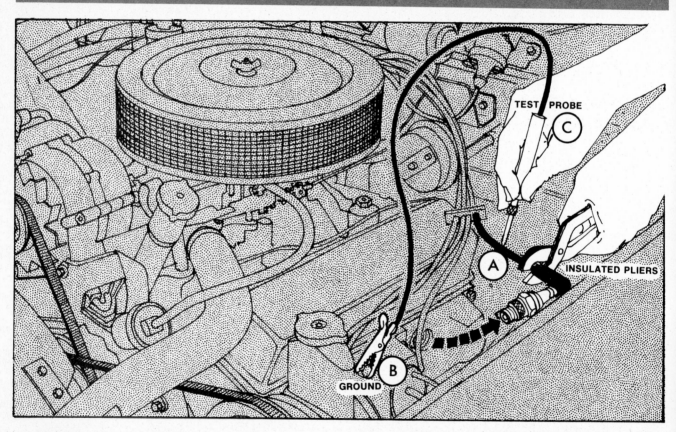

Backing up from the spark plugs, check the fragile silicone-jacketed secondary wires. The higher voltages used today require extra insulation and heat resistance. Silicone does the job admirably, but it stretches easily and must be handled carefully. Disconnect each wire, one at a time from its plug and keep it from grounding (A). Ground one end (B) of your test probe. Start the engine and run the free end of the test probe (C) over the length of the plug wire. If at any point sparks jump from the wire to your probe, there is a break or cut in the silicone insulation.

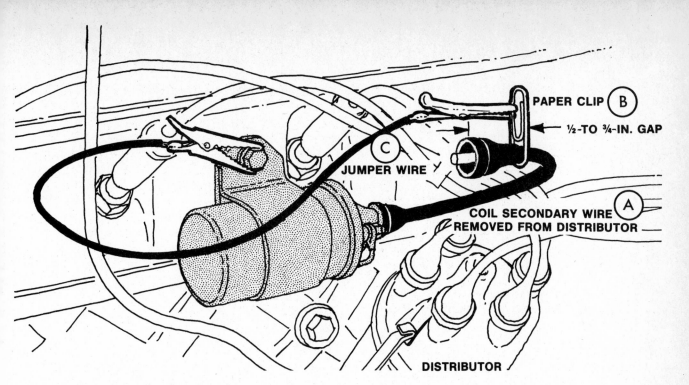

PAPER CLIP Ⓑ

½-TO ¾-IN. GAP

Ⓒ

JUMPER WIRE

COIL SECONDARY WIRE Ⓐ
REMOVED FROM DISTRIBUTOR

DISTRIBUTOR

CHECKING THE COIL OUTPUT

Backing up further, find out if the coil is delivering a good spark. With one of your plug wires still disconnected, crank the engine over and run your probe over the coil wire to check for breaks, just as you did with the plug wires. Now pull the coil wire (A) out of the distributor cap. Slip a paper clip (B) over the wire ½-inch to ¾-inch away from the distributor end and ground the paper clip to the engine with a jumper wire (C). Crank the engine again. You should get a good spark between the paper clip and the end of the wire. If you do, but you *didn't* get a spark from one or more of the plug wires, the problem is in the distributor cap or rotor. If there was no spark on the coil wire, next check to see if the coil is getting the proper voltage. Check your battery with a voltmeter, which should read 12 to 13 volts. Now check the voltage at the coil's positive terminal with the ignition key on. If the coil voltage reads less than the battery voltage, then there is a break in the ignition wires or a problem with the ignition switch.

> **NOTE:** MANY NEW GENERAL MOTORS CARS WITH H.E.I. (HIGH-ENERGY IGNITION) HAVE A SPECIAL COIL WHICH IS MOUNTED INSIDE THE DISTRIBUTOR CAP. SOME OF THE TESTS ASSOCIATED WITH CONVENTIONAL COILS DO NOT APPLY TO THESE COILS. CHECK YOUR FACTORY SHOP MANUAL FOR PROPER TEST PROCEDURES.

Speaking in general about troubleshooting, the conditions under which your car exhibits a tune-up problem may be a clue to the source of trouble. For instance, if the engine only runs roughly at idle, the problem is probably not in the ignition system. A vacuum leak is the most common minor problem with late-model cars, so check the many vacuum hoses for leaks and tighten the intake manifold bolts and carburetor mounting bolts to their proper torque values.

If, on the other hand, the engine runs roughly at all speeds or at partial throttle and higher speeds, there may very well be trouble in the ignition system. Of course, that's assuming that the carburetion tests out okay. If you've narrowed the problem down to the ignition system and the tests outlined above lead you to believe that the fault is not in the coil, plugs, cap or rotor, it's time to visit your dealer. His oscilloscope and testers can pinpoint the problem.

> **WARNING:** DO NOT LEAVE THE IGNITION SWITCH IN THE "ON" POSITION WHEN MAKING UNDER-HOOD TESTS UNLESS YOU PLAN TO START THE ENGINE. THE "BLACK BOX" MODULE AND PICKUP UNIT IN MOST ELECTRONIC SYSTEMS ARE *ON* WHEN THE KEY IS ON, SO A SPARK CAN BE GENERATED WHEN THE KEY IS TURNED OFF OR WHEN THE DISTRIBUTOR CAP IS REMOVED, POSSIBLY CAUSING UNWANTED ENGINE ROTATION.

TROUBLESHOOTING THE CHARGING SYSTEM

As you have seen in the chapters on the starter and ignition systems, the battery is the heart of the electrical network of any automobile. This chapter deals with the mechanical/electrical means by which the battery is kept in a state of charge while the engine is running.

The charging system actually does more than charge the battery. It supplies the electricity for running the ignition system and all the electrical accessories. Besides the battery, the charging system consists of the generator or alternator, the regulator, the ammeter or a warning light on the dashboard and the wiring between these parts.

HOW THE CHARGING SYSTEM WORKS

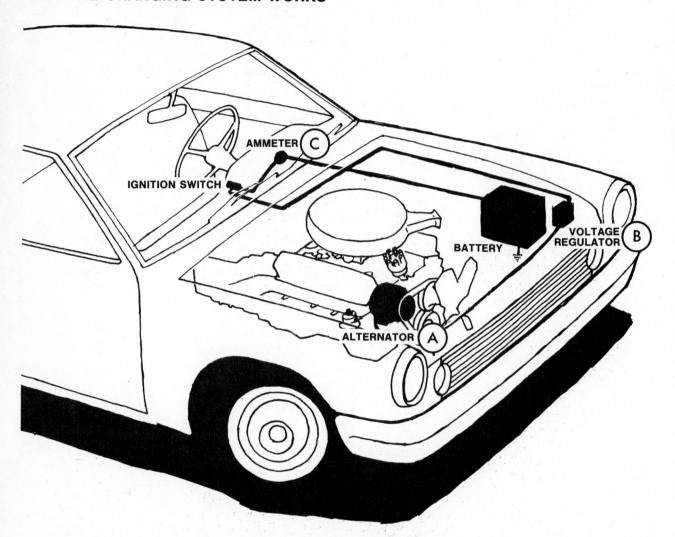

The charging unit, either a generator or alternator (A), is operated by a belt running from the pulley on the engine crankshaft. When the engine is running, the rotation of the crankshaft turns the charging unit at a speed high enough to produce sufficient electrical energy to charge the battery and run all other electrical parts.

NOTE: NOT ALL CHARGING SYSTEMS ARE COMPLETELY EFFICIENT AT LOW ENGINE SPEEDS. IDLING MAY CAUSE REDUCED OUTPUT.

As engine speed varies, the output of the charging unit varies. The regulator (B) is a device which controls two major functions. First, it controls the amount of current being returned to the battery to charge it. Second, it controls the voltage output of the charging unit to prevent damage to the system. The ammeter (C) or warning light, a meter that measures amps (units of charging current), is mounted inside the car where it is visible to the driver.

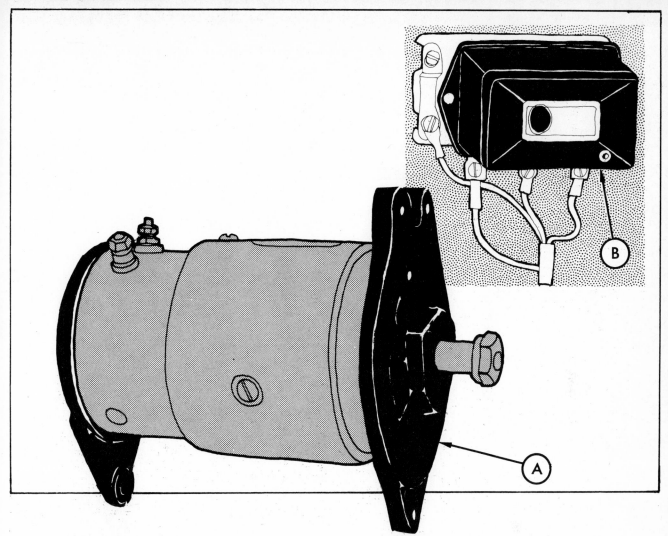

The automotive generator (A) is a mechanical device that produces a supply of electricity. As electrical equipment goes, it is a fairly simple machine. Let's take a look at the operation of the ignition coil again. When the ignition points open, the collapsing magnetic field in the primary side of the coil induces a high voltage and a flow of current in the secondary side of the coil. This is true even though there is no direct electrical connection between the two. The process is called induction.

In the generator, this process takes the form of a coil which rotates past the magnetic field to produce the effect of a rising and falling magnetic field, as though it were being turned on and off like the primary side of an ignition coil. Each time the coil of wire moves through the magnetic field, a voltage is produced and current flows. By using a number of magnetic fields and a number of loops of wire, it is possible to produce the amount of electric voltage and current needed to charge the battery and power the electrical equipment of the automobile.

The rotating coils of wire inside the generator are called the armature. Along with some small magnets to provide the initial magnetic field, there are electromagnetic coils attached to the case of the generator. These are known as field coils. Once the generator is in motion, part of the electricity developed is fed back to the field coils to increase the magnetic fields, thereby increasing the output of the generator.

If there were no controlling force, the generator would produce a higher and higher voltage as engine speed increased. The voltage regulator is designed to prevent this. The voltage regulator (B) controls the electricity fed back to the field coils and keeps the output of the generator constant over a wide range of engine speeds. The voltage regulator also has two other functions. First, it controls the amount of current directed to the battery to prevent overcharging the battery, and second, it cuts off the circuit when the engine is not running. In generator systems, the voltage regulator is a separate unit.

THE ALTERNATOR

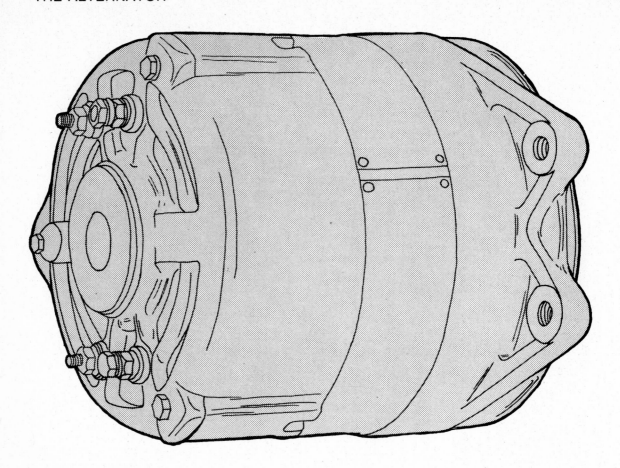

After the kind of generator just described had been in use for many years, another form of generator was designed. It's called an alternator. This unit, used in most modern automobiles, is much more efficient. It is generally lighter and smaller than a generator but capable of delivering the same amount of power.

The alternator works on the same physical principles as the generator, but the mechanical arrangement is different. Instead of fixed magnetic fields and rotating armature coils, the alternator used fixed coils inside the case, and the magnetic field is produced in the rotating shaft at the center of the alternator.

In both the generator and the alternator, the movement of the coils relative to the magnetic field (it makes no difference which actually moves as long as there is a movement of one relative to the other) produces a voltage which rises and falls. As it rises and falls, the polarity of the voltage changes. This produces an alternating (AC) current (one that reverses direction) exactly like that used in house lighting and appliances. This current cannot be used by the battery or other automobile equipment, as they all work on direct current (DC).

In the generator, this difference in currents is taken care of by the way the electricity is picked off the armature. The contacts in the generator are called brushes. They ride on a rotating contact on the end of the armature called the commutator. The commutator is divided into segments so that at any one time, the brushes are only in contact with the output of one coil. This arrangement allows current to be drawn in only one direction, converting the AC output to a DC output.

In the alternator, since the coils which produce the electrical current are fixed and do not rotate, some other method had to be found to convert the AC output to DC. It was accomplished by a solid-state device called a rectifier. In early alternators, this was a separate piece of equipment, but in later models, it is physically part of the alternator unit.

The voltage regulation of the alternator is handled by a separate regulator, but unlike the regulator of the DC generator, the one for the alternator is often a solid-state (transistorized) unit.

TROUBLESHOOTING THE GENERATOR CHARGING SYSTEM

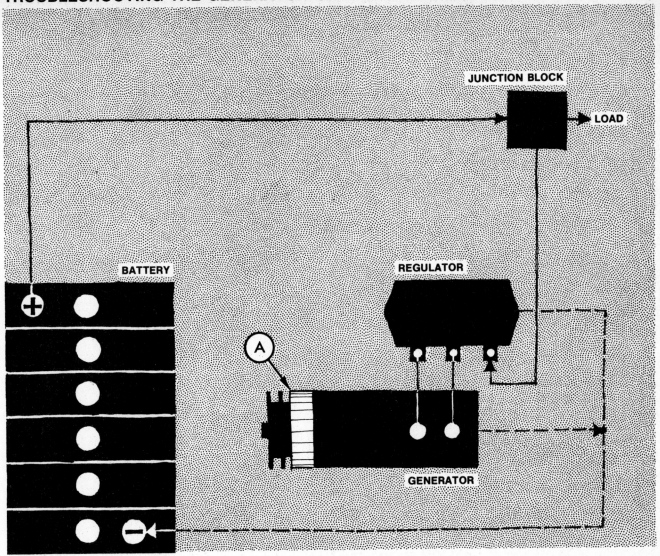

Even without any test equipment you can often locate troubles in the charging system of your automobile. Remember, *check the obvious first!* Symptoms of charging system trouble are: hard starting (check starting system also) and a low ammeter reading or warning light that comes on or stays on at all times. Also, a battery that frequently requires charging is a good sign of a charging system malfunction, but the battery itself should always be checked first. If instrument lights burn out frequently, it can mean that the voltage is too high. Headlights that brighten and dim as engine speed varies are a sign of charging system problems too.

One of the most common problems in the charging system is a drive belt that is too loose. These belts stretch with use and can become loose enough to slip, allowing the generator to slow down past the point where it can deliver the required amount of current to the system. Look for shiny or glazed sides on the belt where it comes in contact with the sides of the pulleys. The generator is mounted in such a manner that it can be adjusted to increase or decrease the tension on the belt. The shop manual will give the required tension. Don't tighten the belt too much. This can cause generator bearing failure by imposing too heavy a side load on the armature shaft. If the belt appears to be torn or cracked, replace it. If it has been slipping and the surfaces have been glazed by heat, consider changing it. The price is low, and a glazed belt is sure to fail at some later time.

Check all wiring connections, starting with the battery cables. Look for corrosion, loose connections and frayed or broken wires between the battery, generator and voltage regulator. If the car will run, start it and listen to the generator for possible noisy, dry bearings or the sound of something rubbing, such as the cooling fan blades (A) on the front of the generator.

If everything appears okay, you can then eliminate the battery as a source of trouble by performing the cranking voltage check as outlined in the chapter on starting systems.

SINGLE CONTACT

DOUBLE CONTACT

A quick check of the generator charging system is possible, using a multimeter to measure the output of the generator. By connecting a jumper wire to the FLD terminal on the voltage regulator (see the test opposite), then connecting the other end of the jumper wire to ground, the voltage to the field coils in the generator is cut off. This step makes it easy to determine if the problem is in the regulator or in the generator itself.

There are two different voltage regulator designs. These are called "A" circuit regulators and "B" circuit regulators. Most General Motors cars (Chevrolet, Buick, etc.) have the A circuit. Ford cars usually have the B circuit regulator.

Both kinds of regulators are available in two styles, a single-contact model and a double-contact model. The double-contact voltage regulator is usually associated with a heavy-duty generator system, but it is becoming more common on standard automobiles, especially those with accessory equipment such as air conditioners or power seats and windows. This gives the troubleshooter a total of four different types of regulator that he may have to check. If you are uncertain which type your car has, check the outside cover. Many regulators are so marked on the outside. If the voltage regulator is unmarked, refer to the shop manual for your car or remove the cover and examine the voltage limiter relay (B). The voltage limiter relay is usually on one end of the regulator rather than being in the middle. Examine the contacts (A). If there is more than one set of contacts on the voltage relay, it is a double model.

CAUTION: REMOVE THE GROUND (-) CABLE FROM THE BATTERY BEFORE RE-MOVING THE REGULATOR COVER TO AVOID ELECTRICAL SHOCK OR DAMAGE TO THE REGULATOR.

TESTING THE "A" CIRCUIT SINGLE-CONTACT SYSTEM

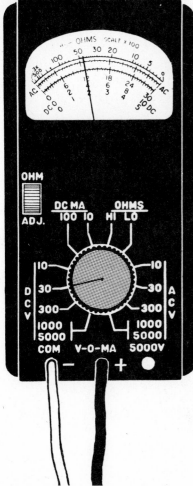

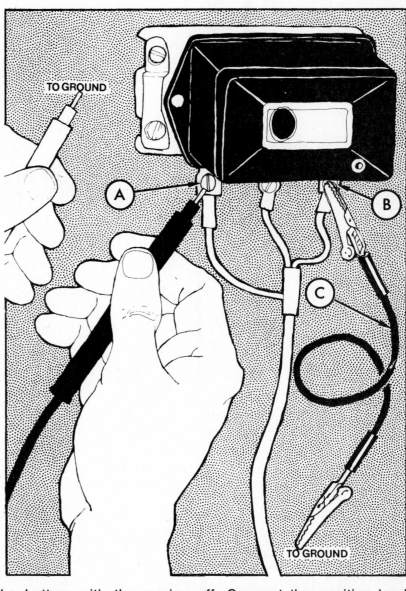

The multimeter shown here and elsewhere in this book is designed to represent a multiple-function volt/amp/ohm/meter. There are several types of such multimeters available through auto parts stores and tune-up equipment sales outlets.

Using the multimeter, check the battery with the engine off. Connect the positive lead (+) of the multimeter to the positive post of the battery. Connect the negative lead (-) of the multimeter to the negative post. Measure the battery voltage. The voltage should be between 11.5 and 12.5 volts (for a 12-volt battery).

Connect the positive lead of the multimeter to the BAT terminal (A) of the regulator. Attach the negative lead to a good ground on the engine, and connect a jumper wire (C) from the FLD terminal (B) to ground. Set the meter selector switch to read in the 15- to 20-volt range.

CAUTION: DO NOT EXCEED THE FOLLOWING VOLTAGES BY MORE THAN ONE VOLT. BRING THE ENGINE RPM UP SLOWLY TO AVOID OVERVOLTAGE.

Start the engine and accelerate it until the voltage reads 15.4 volts for a 12-volt system or 7.8 volts for a six-volt system.

If attaching the ground to the FLD terminal of the voltage regulator brings the charging voltage up to the required voltage, the regulator is bad. If grounding the FLD terminal seems to have no effect on the measured voltage, the generator is at fault.

TESTING THE "A" CIRCUIT DOUBLE-CONTACT SYSTEM

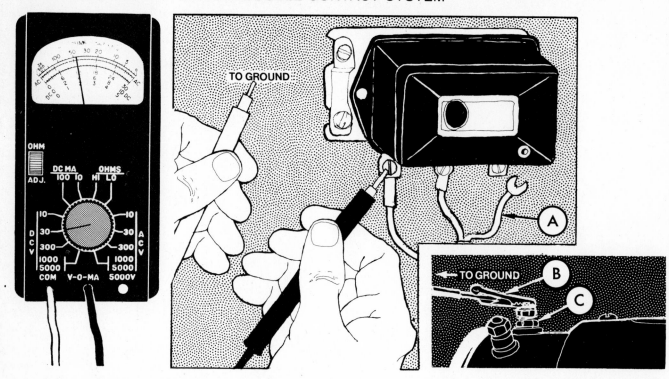

Connect the multimeter in the same manner as in the single-contact check. *Do not* ground the FLD terminal of the regulator. Disconnect the FLD lead (A) from the regulator. Then connect a jumper wire (B) from the FLD terminal on the generator (C) to a good ground. Perform the rest of this check as in the single-circuit check. The voltage readings obtained in this test should be the same as for the single-circuit check.

TESTING THE "B" CIRCUIT SINGLE-CONTACT SYSTEM

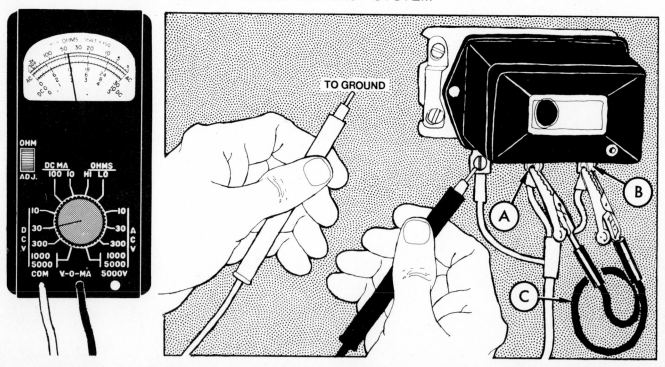

Connect the multimeter as in the previous two tests. Connect a jumper wire (C) between the OUT (A) and FLD (B) terminals of the regulator. Then proceed as in the first two tests. The voltage readings obtained should be the same as in the above two tests too.

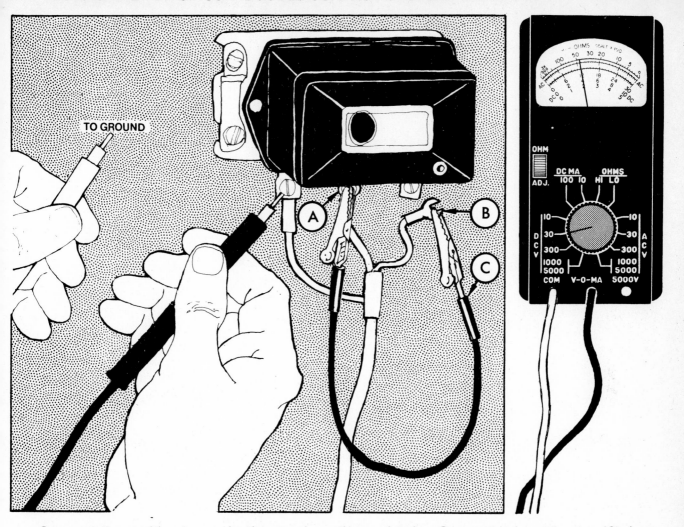

Connect the multimeter as in the previous three checks. Connect a jumper wire (C) from the OUT terminal (A) to the end of the field lead (B) that is disconnected.

NOTE: THE ARMATURE TERMINAL ON THE VOLTAGE REGULATOR MAY BE MARKED "ARM" OR "OUT."

This check is done in the same manner as before, except for the test connections shown. The voltage readings obtained should be the same as in the first check.

After you are satisfied which of the two units is at fault, the generator or the voltage regulator, refer to the shop manual for repair instructions.

TROUBLESHOOTING THE ALTERNATOR CHARGING SYSTEM

The alternator does the same job as the generator; it charges the battery and provides all electricity for the automobile while it is running. Because of physical differences in the construction of alternators and generators, the alternator cannot be handled and checked in the same manner as the generator. Care must be taken to avoid damage to the diodes, which change the alternating current (AC) produced by the alternator into direct current (DC) for use in the electrical system.

NOTE: NEVER GROUND OR SHORT THE TERMINALS ON ANY ALTERNATOR CHARGING SYSTEM.

After carrying out all of the normal visual checks of the system described in the generator section, you can perform an output check of the alternator which is similar to the ones just performed on the generator.

ALTERNATOR CHARGING CHECK

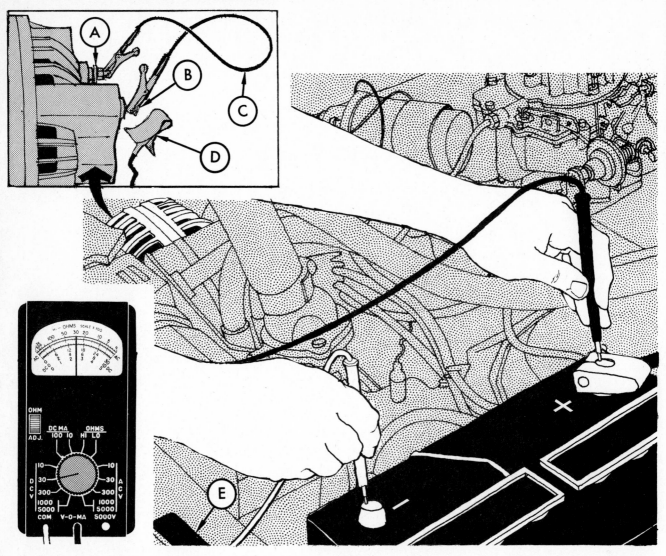

Before starting the hookup of the multimeter for the check, disconnect the ground (-) cable from the battery to remove all electricity from the charging system.

On alternators with separate voltage regulators, remove the FLD lead (D) and tape it to prevent accidental grounding of the wire. Connect a jumper wire (C) between the FLD terminal (B) on the alternator and the alternator OUT terminal (A).

NOTE: THE OUTPUT TERMINAL MAY BE MARKED ''BAT,'' ''B'' OR '' + ''

On models that have a protected wiring harness (the connections are inside a plastic plug), disconnect the electrical plug at the regulator and install the jumper wire between the ''F'' receptacle in the plug and the ''3'' or ''A'' receptacle in the plug instead of using the hookup shown.

CAUTION: DO NOT RUN THE ENGINE ABOVE A MEDIUM IDLE WHILE MAKING THIS CHECK. THE ALTERNATOR IS RUNNING WITHOUT PROPER CONTROL AND MAY BE DAMAGED IF ENGINE SPEED GOES TOO HIGH.

Reconnect the battery cable and connect the multimeter as shown in the drawing. Start the engine and test at idle speed or slightly above. The results should be the same as for the generator test hookups. The meter should show 15 volts charging voltage. However, even a reading of 15 volts may still leave the alternator with a short in one of the diodes (an electrical check valve that allows current to flow in only *one* direction) that changes the alternating current to direct current. Alternator voltage may come up to correct specifications with a bad diode, but the alternator won't be charging the battery properly. If after all other checks have been made, no trouble is found and the system is still not charging properly, the problem may be a bad diode. We do not recommend that you attempt to check the diodes. Take the car to a mechanic and have him check them.

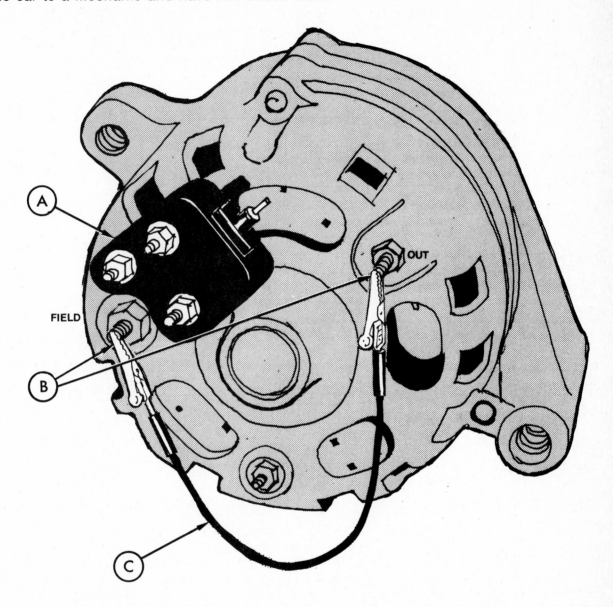

To test an alternator with an enclosed or attached regulator (A), disconnect all wires from the alternator and tape the ends to prevent accidental grounding. Connect a jumper wire (C) to the exposed terminals (B) on the alternator.

If the specified charging voltage is reached with the regulator out of action, the alternator is good. The regulator is the problem.

> **NOTE:** ENCLOSED AND ATTACHED REGULATORS ARE ON THE WAY OUT. ONE OF THE REASONS IS THAT WHEN YOU ATTEMPT TO USE JUMPER CABLES TO START YOUR CAR, YOU WILL BURN OUT THE REGULATOR UNLESS ALL LIGHTS AND ACCESSORIES ARE TURNED ON *BEFORE* DISCONNECTING THE JUMPER CABLES.

After you have discovered which of the units is bad, refer to the shop manual for repair instructions.

TROUBLESHOOTING THE FUEL SYSTEM

Compared to the electrical portions of the automobile, the equipment for storage and delivery of gasoline to the engine is quite simple. Except for the carburetor and some additional equipment installed on late-model cars to reduce emissions, the troubleshooting steps outlined here are sufficient for solving most fuel problems. However, this chapter also goes into some detail on all fuel system parts to help you pinpoint problems other than simple start/no start conditions.

As can be seen in the drawing, the fuel system contains a number of parts. Located at the rear of the car is the fuel tank (A), which contains the supply of fuel for the car. It has a filler cap and a vent (B) to allow air to enter the tank as fuel is withdrawn.

NOTE: WITH THE INTRODUCTION OF EVAPORATIVE SYSTEMS FOR EMISSION CONTROL, VENTING IS NO LONGER HANDLED IN THIS MANNER ON LATE-MODEL CARS. SEE THE SHOP MANUAL FOR SPECIFIC INSTRUCTIONS.

The fuel line (C) runs from the gas tank forward to the engine area, where it connects to a fuel pump (D) on the engine. At some point along this line, either before or after it reaches the fuel pump, there may be some sort of a filter (E) to remove dirt particles from the fuel before it goes into the carburetor. After leaving the fuel pump, the line goes to the carburetor (F), which mixes fuel and air in the correct proportions for burning in the combustion chambers. On top of the carburetor is an air filter (G), which removes dirt and other particles from the air. The action of the carburetor is controlled by a mechanical linkage (H), which runs from the carburetor into the driver's compartment and to the accelerator pedal.

TROUBLESHOOTING THE FUEL TANK AND LINES

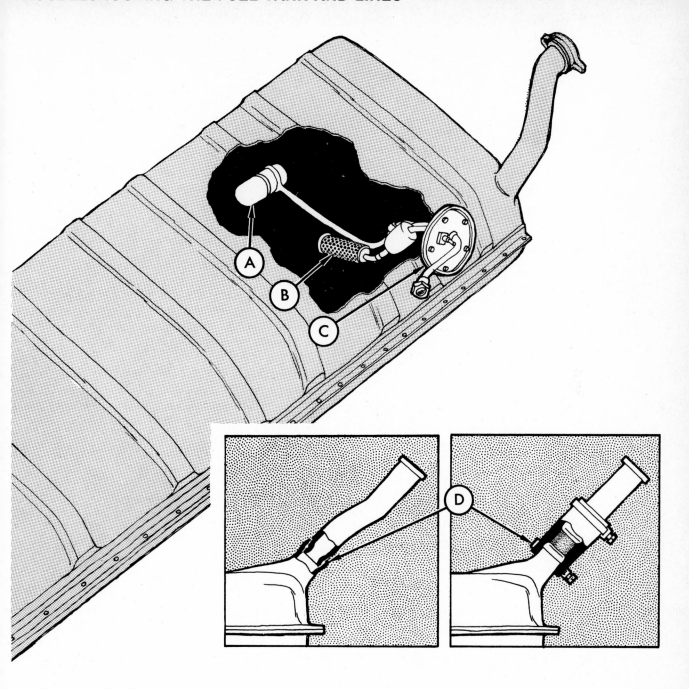

There is very little that can go wrong with the fuel tank. The tank is a metal container with a pickup unit (C) suspended in the top center of the tank. Along with this pickup is a float (A), which signals the level of the fuel to the gas gauge. These units are not normally repairable. They can be replaced, although removal of the fuel tank is required in many cases.

Actual leakage of fuel from the metal portion of the tank is rare, but leakage can occur around the attachment point of the filler neck (D) to the tank. In such cases, the repairs should be done by a qualified mechanic. Fuel flow stoppage, as outlined in the fuel system logic tree in the back of the book, is usually associated with the filter or screen (B) on the fuel pickup or inside the fuel line.

Indications of fuel leakage are the smell of gasoline around the bottom of the fuel tank and lines or discoloration caused by gas leaking down the frame of the car. On new cars with evaporative control systems, there may be several lines leading to and from the gas tank or other containers which hold gas vapors. See the shop manual for your car for specific information on troubleshooting and repairing these evaporative control systems.

TROUBLESHOOTING THE FUEL PUMP

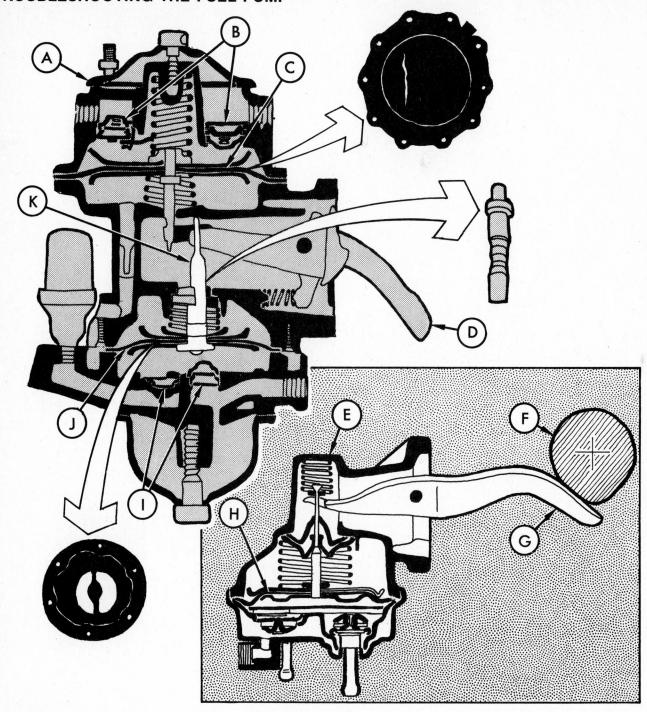

The normal fuel pump used on modern automobiles is the mechanical type (E). Some common mechanical problems that can occur in a fuel pump are:

- Worn vacuum valves and seat—diaphragm type (B)
- Punctured vacuum diaphragm (C)
- Punctured fuel diaphragm (J)
- Worn fuel valves and seats (I)
- Worn pull rod (K)
- Worn linkage (D)

Without the fuel pump to pull gas from the tank to the float bowl of the carburetor, the engine would quickly run out of fuel and stop running.

Most fuel pumps work by mechanical action through a lever (G) which contacts a portion of the camshaft (F). As the camshaft rotates inside the engine, the lever is moved up and down by the camshaft. This lever action operates a rubber diaphragm which creates suction, pulling fuel through the lines from the tank. On one stroke of the diaphragm (H), fuel is pulled into the pump through a one-way valve. On the other stroke of the pump, the fuel, which cannot return to the tank through the one-way valve, is forced out of the fuel pump to the carburetor.

On many fuel pumps, there is also a separate section (A) devoted to producing a vacuum to operate windshield wipers.

> **NOTE:** FUEL PUMPS THAT CREATE VACUUM TO RUN WIPERS ARE COMMON ON OLDER AUTOMOBILES BUT NOT ON LATE MODELS.

Many modern fuel pumps are designed to be non-repairable. These types have a crimped shell rather than a bolted shell and must be replaced if they go bad. Those types with a bolted shell can be repaired. The most common problems are a ruptured fuel diaphragm (H) or (J) or a lever (G) which is worn to such a point that it is not capable of delivering a full stroke. If the fuel pump is removed to check the lever for wear and the engine is the type that uses a small pushrod as a connection between the cam and the fuel pump, carefully check the pushrod for wear.

Carefully check all connections at the fuel pump. A leak in a line leading to or from the pump will reduce pump pressure. Steel lines can develop cracks from vibration and flex lines can rot. Below are three checks you can perform to further test the fuel pump for proper operation.

FUEL PUMP VOLUME TEST

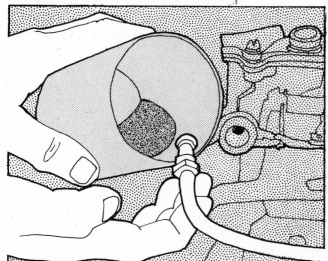

The method for checking the amount of fuel being delivered by the pump is the same as outlined in the fuel system logic tree. Remove the inlet fuel line from the carburetor. Use a container of reasonable size. Position the line so that the fuel that is pumped into the container will not spill on any hot part of the engine.

> **WARNING:** WHEN WORKING WITH DISCONNECTED FUEL LINES, A POTENTIAL FIRE HAZARD EXISTS. DISCONNECT THE HIGH-TENSION LEAD (THE CENTER LEAD) FROM THE IGNITION COIL TO PREVENT THE ENGINE FROM STARTING.

Crank the engine over while watching the fuel line (you will need a helper here). Most automobile pumps are capable of filling a pint container in 30 seconds.

> **NOTE:** MANY HIGH-CAPACITY PUMPS ON MODERN AUTOMOBILES WILL DELIVER CONSIDERABLY MORE THAN 1 PINT IN 30 SECONDS. BE SURE TO USE A CONTAINER CAPABLE OF HOLDING AT LEAST A QUART.

Measure the elapsed time and compare it to the manufacturer's specifications (see the shop manual). While the container is filling, submerge the end of the line in the fuel to see if any air bubbles are present. If there are bubbles, this is an indication of air leaks in the pump or in the lines. If your engine is equipped with a metal line between the fuel pump and the carburetor, you may have to attach a piece of flexible line to the end of the metal line in order to submerge it in the container. If the pump volume is low (pump puts out ½ pint or less in 30 seconds), the pump may be bad or there may be a restriction in the line leading from the fuel tank to the pump. Check the line carefully for signs of leaks. Then go on to the second fuel pump check: inspecting the pressure output of the fuel pump.

FUEL PUMP PRESSURE TEST

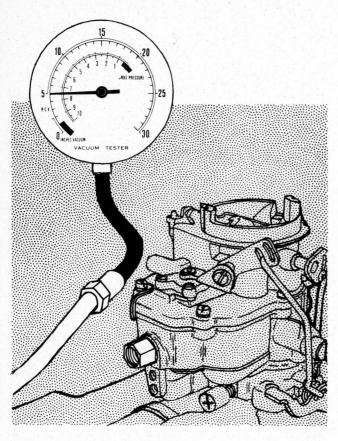

The vacuum gauge can be used to check the pressure output of the fuel pump by employing its pressure scale. Remove the fuel line at the carburetor and connect the vacuum gauge to the line. Crank the engine over and watch the gauge. The gauge should indicate the following:

- V-6's = 3.0/4.5

- Ford = 3.5/6.5

- Pinto = 3.5/4.5

- Chevy V-8, pre-1970 = 5.0/6.5

- Chevy V-8, after 1970 = 7.0/8.5

- Vega = 3.0/4.5

- Chrysler = 3.0/8.5

For all other cars, you should consult the shop manual.

On older model fuel pumps, the pressure will hold for several minutes after the engine stops, but modern fuel pumps are equipped with a pressure bleed valve which vents pressure when the engine is not running to prevent flooding the carburetor.

VACUUM TEST

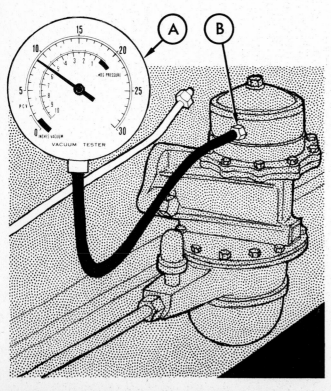

On automobiles with vacuum-assisted windshield wipers, a booster may be incorporated on the fuel pump. (Automobiles equipped with electric windshield wipers will not have this type of vacuum booster on the fuel pump.) Pumps with such a booster look like two fuel pumps, one on top of the other.

To test the vacuum side of the fuel pump, disconnect the vacuum line at the vacuum inlet (B—see the shop manual for location) and connect the vacuum gauge (A) to the inlet. Start the engine and run it at a fast idle (1,000 rpm). The gauge should show a reading of 8 to 10 inches of vacuum. Stop the engine. The vacuum reading should fall off slowly.

Rapid decline of vacuum indicates a leak in the pump or vacuum system. If windshield wiper action in vacuum-powered wipers is sluggish, the check shows a rapid reduction of vacuum after the test or the test fails to provide the proper vacuum reading, the vacuum section of the fuel pump is bad or there is a leak in the lines. Consult the shop manual for information on repairing or replacing the vacuum booster section or the entire fuel pump.

TROUBLESHOOTING FUEL FILTERS

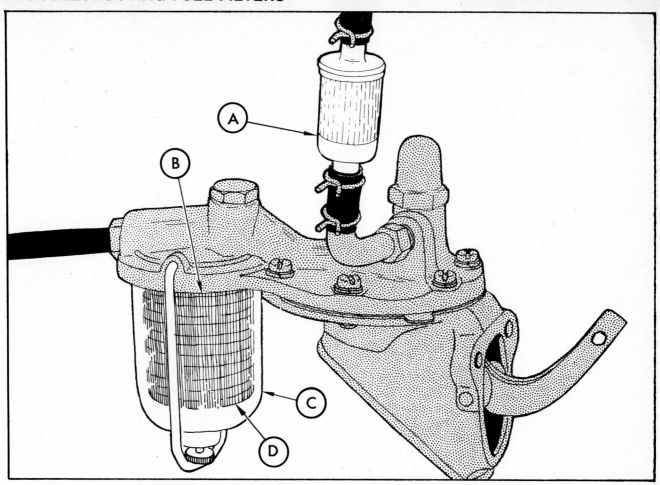

Fuel filters generally come in two types: an in-line filter (A), which is put into the line between the fuel pump and the carburetor; and a sediment-bowl kind (B), which is part of the fuel pump housing. In either case, clogging by dirt or sediment can block the flow of fuel to the engine.

In-line filters are designed to be a throwaway item. The cost of replacement is low, and if clogging is suspected, the filter should be removed and a new one installed.

The sediment bowl is a glass bowl (C) held in place on the fuel pump by a clamp and hold-down screw. Inside the bowl is a filter element (D) which, in most cases, is washable in gasoline.

NOTE: USE CAUTION WHEN REPLACING THE SEDIMENT BOWL FILTER. THE GASKET MUST PROVIDE A PERFECT SEAL TO PREVENT GAS LEAKAGE.

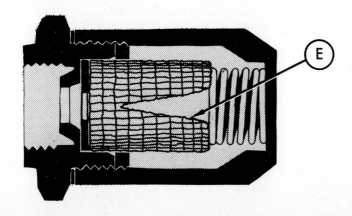

Another washable fuel filter (E) is often found in the fuel inlet fitting of many modern carburetors. This is a short filter of fine brass mesh which will filter out large particles of dirt and grit to prevent them from entering the carburetor. In many cases, the inlet fitting on the carburetor must be removed to get at the filter element. Check the shop manual for information on cleaning or replacement.

TROUBLESHOOTING THE CARBURETOR

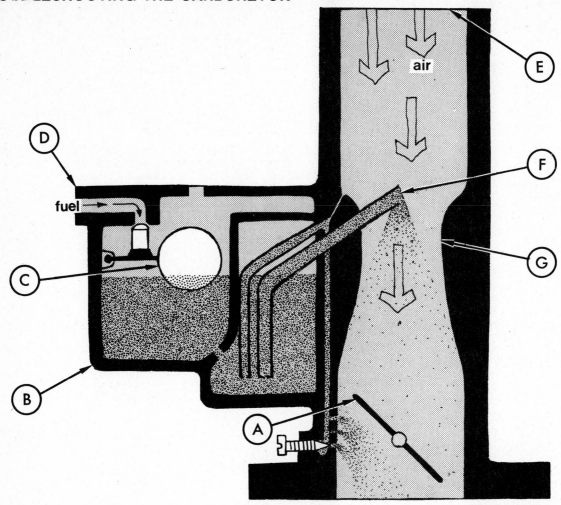

The most important single element in the fuel system is the carburetor. Its job is to provide the engine with the proper air/fuel ratio for a wide range of operating conditions.

The carburetor operates on a simple physical principle. Air drawn into the engine by the downward suction of a piston in a cylinder enters the top of the carburetor bore (E). As the air travels downward in the bore, it passes through a slight narrowing of the bore known as the venturi (G). As the air passes through the venturi, it speeds up. This speedup of the air causes a slight drop in pressure in the venturi. The drop in pressure pulls gas from the float bowl (B) through a nozzle (F) into the bore of the carburetor. At this point, the fuel mixes with the air, forming a fine spray of atomized particles. This air/fuel mixture passes through the carburetor into the intake manifold, which distributes the mixture to the cylinders for compression and burning.

As pressure is reduced in the venturi, it causes fuel to be pulled from the float bowl (B). The falling level of the gas causes the float (C) to drop. The float controls a valve called the needle and seat (D), which opens to allow more fuel to enter the float bowl from the fuel pump. This self-metering system keeps a constant supply of fuel available to the carburetor.

Below the point where the fuel enters the bore is a movable plate. This throttle plate (A) is controlled by the linkage attached to the gas pedal. The opening and closing of the throttle plate controls the amount of air that can pass through the bore and also controls the fuel that is drawn into the air stream. As the throttle plate opens, the air volume entering the intake manifold increases and draws in more fuel, due to the increasingly low pressure created by the venturi. This action causes the engine to speed up and deliver more power. If the throttle plate closes, the amount of air that can enter the engine drops, causing a lessening of the partial vacuum of the venturi, and less gas is pulled into the bore. This is the basic metering system that controls the overall carburetor operation.

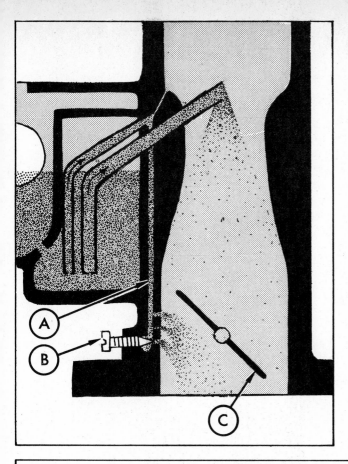

When the engine is running at idle speed or with only slight foot pressure on the gas pedal, the throttle plate is nearly closed. This reduces the intake of air below the point where it will pull fuel from the float bowl through the main metering nozzle. A separate fuel path called the idle circuit (A) is necessary. When the engine is running at idle, the vacuum or low-pressure area is not at the venturi, but is most strongly felt below the throttle plate (C). By providing another route for gas to enter the carburetor bore below the throttle plate, sufficient fuel can enter the engine for idle and low-speed operation.

Fuel is drawn through a passageway from the float bowl by the low pressure to a point below the throttle plate. There is an external adjusting screw, called the idle mixture screw (B), located on the outside of the carburetor near the base. This screw regulates the amount of fuel available at the port. Another adjustment screw, the idle speed screw, is also located on the outside of the carburetor. The idle speed screw controls the position of the throttle plate over a small range to adjust the amount of air that is allowed to enter the engine.

NOTE: THE IDLE SPEED ADJUSTMENT MAY ALSO BE CALLED THE THROTTLE STOP.

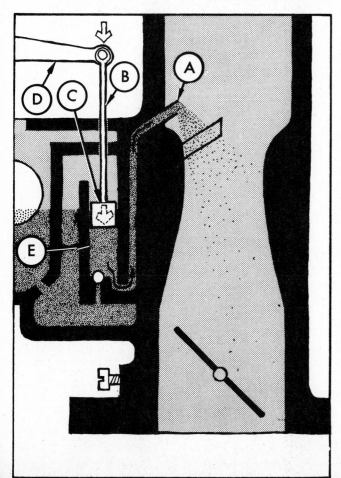

In some carburetors, a slightly different system is used, one that allows the throttle plate to close completely and routes air through a passageway around the plate to provide idle air flow.

When the throttle is opened suddenly while the engine is idling or running at a steady speed above idle, the rush of additional air into the engine upsets the balance of air to fuel. The fuel, being heavier, cannot respond as quickly as the air. To offset this, another system, called the accelerating pump (B), is used. This consists of an external linkage (D) attached to the throttle and a plunger (C) inside a well (E) filled with gas from the float bowl. When the gas pedal is depressed, the action of the linkage forces the fuel in the accelerator pump well to shoot out of a port (A) into the air stream in the bore. This momentary addition of fuel corrects the imbalance and permits the engine to function normally until the increased suction in the venturi starts drawing more gas from the main nozzle.

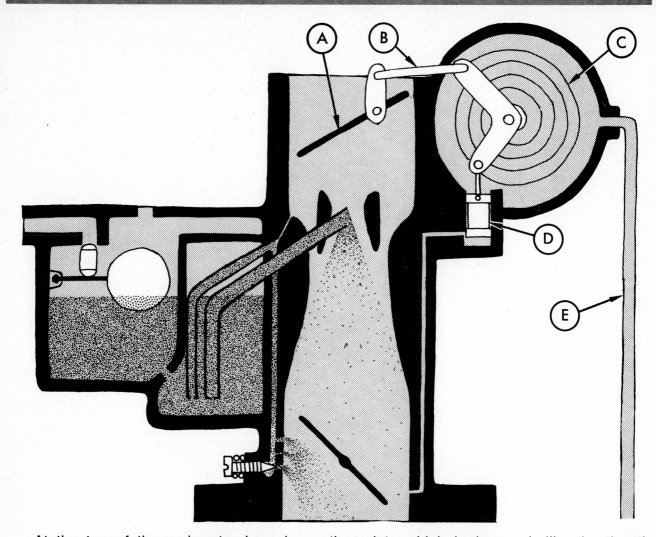

At the top of the carburetor bore is another plate which looks much like the throttle plate. This is the choke plate (A). The choke is used to help the engine start when it is cold and keep it running until the engine warms up to operating temperature.

When the engine is cold, the fuel tends to drop out of the air/fuel mixture and cling to (condense on) the interior surfaces of the intake manifold and the carburetor. This disturbs the balance of air to fuel. To prevent this problem from affecting the engine, the choke plate closes, cutting down on the intake of air. This creates a mixture richer in fuel and aids starting. The choke can be manually or automatically operated. Some older cars and trucks may have a manual choke controlled by a knob on the dashboard, but modern vehicles have an automatic choke. The automatic choke shown has a choke plate (A) which is connected to the thermostatic coil spring (C) by a linkage (B). On the other side of the linkage is a choke piston (D). Connected to the body of the choke housing is a tube (E) that runs to the heat stove.

Closing the choke is accomplished by the thermostatic coil (C). The spring is made of a material which relaxes when heated. To set the choke on most cars (when starting a cold engine), depress the gas pedal firmly, all the way to the floor. This positions the linkage to shut the choke plate in the carburetor bore. It also slightly increases the idle speed for cold engine warmup. While the engine is starting, the choke remains closed to block off most of the incoming air. This provides the engine with a rich fuel mixture. As soon as the engine starts, the choke must be opened partway to allow enough air for idle operation. The choke piston does this. By using the vacuum in the lower part of the throttle bore, the choke piston is pulled down, moving the linkage to open the choke slightly. As the engine warms up, the thermostatic spring is warmed by air coming from the heat stove, which is a metal box close to one exhaust manifold. The spring relaxes and opens the choke all the way once the engine has reached operating temperature.

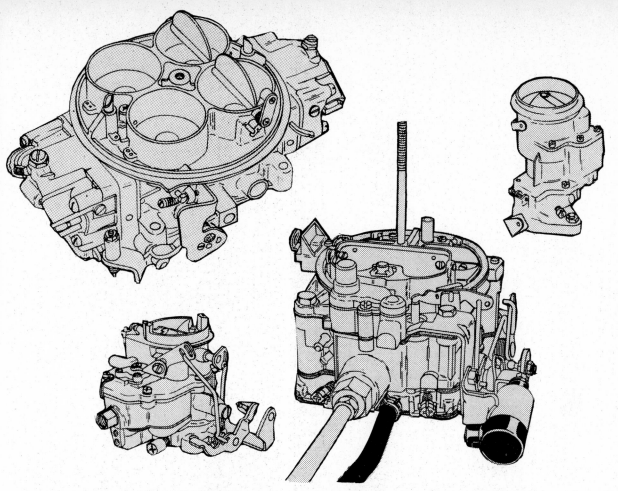

Generally, this is how the carburetor functions. Each automobile uses a different type of carburetor. It may have a combination of one, two, three or four barrels or bores and many extra parts, due to the requirements of fuel metering and emission controls. For more information, see Petersen's BASIC CARBURETION AND FUEL SYSTEMS or consult the shop manual for your particular car.

Because of the complexity of the carburetor and the fact that many of the adjustments are sealed to prevent upsetting the emission control system, most carburetor work is beyond the scope of this book. However, we have included a few simple checks to help you determine if your carburetor is in good working order.

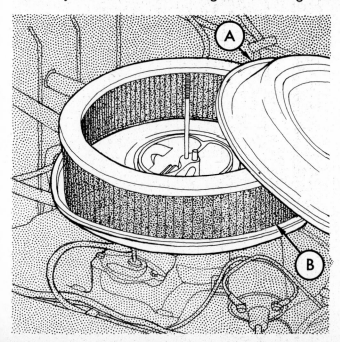

1. To gain access to the carburetor, remove the air cleaner cover (A). This is the large metal cover on top of the carburetor. Usually the air cleaner is fastened by a single bolt or nut in the center. There may be several hoses or other connections to the air cleaner that must be removed. These are parts of the emission control system. Examine the filter element (B) in the air cleaner. If it is dirty or oily, it may be a cause of carburetor problems. Look carefully at the outside of the carburetor and check the linkage to see that it moves freely. Stains of gas or buildups of grease or dirt on the outside of the carburetor can indicate leaks in the gaskets. If the inside of the carburetor bores are extremely dirty, the carburetor is in need of disassembly and cleaning. Examine all lines, rubber and metal, that lead to the carburetor for cracks or crimps that may cause fuel flow problems to the carburetor.

TROUBLESHOOTING THE FUEL SYSTEM

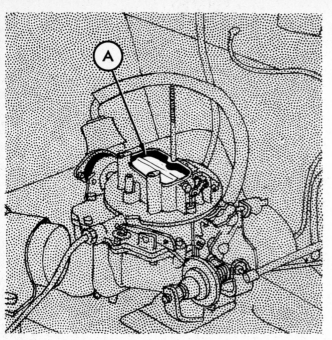

2. A quick check of choke operation may be made by checking the position of the choke plate (A) when the engine is off. The plate should be nearly closed.

> **NOTE:** ON SOME CARS, THE CHOKE MAY BE IN A CENTER POSITION IN THE CARBURETOR WHEN THE ENGINE IS NOT RUNNING. DEPRESS THE GAS PEDAL FIRMLY TO THE FLOOR AND RELEASE IT. THE CHOKE PLATE SHOULD NOW BE NEARLY CLOSED. IF THE CHOKE DOES NOT MOVE FREELY, EXAMINE THE LINKAGE TO SEE IF IT IS BINDING. THE CHOKE LINKAGE IS ADJUSTABLE EITHER BY LOCK NUT OR BY BENDING. SEE YOUR SHOP MANUAL FOR INFORMATION ON ADJUSTMENT.

With the choke closed, start the engine and let it warm up to normal operating temperature. As the engine warms, the choke should slowly open to allow more air to enter the engine.

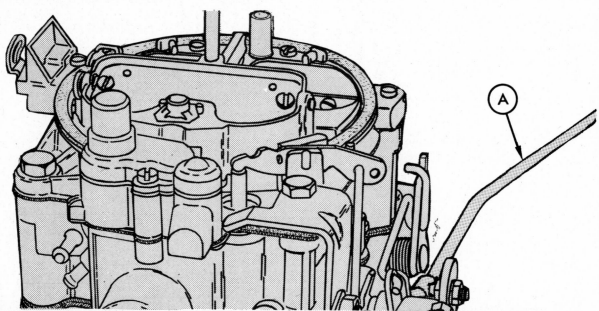

> **WARNING:** THE ENGINE SHOULD BE TURNED OFF WHEN YOU CHECK THE ACCELERATOR PUMP TO PREVENT POSSIBLE ACCIDENT OR INJURY FROM ENGINE FIRE.

3. The action of the accelerator pump may be checked by grasping the throttle linkage (A) and operating it quickly while looking into the carburetor. If a spray of gas can be seen when the linkage is pulled, the accelerator pump is working.

> **NOTE:** IF NO GAS IS OBSERVED SQUIRTING INTO THE BORE, THE TROUBLE COULD ALSO BE THAT THERE IS NO GAS IN THE FLOAT BOWL. CHECK THE FUEL PUMP AND FUEL LINES TO SEE IF GAS IS REACHING THE CARBURETOR.

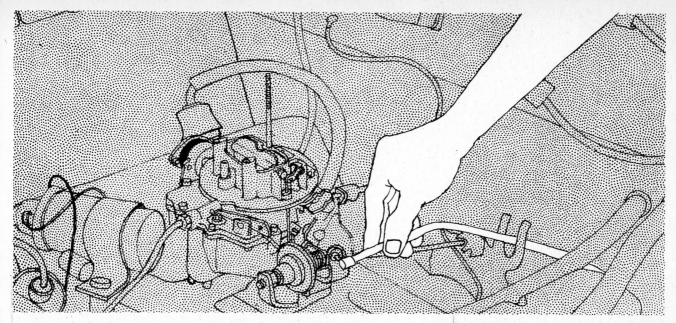

4. Checking the air/fuel ratio of the carburetor requires a specialized piece of test equipment called an exhaust gas analyzer (see Petersen's AUTOMOTIVE TUNE-UP AND TEST EQUIPMENT). However, the following simple check can give you a good idea of whether your carburetor is performing correctly and if it needs adjustment or overhaul.

Remove the air cleaner to expose the top of the carburetor. Put the transmission in neutral and set the emergency brake. Start the engine and let it warm up to operating temperature. In one hand, grasp the throttle linkage and pull until the engine speed comes up to about what it would be at a road speed of 30 mph (this does not have to be exact). Place your other hand or a piece of stiff cardboard over the carburetor and slowly lower it to close off part of the carburetor's flow of air. If the engine slows down very slightly, the carburetor is properly adjusted. If the engine speeds up slightly, it is too lean (not enough fuel). If it doesn't speed up at all, the mixture is too rich (too much fuel). Either of the second two conditions indicates that the carburetor needs adjustment or work. See your shop manual or your local mechanic.

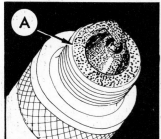 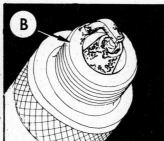

5. Spark plugs can also be an indicator of air/fuel ratio. This ratio should be roughly 12.5:1 to 14.5:1 (air to fuel). Spark plugs that are white or show evidence of burning (A), indicate a lean condition. Plugs that are covered with a soft, black, sooty deposit of imperfectly burned fuel show a too rich condition (B).

NOTE: THESE SPARK PLUG READINGS CAN ALSO BE CAUSED BY OTHER PROBLEMS. REFER TO THE CHAPTER ON IGNITION SYSTEMS.

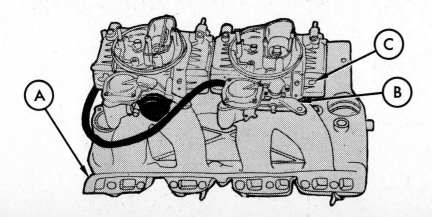

6. A persistent lean reading accompanied by low power may indicate a vacuum leak at the base of the carburetor (B) or around the intake manifold on top of the engine (A). Leaking vacuum lines, clogged vents for the float bowl (C) and the wrong internal metering parts in the carburetor can also cause the car to run lean.

TROUBLESHOOTING EMISSION CONTROLS

Emission control systems or smog controls are subject to certain problems, like all other engine components. There are several basic systems, but each manufacturer approaches the solution to pollution problems in a slightly different way, so each different brand of car may have emission control equipment that looks totally unlike that found on an automobile of another manufacturer.

Another problem that the troubleshooter should be aware of is that in many instances, the equipment is factory-adjusted. Attempts to work on the emission control system may be a violation of state or federal laws.

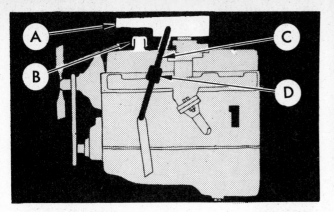
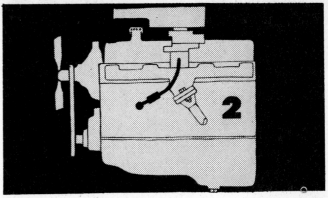

The simplest emission control system is the positive crankcase ventilation system (PCV). Before emission controls came into being, blowby fumes in the crankcase were vented to the outside atmosphere through a road breather tube. Since a large part of these fumes are unburned hydrocarbons (incompletely burned gasoline), this tube was a major source of smog. The PCV equipment stops this by routing fumes from the crankcase through a hose (C) which is equipped with a one-way valve (D) to the air cleaner (A). The oil filler cap (B) is vented to let outside air in. When the engine is running, fumes are extracted from the crankcase by engine vacuum. They are sucked into the hose, through the one-way valve and into the carburetor. They then enter the cylinders, where they are burned along with the air/fuel mixture. This system is known as the Type 1 PCV system. The Type 2 PCV system is the same except that the oil filler cap is designed to limit the intake of air to the crankcase. The valve in the Type 2 system is a diaphragm type that regulates the amount of flow according to crankcase vacuum. The Type 2 system valve keeps the crankcase at a mild vacuum to make sure all fumes are extracted under all running conditions.

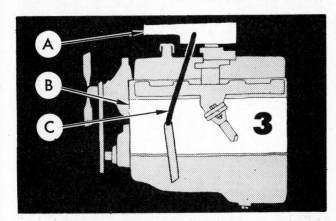
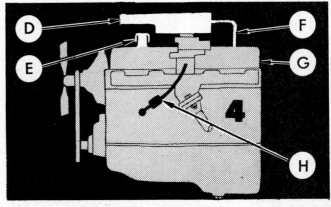

The Type 3 system is simpler in that it has no valve, simply a hose (C) running from the crankcase (B) to the air cleaner (A). The latest type, Type 4, is a combination of Types 1 and 3. A sealed oil filler cap (E) prevents fumes from escaping under zero vacuum conditions (a fault of the earlier systems). A tube (F) from the air cleaner (D) to the valve cover (G) routes fresh air to the crankcase. Air is pulled through the crankcase and into the hose connection (H) of a regular PCV tube and valve for routing back to the carburetor. When the Type 4 system is under zero vacuum (engine accelerating wide open) the flow of fumes through the PCV valve stops. Fumes are then able to enter the carburetor by flowing back up the fresh air inlet in the air cleaner.

A quick check of PCV systems is included in the section on excessive oil consumption. If you suspect malfunction of a PCV system, this check will help you be sure.

Because the PCV system picks up considerable oil fumes along with the products of blowby, the hoses, valves and flame arresters are prone to clogging. The rubber hoses themselves wear out at some point, and they can become restricted by collapsing internally or by cracking. PCV valves on some types can be checked by removing them and shaking them to see if the check ball rattles. On the types which take in fresh air through the oil filler cap, clogging of the air passage in the cap can cause problems. They should be checked and cleaned in solvent. The air cleaner is an item which should also be checked. Oil vapors entering the air cleaner housing can saturate the filter element, causing a restriction on incoming air to the carburetor.

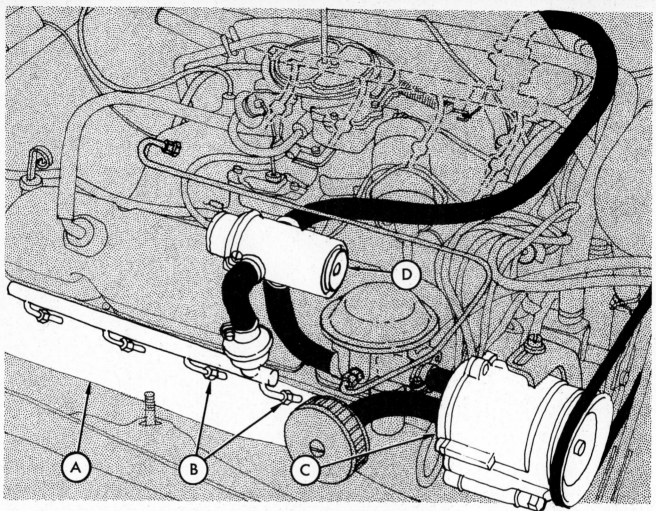

A newer form of emission control is the air injection reactor (AIR). In this system, a belt-driven pump (C) provides a flow of fresh air at approximately 1 psi (pounds per square inch). The air is directed to injection tubes (B) located on the exhaust manifolds (A). The purpose of the AIR system is to direct a stream of fresh, oxygen-filled air to the point at which the exhaust gases exit the combustion chamber.

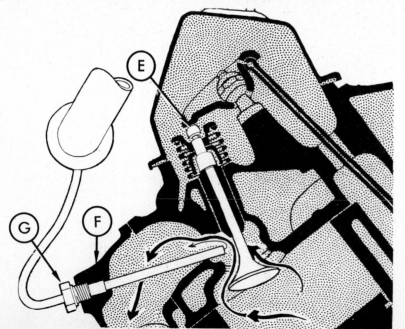

When the exhaust gases pass around the open exhaust valve (E) into the exhaust manifold (F), the stream of air entering the manifold from the air delivery tube (G) near each port mixes with it and causes it to reburn at an extremely high temperature, reducing the amount of unburned hydrocarbons. Incorporated in this system is a check valve (D), which prevents exhaust gases from getting back to the pump and damaging it.

Also a part of the AIR unit is an anti-backfire valve (A). This redirects the air from the pump when the driver lifts his foot from the throttle and prevents backfiring in the exhaust manifolds. When the gas pedal is released, the engine gets a rich mixture of fuel, which it does not burn well. This rich mixture is present in the exhaust manifolds, and if combined with the fresh air, would result in an explosion inside the exhaust manifold or pipe. The valve only operates for a moment as the driver lifts his foot from the pedal. The valve cuts off the supply of air coming into the exhaust manifold from the AIR pump until the brief period of extra-rich gas mixture passes. The system then returns to normal operation.

Troubleshooting the AIR system is not hard. The first step is to examine the belt which drives the air pump. It should be in good condition, without any glazing, cuts or signs of fraying or rotting. It should also be adjusted correctly for tension (see shop manual).

NOTE: BEARING NOISES IN AIR PUMPS ARE OFTEN DIFFICULT TO DISTINGUISH FROM NOISES IN GENERATORS AND POWER STEERING UNITS, WHICH MAY BE LOCATED NEARBY.

Some models of the pump have provisions for oiling. If so, it should be oiled periodically to be sure it turns freely. Air coming into the pump is filtered either by a small filter (B) located on the pump or by routing the air through the main air cleaner filter element on the carburetor. Pump sucking power can be checked by removing the filter and using a cigarette or match to see if the pump will draw in smoke when the engine is idling. The air pump is not an easy unit to work on. Many models cannot be disassembled without special tools. If you have a major problem, see your local mechanic.

There are a number of other emission control systems on the modern automobile engine. Some affect the operation of the ignition, others cycle exhaust gases back to the cylinders for burning. Because of the complexity of these systems and the specialized tools and knowledge involved in troubleshooting and repairing these systems, we recommend that the reader consult the shop manual on his car or see a mechanic for emission control work.

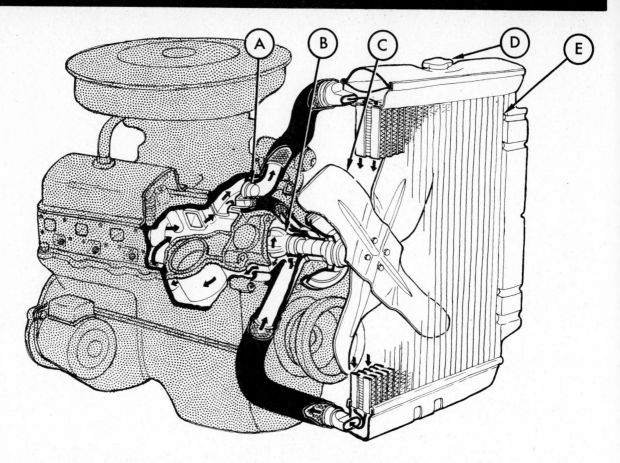

The parts of the engine cooling system are: the radiator (E), the radiator cap (D), the water pump and fan (B and C), the thermostat (A) and the hoses which connect the radiator to the engine. The water pump is driven by the same drive belt that turns the fan. Water is pumped from the bottom of the radiator into the engine by the water pump, circulated through internal passageways inside the engine block and heads to remove excess heat from the engine, then pumped out through the thermostat and upper radiator hose to the reservoir at the top of the radiator. The hot water then flows slowly down through a system of tiny tubes surrounded by fins. This is known as the radiator core. Heat is transferred from the water to the surrounding air by the fins. When the cooled water reaches the bottom of the radiator, it is again picked up by the pump and sent through the engine.

The fan assures a sufficient flow of air through the radiator fins when the car is stopped at idle or moving slowly. Without the fan to draw air over the radiator when the car is not moving fast enough for motion to do the job, the radiator would be unable to pass enough heat into the air, and the coolant would soon heat up.

The major problem in cooling systems is the buildup of rust and scale inside the cooling system. This robs the system of the ability to conduct heat away from the engine (by plugging up the tiny tubes in the radiator and jamming the thermostat closed). Scale and corrosion can be reduced by the use of special coolant mixtures (antifreeze and water) which have chemicals to reduce or prevent this buildup.

In troubleshooting the cooling system, *check the obvious first*. A breakdown of the system usually shows up first as a loss of coolant. If the temperature warning light on the dashboard or the temperature gauge show a high temperature indication, check the level of the coolant in the radiator.

WARNING: USE EXTREME CARE WHEN CHECKING THE COOLANT LEVEL IN THE RADIATOR. LET THE ENGINE AND COOLING SYSTEM COOL DOWN TO A SAFE LEVEL (LUKEWARM TO THE TOUCH) BEFORE LOOSENING THE CAP. FAILURE TO DO SO CAN RESULT IN SEVERE BURNS FROM HOT LIQUID.

If the coolant level is down, visually check the hoses and radiator for leaks or rust marks which might indicate the presence of leaks.

> **NOTE:** SOMETIMES A RADIATOR OR HOSE WILL LEAK WHEN THE ENGINE IS RUNNING AND THE SYSTEM IS UNDER PRESSURE BUT WILL NOT LEAK WHEN THE ENGINE IS SHUT DOWN.

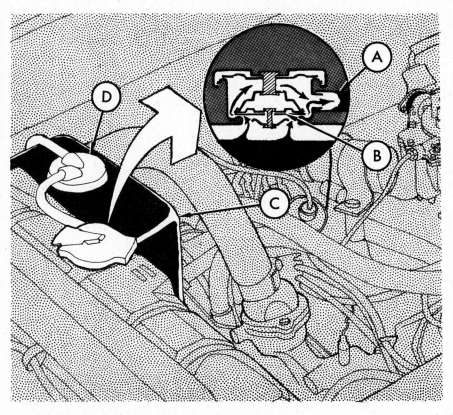

Pressure caps used to seal the cooling system maintain the closed system until pressure reaches the maximum. Then the cap opens a relief valve (B) that releases pressure to an overflow tube (A).

A newer system used on many new cars is the coolant recovery system (D). The radiator is closed at all times and under pressure. As the pressure builds up in the system (engine running), the radiator cap pressure relief valve opens and coolant escapes to a holding tank (C), instead of being lost out the drain tube. When the temperature drops in the radiator (engine off), the slight vacuum created by the drop in pressure draws the coolant back into the system.

TESTING THE RADIATOR FOR LEAKS

The radiator and hoses can be checked for leaks by using a radiator pressure tester (A). It connects to the radiator filler opening (C) and is pumped up like a tire pump. On the tester is a gauge (B) which indicates whether or not the system is holding pressure. Pay particular attention to the area of the reservoir tanks (the upper and lower portions of the radiator) for evidence of leaks around the hose connections and soldered seams.

TROUBLESHOOTING COOLING SYSTEMS

TESTING FOR INTERNAL RADIATOR LEAKS

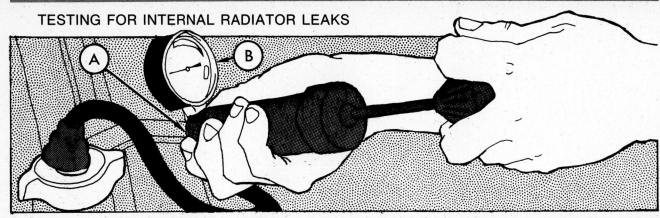

A blown head gasket or a crack in a head or cylinder wall can allow combustion gases to enter the cooling system and let coolant leak away into the cylinders. If the hot combustion gases enter the coolant, it may cause the coolant to heat up faster than normal or even boil. Using the pressure tester (A), pressurize the system to about 7 psi (B) and run the engine. Run the engine at high rpm and watch the gauge for signs of a pressure fluctuation. Fluctuation indicates a combustion leak. On V-8 engines, you can track the problem to one bank or the other by disconnecting all the wires from the spark plugs on one bank. ("Bank" refers to one cylinder head on a V-8 engine. There are four cylinders in each bank or side of the engine.) Run the engine on the other bank. (It will just barely run, but well enough for the test.) If the gauge still fluctuates, the problem is in the running bank. If the gauge does not fluctuate, the problem is in the disconnected bank of cylinders.

TESTING THE PRESSURE CAP

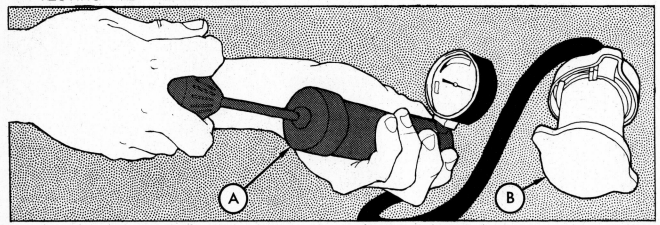

The same tester (A) used to check the radiator for leaks can be used (with a suitable adapter) to check the pressure cap (B).

TESTING THE THERMOSTAT

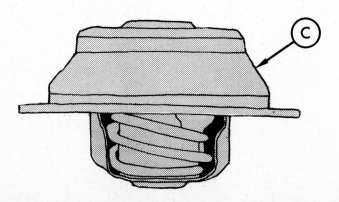

The thermostat (C) maintains the desired temperature level in the cooling system. It restricts the flow of water through the main portion of the system until the water temperature in the engine reaches the desired level. Then it opens to allow all of the coolant to circulate through the radiator. Different engines require different thermostats, each with a specific temperature range.

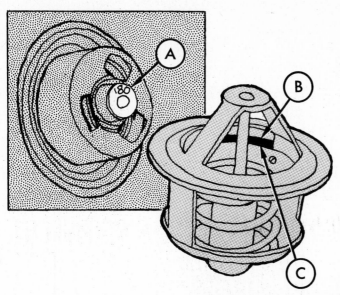

To test the thermostat, remove it from the engine (see the shop manual for removal instructions). Suspend the thermostat in a container of hot water. Use a thermometer to read the water temperature. See your shop manual for the operating temperature of the thermostat. When the water reaches this temperature, as indicated on the thermometer, the thermostat should open. To check, place a .003-inch feeler gauge between the valve (C) and seat (B) of the thermostat. When the gauge becomes loose, the water temperature should be within a few degrees of the rated temperature on the thermostat (A). If the temperature of the water rises several degrees more, the valve should open all the way (about ¼-inch). When allowed to cool, the thermostat should close. If it does not work easily, replace it.

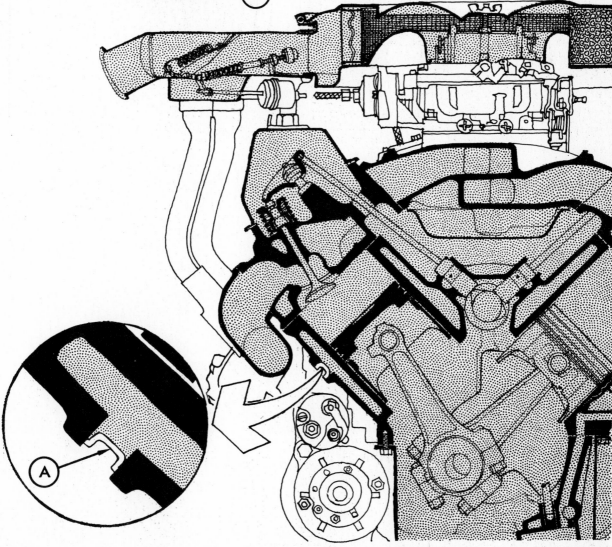

Another part of the cooling system that should be checked for signs of external leakage is the freeze plugs (A). These are small metal plugs fitted into the sides of the engine block to fill holes left by the manufacturer's casting operation. In time, these may corrode or rust and may leak. Check the shop manual for the location of these plugs and inspect them carefully.

TROUBLESHOOTING COOLING SYSTEMS

COOLING SYSTEM—COLD WEATHER OPERATION

During winter months, when temperatures fall below freezing, the cooling system should be protected from freezing by the addition of an antifreeze compound. Most of the coolants sold in automotive stores and dealerships have some antifreeze protection, but in severe weather you may need to increase the protection afforded by your coolant by adding more antifreeze. See the shop manual or owner's manual for specific information about your car's requirements.

During extended sub-zero cold, hoses and drive belts may become brittle. Both should be inspected at reasonable intervals for damage. Under certain conditions, the temperature of the coolant in the radiator may drop low enough to freeze (this is especially true if plain water or antifreeze with a high water content is being used). If your car overheats in very cold weather without any external signs of cooling system problems, this may be the reason. The answer may be to increase the concentration of antifreeze. A temporary aid to use until you can obtain additional antifreeze is to block off a part of the radiator with cardboard to restrict the flow of air through the cooling fins. This will raise the temperature of the coolant already in the radiator enough to prevent freezing.

CAUTION: BE CAREFUL WITH THIS TEMPORARY METHOD. DO NOT BLOCK SO MUCH OF THE RADIATOR THAT THE ENGINE OVERHEATS.

TROUBLESHOOTING THE WATER PUMP

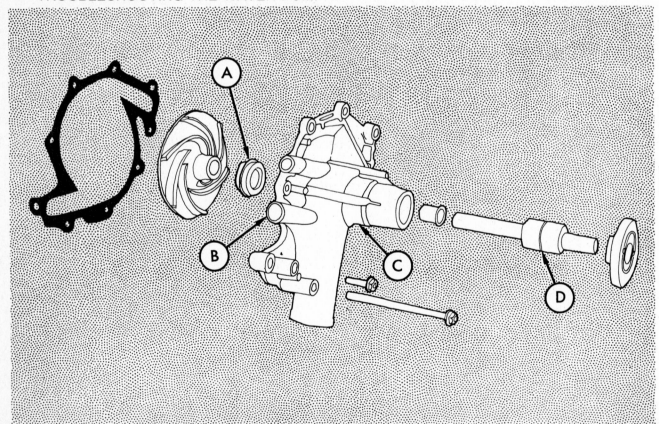

The water pump (B) on most engines is highly reliable. There isn't much that can go wrong with it except wear of the bearings (D) or loss of a seal (A), allowing the pump to leak. If you are experiencing coolant loss and cannot find any leaks in the radiator or hoses, examine the bottom of the water pump. There is a small drain hole (C) on the underside of most pumps. If the pump has a bad seal, traces of water can be seen on the front of the engine under the pump. Water pumps are not repairable without special tools. If the pump malfunctions, replace it. Also check the fan belt. A loose belt will cause the pump and fan to run more slowly than is needed for good cooling.

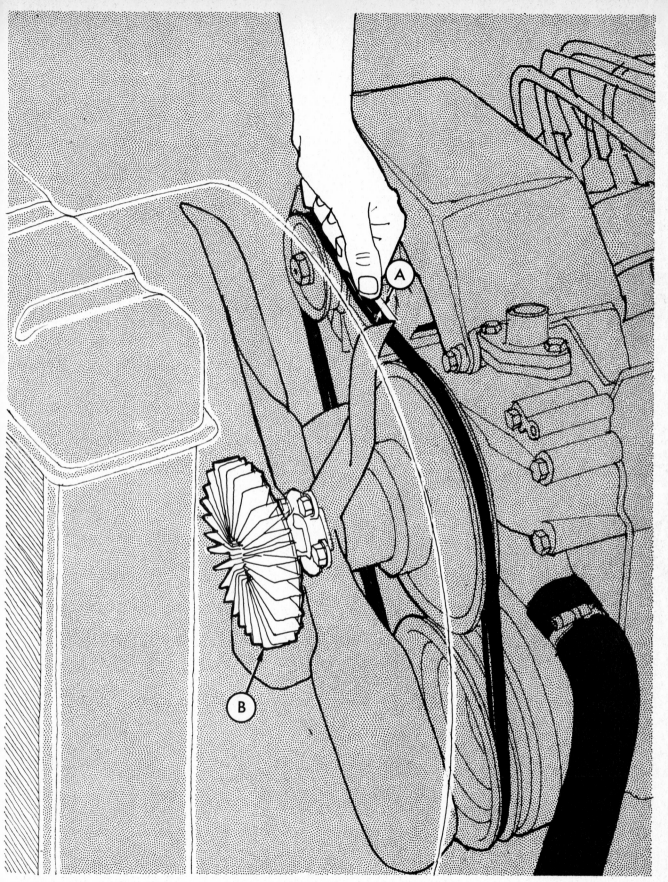

Adjust the fan belt tension according to the owner's manual or shop manual for your car. A simple rule of thumb is to keep the belt tight enough that you can move it only about ½-inch (A). Both the belt and the pump itself will often give an indication of trouble by making squealing noises. The fan itself usually causes no problem, but many fans are attached to a drive (B) that disconnects the fan when the engine is running at high rpm. If the drive fails, it can cause overheating by preventing the fan from turning at low engine rpm.

TROUBLESHOOTING FRONT SUSPENSION

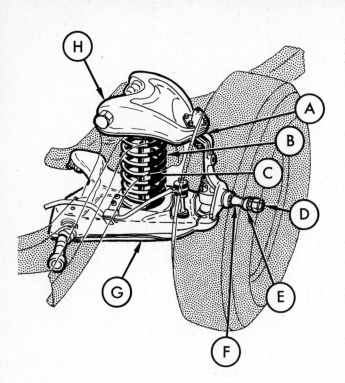

The front suspension attaches the front wheels to the frame of the car. It permits each front wheel to turn and to move up and down independently when going over bumps and dips in the road surface. Springs (B) suspend the frame and body and allow the wheels to move up and down while maintaining a ride that's as nearly level as possible. The shock absorbers (C) are designed to dampen the shock of a bump and isolate the passengers from impact. They also help keep the car level on turns.

With modern independent front suspension, the car's weight is supported by ball joints (A). These work like knee joints, allowing the suspension to flex and the front wheels to pivot. The portion on which the wheel actually rides is known as the spindle (F). The wheel is supported by bearings (E) which go over the spindle, and the wheel is retained by a large nut (D). The pivoting portions of the suspension are called control arms. These are attached to the frame and the ball joints. There is an upper control arm (H) and a lower control arm (G).

NOTE: THERE ARE MANY DIFFERENT FORMS OF SUSPENSION USED ON AUTOMOBILES. SOME DO NOT HAVE THESE KINDS OF CONTROLS; OTHERS MAY HAVE ONLY ONE CONTROL ARM. BE SURE TO EXAMINE YOUR SUSPENSION CAREFULLY OR CHECK THE SHOP MANUAL FOR FURTHER INFORMATION. ALSO SEE PETERSEN'S BASIC CHASSIS, SUSPENSION AND BRAKES.

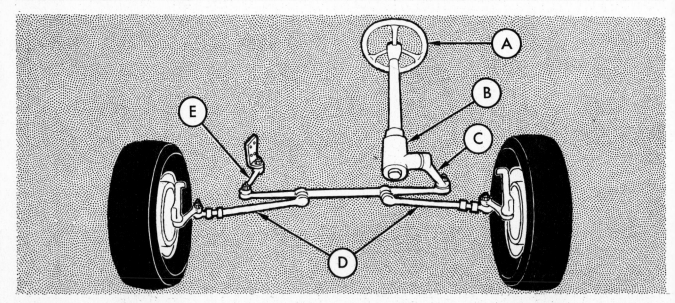

The steering system, which is connected to the front suspension, is made up of several parts. The steering wheel (A) is attached to a shaft, which runs to a gearbox called the steering box (B). The steering box transforms the movement of the steering wheel into car motion by means of the pitman arm (C). The pitman arm is attached to the spindles of both wheels by a series of rods called tie rods (D). Extra support for the steering linkage may be added by an idler arm (E).

For our purposes, it is enough to say that the wheels are controlled simultaneously by the steering mechanism and that both move in the same direction. Actually, the front wheels move in a complicated path that requires considerable automotive engineering experience just to understand, but it is not necessary to know all this to troubleshoot the suspension and steering.

The most obvious indicator of a front suspension problem is the way the car handles. Such things as poor directional stability or hard steering are easy to recognize. A quick check for front suspension problems is best accomplished by test driving the car. Select a place where you can maneuver the auto without risk of an accident. A large, empty parking lot is a better choice than the highway unless you have access to a section of lightly-traveled road.

For the test, drive the car at a speed of about 20 mph. Loosen your grip on the steering wheel so that the car is not being directed by your actions.

WARNING: IF YOU CAN SEE THE STEERING BOX MOVE WHEN THE STEERING WHEEL IS TURNED, THE BOLTS HOLDING THE STEERING BOX TO THE FRAME ARE LOOSE. THIS IS A COMMON PROBLEM ON SOME CARS AND CAN BE VERY DANGEROUS.

NOTE: DO NOT HOLD YOUR HANDS TOO FAR AWAY FROM THE STEERING WHEEL; YOU MAY NEED TO GRAB IT QUICKLY.

The car should maintain a straight course. This test is best performed where the road surface is perfectly flat. Most highways have a slight hump or "crown" in the center for water drainage. This crown will cause the car to steer to the low or outer side. Carefully notice if any vibration or chattering is fed back to the steering wheel by the suspension. A constant chatter or side-to-side movement of the steering wheel indicates that the tires are out of balance. With the car going in a straight line, make a normal turn to one side, then release pressure on the steering wheel. The car should straighten out and the steering wheel should return to center. If this doesn't happen, it could mean you have binding linkage, insufficient caster (a built-in steering angle) or insufficient steering axis inclination (another built-in steering setting). A careful check of tire surfaces will help you further diagnose front suspension problems.

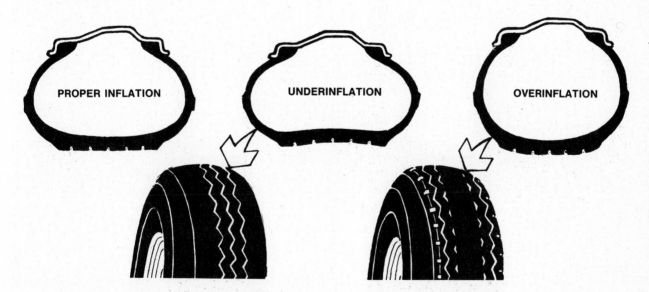

PROPER INFLATION   UNDERINFLATION   OVERINFLATION

Tire wear patterns, such as those shown in the tire wear chart, can be a helpful guide to troubleshooting suspension problems. Keep in mind that different brands and tread styles may show different wear patterns on your automobile. Make sure that the tires themselves are not part of the problem. Incorrect tire pressures, tires too wide or too narrow for the rim they are mounted on or tires that are not properly rated for the load of the vehicle can cause considerable change in wear patterns.

TROUBLESHOOTING FRONT SUSPENSION

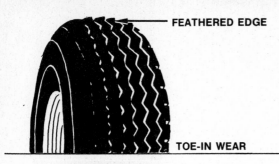

FEATHERED EDGE

TOE-IN WEAR

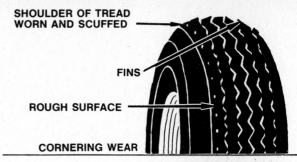

SHOULDER OF TREAD WORN AND SCUFFED

FINS

ROUGH SURFACE

CORNERING WEAR

ONE SIDE OF TREAD WORN

CAMBER WEAR

IRREGULAR DEPRESSIONS

MULTI-PROBLEM

Driving the car over a bumpy surface can give an indication of spring and shock absorber quality. A car that bounces and dips going around a corner probably has worn shock absorbers. Complete suspension travel or "bottoming out" of the suspension when going through a dip at a reasonable speed means that the car should be checked for weak springs and worn shock absorbers. Remember that most American autos have a soft suspension to give a more comfortable ride, so care must be excercised in making a judgment about suspension problems. What seems sluggish or soft may be normal ride qualities.

Excess movement or slack in the steering wheel is a trouble sign. The normal steering wheel should only move an inch or so before the car reacts. Too much "play" is a sign of a worn steering box or steering linkage.

> **NOTE:** EXCESS STEERING WHEEL PLAY CAN OFTEN BE CORRECTED BY ADJUSTING THE STEERING BOX ITSELF.

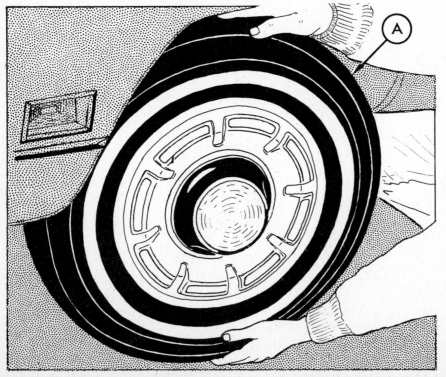

(A)

To further check the suspension, place the car on axle stands or a hydraulic hoist. Then examine the front suspension components for signs of failure or wear. One of the easiest things to check is front wheel bearing wear. Grasp the tire (A) at the top and bottom and try to move it in and out in a vertical plane. If the wheel bearing clearances are excessive, there will be obvious movement and sometimes a clunking sound as the front wheel and drum move on the spindle. Badly worn ball joints can also show up in this check, but they aren't as noticeable.

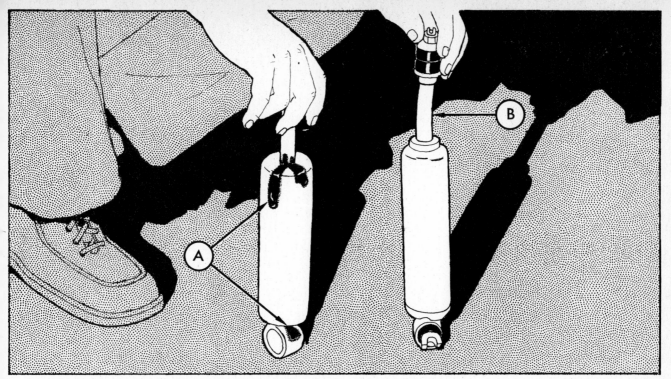

With the car raised, check the exterior of the shock absorbers for signs of oil leakage (A) or broken or bent connecting ends (B). A final check of shock absorbers can be made by removing the shock absorber from the car and testing it by hand. (See the shop manual for instructions on removing the shock absorber.) Once you have the shock removed, it can easily be tested. Grasp each end of the shock and pull or push the shock from the open position to the closed. The shock should have a smooth action but be very hard to move. If the shock is easy to operate, it is probably worn out and should be replaced.

All the steering linkage should be checked visually to determine if any components are worn or broken. If it is possible to get the automobile raised on a hydraulic rack at a service station, you may be able to check the front steering components by having one person turn the steering wheel while another watches the suspension. If you are alone, you can turn the wheels from underneath, but it is very hard.

In cases where turning the steering wheel while driving produces an audible clunking sound or a binding feeling, raise the hood and have somebody turn the steering wheel while you watch the steering box.

WARNING: IF A SEVERE FRONT SUSPENSION PROBLEM IS SUSPECTED, DO NOT TEST DRIVE THE CAR YOURSELF. TAKE IT TO A QUALIFIED MECHANIC AND LET HIM TEST DRIVE THE CAR OR CHECK IT ON HIS EQUIPMENT. FAILURE TO DO SO MAY RESULT IN AN ACCIDENT.

Some tire wear problems cannot be blamed on the suspension. If severe tire wear indicates a problem, first satisfy yourself that tire inflation is correct and that the wheels themselves are not at fault. A steel rim may become deformed after coming in contact with a curb or other solid object without the driver being aware of the problem. Out-of-round tires or out-of-balance tires and wheels can not only cause severe tire wear but can increase wear of the front suspension parts. One not too common but possible problem is nonuniform tire sizes. This can result in a car that wanders or pulls to one side and unusual tire wear. This usually occurs when the spare tire is a different size than the regular tires and is installed on one of the front wheels.

One of the most important things governing front suspension wear is lubrication. All the moving parts of the front suspension and steering systems are subjected to dirt, water and the effects of road salt in Eastern states. All joints and fittings that require lubrication should be checked carefully for fresh lubrication and should be serviced if necessary. Failure to provide adequate lubrication can result in early failure of your car's suspension and steering components.

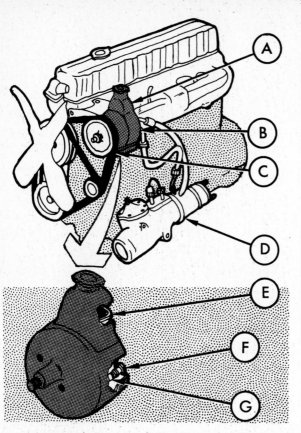

The power steering unit assists the driver by reducing the fatigue or strain of turning the steering wheel, especially at low speeds or in tight spaces where the requisite physical force may be quite high. The system consists of two basic units: the hydraulic fluid pump (A) and the steering unit (D). The power steering pump is driven by a belt (C) that may drive the air conditioning pump too. Power steering pumps usually deliver between 650 and 1,300 pounds pressure, depending on the design and type of the pump. The fluid used is a special fluid developed for this one use. In some cases, however, Type "A" automatic transmission fluid is used.

> **NOTE:** CHECK THE SHOP MANUAL OR LOOK FOR A SERVICING TAG ON THE UNIT BEFORE ADDING FLUID. NEW FLUID SHOULD ALWAYS BE OF THE TYPE RECOMMENDED BY THE MANUFACTURER.

Part of the pump assembly is taken up by a reservoir (B), which holds fluid for the system. It also incorporates a filter screen (E) inside to remove unwanted particles and foreign matter from the fluid before it goes to the steering unit.

Hoses carry the fluid from the pump to the steering unit. The smaller hose is the high-pressure hose, while the larger hose is the return line for fluid coming back to the reservoir. When fluid circulation reaches about 2 gallons per minute, the flow control valve (F) opens to form a passageway between the inlet and outlet sides of the pump, permitting excess oil to recirculate through the pump. When oil pressure exceeds a pre-set pressure limit, a relief valve (G) opens and allows fluid to flow to the inlet side of the pump and recirculate without raising the pressure in the rest of the system.

In checking out a power steering unit, be sure that any steering or handling problems are not the fault of some other part of the front suspension or steering mechanism. Once that portion of the check is satisfied, you may then turn your attention to the power steering system itself. (See the chapters on suspension and brakes.)

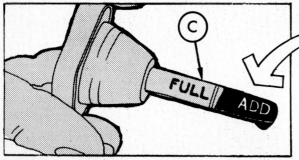

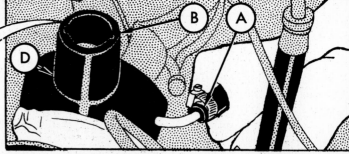

The first step is to check the power steering fluid reservoir (D). Wipe the cover before opening to prevent dirt from getting into the reservoir. Most power steering units have a small dipstick (C) built into the reservoir cap. The dipstick will show you the exact fluid level in the reservoir. If there is no specific filling level indicated on the pump or the dipstick is not legible, check the shop manual or maintain the level about 1 inch below the top of the filler opening (B). If the fluid level is very low, check the system carefully for leaks. Check all connections, hoses and joints for signs of fluid leaking out. Coverings on hoses (A) should not be frayed or cut. After you are satisfied that the system is not leaking, the next step is to check drive belt tension.

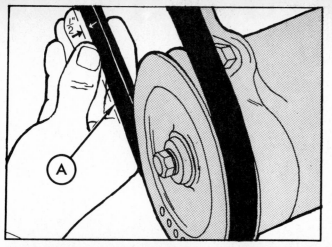

Examine the belt just as you did when checking the drive belt for the charging system (it may in fact be the same belt on some cars). Look for worn or frayed material or glazing of the sides of the belt which would indicate the belt is slipping into the drive pulleys. Belt tension (A) should be maintained at the factory recommended settings. If you can find a belt tension gauge, use it to set the tension. If not, set the belt tension just tight enough (approximately ½-inch deflection [A]) so that it doesn't slip when the steering wheel is turned all the way from side to side with the engine running.

WARNING: DO NOT REACH INTO THE ENGINE COMPARTMENT NEAR THE FAN BELTS AND PULLEYS WHEN THE ENGINE IS RUNNING. SERIOUS INJURY CAN RESULT FROM CLOTHING OR HANDS BEING CAUGHT IN MOVING PARTS.

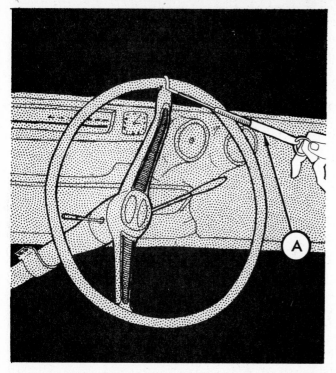

The effort required to turn the steering wheel is a good indicator of the way the system is working. Park the car on a smooth surface (garage floor or smooth concrete driveway), place the emergency brake on and run the engine with the transmission in "N" or "P." Using a spring scale (A), find out how many pounds of pull it requires to turn the steering wheel.

NOTE: IT IS IMPORTANT THAT PROPER TIRE INFLATION PRESSURES BE MAINTAINED FOR THIS STEERING CHECK.

The usual reading for a good system will be in the range of 3½ to 12 pounds. In all cases, the effort required to turn the steering wheel should not exceed 20 pounds. A distributor point tension scale will work for this check. A scale of the type used for weighing game fish will do in a pinch.

You can check the fluid volume and pressure valves by turning the steering wheel full left and full right with the engine running. All other test conditions should be the same as in the previous check for steering force. If these valves are working normally, you should be able to hear a slight buzz as the wheels approach full deflection to one side. If no buzzing noise can be heard during the test, a sticking or otherwise malfunctioning valve should be suspected.

CAUTION: DO NOT HOLD THE STEERING WHEEL IN THE EXTREME RIGHT OR LEFT POSITION FOR MORE THAN A FEW SECONDS. IF EITHER OF THE RELIEF VALVES ARE NOT WORKING, THE HIGH PRESSURES BUILT UP MAY DAMAGE THE SYSTEM.

Because of its complexity, we do not recommend that the reader attempt to repair any part of the power steering other than adjusting the drive belt, tightening loose bolts and replacing hoses. If the troubleshooting procedure shows a possible problem, take the car to a qualified mechanic for repair.

TROUBLESHOOTING HYDRAULIC BRAKES

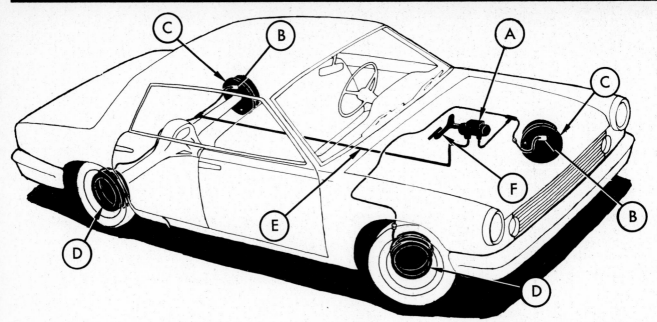

There are three basic types of hydraulic brakes on automobiles: drum or "conventional" brakes, disc brakes and brakes (either drum or disc) that are assisted by a power booster (power brakes). The brake system parts are shown in this drawing. The master cylinder (A) contains the reservoir of fluid used in the system, and the brake pedal (F) is connected to the master cylinder by a mechanical linkage. When you depress the brake pedal, hydraulic fluid under high pressure is forced out of the master cylinder into the brake lines (E) and directly to the four slave cylinders (B) inside the brake housings. These slave cylinders (normally referred to as wheel cylinders), acting under the pressure of the fluid, move the brake linings (D) so that they come in contact with the inside of the four brake drums (C). The friction between the brake linings and the drums is the force that slows the car down.

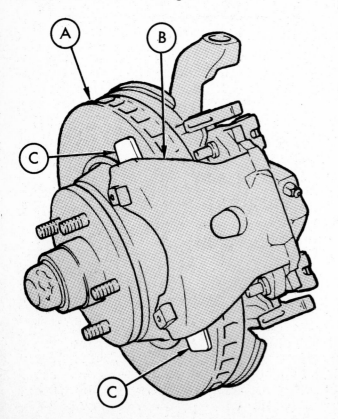

The disc brake system works on the same general principle, but instead of having the brake linings inside a drum as in the conventional brake system, the disc brake system uses a steel disc (A) which replaces the drum. This disc or "brake rotor" is attached to the hub where the wheel bolts on. Small patches of brake lining in pads are held inside a cast metal part called a caliper (B). This caliper performs the same function as the wheel cylinder: It supports the brake linings. When pressure is applied to the brake pedal, fluid forces the pads (C) against the brake rotor, providing the same friction process as with conventional brake systems to slow the car down. The caliper is held in a mounting which prevents the caliper from rotating but allows it to move from side to side slightly to self-align with the brake rotor.

Disc brakes are generally found only on the front wheels of a car, though many sports cars have disc brakes on all four wheels. The discs are more efficient than drum brakes and are becoming more common. Since the usual pattern is to have disc brakes on the front wheels only, some form of adjustment is necessary to balance the braking action between front and rear wheels.

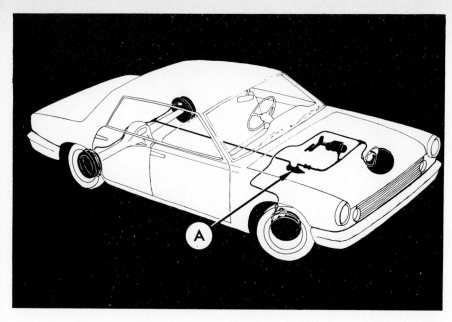

This adjustment is done by installing a proportioning (metering) valve in the line to vary the pressure felt by the two types of brakes. The proportioning valve (A) limits the pressure to the rear wheel cylinders to decrease the braking action slightly. This is necessary to prevent skidding of the rear wheels. When stopping quickly, the weight of the car is transferred (thrown forward) to the front suspension. This makes the rear of the car lighter than the front. Equal braking action would cause the rear wheels to lock up and skid.

Power brakes may be drum, disc or the highly popular combination of the two. Power brakes utilize engine vacuum to apply added pressure to the master cylinder linkage just as if you were pressing harder on the pedal. When the pedal is depressed, the vacuum booster (A) aids and multiplies the force of your leg to apply hydraulic pressure to the braking system. This is a definite aid in stopping large, heavy, late-model automobiles. Failure of the power portion of the power brake system does not destroy braking entirely, but it can mean uncomfortably hard pedal pressures are required to stop the car.

TROUBLESHOOTING HYDRAULIC BRAKES

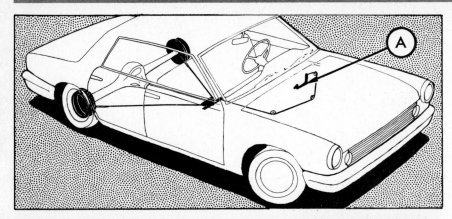

Another linkage which is associated with the brakes is the mechanical emergency brake. This is actuated by a hand or foot handle (A) inside the driver's compartment. The emergency brake (when applied) causes the rear brakes to lock and hold the car in position (until released by the driver) when the car is parked.

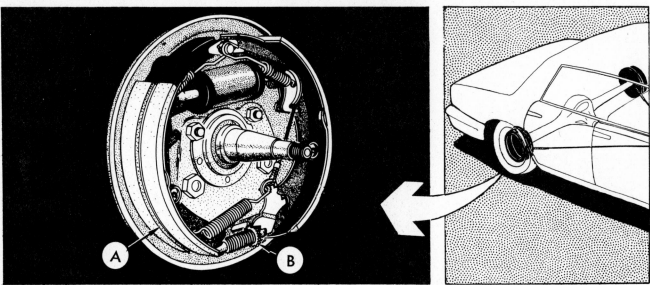

The most common problem associated with brakes of all types is a simple lack of braking ability. This is normally due to wear. The brake lining material (A), which is either riveted or chemically bonded to a steel brake shoe, wears down through use. This increases the distance the lining must travel before it contacts the inside of the drum. It also requires that the pedal move farther to produce the pressure to stop the car.

> **NOTE:** LINING WEAR IS NOT NEARLY AS CRITICAL A PROBLEM WITH DISC BRAKES, DUE TO THEIR SELF-ADJUSTING FEATURE.

All automobiles with drum brakes are equipped with an adjusting mechanism (B) to reduce the distance the linings must travel to reach the drums. Most are adjusted with a special tool from the outside of the car, but some cars are fitted with a special linkage inside the drum which performs the adjustment automatically each time the car is driven backward for a short distance.

TROUBLESHOOTING DRUM BRAKES

There are many brake troubles that can occur other than total failure of the brake system. Not all are dangerous, but any brake problem should be checked immediately to make sure there is not some serious trouble developing. We will take the common problems one at a time and give troubleshooting procedures for each situation. Remember: *check the obvious first!* A careful visual inspection of the brake components is the first step to troubleshooting the system when a problem is suspected. You need not remove the wheels and drums to get a good idea of the condition of the brakes. Unless the brakes are worn beyond the adjustment point, the problem is usually associated with some form of brake fluid leak from the system. This can usually be seen without removing any parts.

Inspect the fluid level in the master cylinder (A) first. If it is low, fill it with the correct type of fluid recommended in the shop manual for your car. Carefully examine all of the lines leading from the master cylinder to each wheel. Look for signs of leakage. These are usually apparent as stains or greasy-appearing areas on brake lines or on the body or frame directly under lines. Examine the wheel backing plates (B) and the insides of the tires on each wheel for fluid stains. Such stains indicate that there is a leak in one of the wheel cylinders.

You can confirm the leak by removing the wheel and drum to inspect the cylinder. At the same time you may also inspect the brake linings to see if they are worn to the point where they require changing (approximately ⅛-inch remaining on the brake shoe). It is better to inspect the front wheel linings first, as they wear more quickly than the rear. Jack up the front end of the car and place an axle stand under the frame or front suspension before removing the wheel.

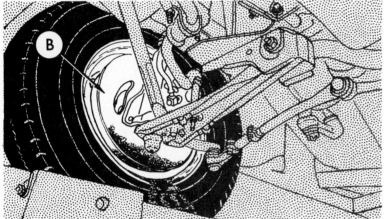

WARNING: DO NOT INSPECT OR SERVICE ANY PORTION OF THE UNDERSIDE OF THE CAR WITHOUT INSTALLING A SAFETY LIFT SUCH AS A JACKSTAND. DO NOT RELY ON A BUMPER JACK TO SUPPORT THE AUTOMOBILE SAFELY. SERIOUS INJURY CAN RESULT.

Remove the hubcap to gain access to the dust cover (A) over the wheel retaining nut (B). This nut is held by a cotter key (C) to prevent the nut from loosening. The cotter key can be removed with pliers. Remove the nut and slide the wheel and drum off the spindle. The wheel bearings will often come off the hub along with the wheel. The bearings should then be wrapped in a clean cloth to prevent them from getting dirty.

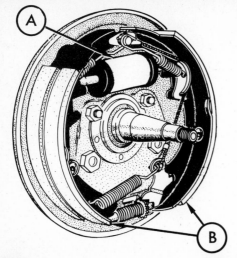

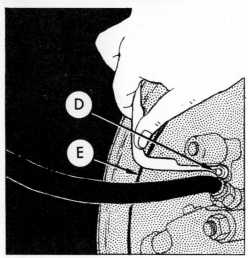

After examining the wheel cylinders (A) for leakage of fluid, check the brake linings (B) for wear. If severe lining wear is evident, the brake drums may be worn or scored to the point where they must be repaired or replaced. (This happens when the lining wears down to the metal shoe and the shoe rubs on the drum.) Look at the inside of the drum. The area where the brake lining contacts the surface of the drum should be smooth and free from scratches or grooves (C). Worn areas that only show on one part of the drum surface indicate that the drum is out of round. Drums can be repaired by having a mechanic turn them on a lathe. This cuts a new face on the inside of the drum that is perfectly round and true. New brake linings can then be installed. Whenever brake replacement or repair is done, the wheel cylinders should be rebuilt with new parts. This is not a hard job and can be undertaken by the average auto owner without too much trouble. Consult the shop manual or Petersen's BASIC AUTO REPAIR MANUAL or THE BIG BOOK OF AUTO REPAIR for complete information on doing your own brake jobs.

If the wheel cylinders or any of the brake lines are loosened for inspection or maintenance, the brake system must be "bled." Bleeding the brake system is accomplished by opening a small valve (D) located on the back of each wheel backing plate (E). When open, this valve allows brake fluid to escape to remove any air bubbles that may have gotten into the system. To bleed brakes you need a supply of brake fluid to refill the master cylinder as fast as fluid is lost at the wheel cylinder. This will prevent more air from entering the system (by allowing the reservoir to empty) while you are bleeding it.

Most professional mechanics use a pressure bleeder, which provides air-free fluid to the top filler cap of the master cylinder. You can get by without the pressure bleeder if you are careful not to let the reservoir run dry. Do not allow the fluid to run for more than a couple of brake pedal cycles before shutting the valve. Bleeding is a two-man job. One man opens and closes the valve at each wheel to allow fluid and trapped air to escape while the other man applies pressure to the brake pedal to force the fluid and air out of the system.

Some major drum brake troubles are: PEDAL GOES TO FLOORBOARD

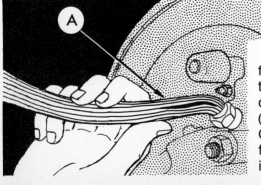

If brake pedal travel is excessive or it goes to the floorboard slowly, with a loss of braking effectiveness, the most probable cause is a leaking brake line or wheel cylinder(s). Inspect all lines, particularly those flex hoses (A) which connect the metal lines to the wheel cylinders. Carefully check the backing plates and tires for signs of fluid leaking. If necessary, remove the drums and examine the inside of the brakes for leaks and lining wear.

Check the level of the fluid in the master cylinder. If the fluid level is near normal and there is no sign of leakage in the lines or wheel cylinders, the master cylinder may be at fault. The seals inside the master cylinder may be worn, allowing fluid to seep back past the plunger. Air in the system (causing a spongy pedal) may also be the problem. Bleed the brakes to see if that will restore brake pedal firmness. Adjust the brakes.

BRAKE PEDAL FEELS SOFT

A soft or spongy pedal feeling is most often caused by air in the system. Check for signs of leakage, bleed the system and adjust brakes. Another cause may be worn brake linings.

BRAKE PEDAL FEELS HARD

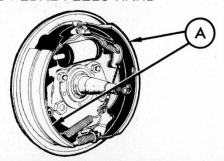

If it requires hard pedal pressure to stop the car (non-power brakes), the problem is usually burned or glazed brake linings (A). This is caused by excessive heat buildup during braking. Once the surface of the brake lining has become glazed, it will not work well until the brake linings are shaved (roughed up) to uncover unglazed brake lining material.

CAUTION: SHAVING LININGS CAN BE ACCOMPLISHED EASILY AT HOME BY REMOVING THE WHEEL AND DRUM AND SANDING DOWN THE LINING WITH A ROUGH PIECE OF SANDPAPER. BE SURE TO SAND LIGHTLY AND COMPLETELY AROUND THE ARC OF THE BRAKE LINING. FAILURE TO DO SO WILL CAUSE FLAT SPOTS ON THE LINING AND UNEVEN BRAKING POWER.

Check the shop manual for information or take the linings and drums to a mechanic for work. If your type of driving places a great demand on the brakes, your mechanic may suggest a switch to a different type of lining that resists glazing.

ONE BRAKE DRAGS

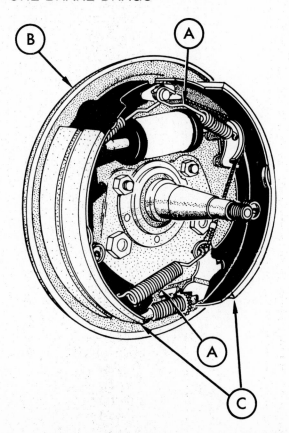

A single brake which does not release all the way or "drags" will cause extreme wear of the lining. This is usually first noticeable as a hesitation on brake release or a sound heard when the car first starts to move. A dragging brake builds up a lot of heat. The driver may discover it by the smell of burned lining or signs of wheel bearing grease leaking down on the tire. Wheel bearing grease becomes quite hot when a brake is dragging and can run out from under the dust cover. Dragging is usually due to a weak or broken brake return spring (A). It can also be caused by a clogged brake line or a wheel cylinder which is dirty and will not return to the relaxed or off position.

Another problem, an uncommon one, is a brake shoe (C) that hangs up on the edge of the backing plate (B). Though rare, it can happen. A very badly warped or egg-shaped drum can cause the brake to drag, with the lining coming in contact with the drum each time the wheel revolves, even though the lining is retracted to its normal off position.

TROUBLESHOOTING HYDRAULIC BRAKES

ALL BRAKES DRAG

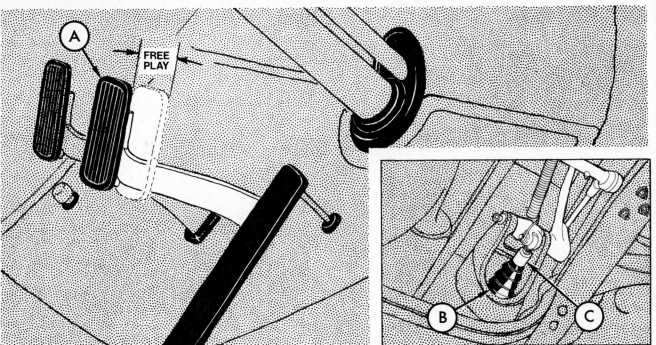

If all brakes drag, the problem is usually a misadjustment in the linkage between the master cylinder (B) and pedal (A). If the linkage (C) is adjusted so that there is no free play when the pedal is not depressed, it can cause the master cylinder to apply a small amount of pressure to the system at all times. If the master cylinder is contaminated with dirt or other foreign material, it can jam the piston in the cylinder so that partial pressure is applied to the system at all times. Finally, if the brake fluid has been replaced with some other type of fluid (such as lubricating oil), it can cause a chemical reaction with the seals, damaging them and causing binding of moving parts inside the master and wheel cylinders.

BRAKES GRAB OR CAR PULLS TO ONE SIDE

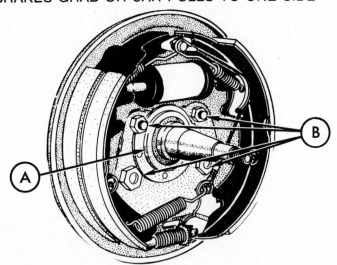

This can be caused by grease or brake fluid seeping onto the linings. Any of the problems listed above for dragging brakes can create a similar effect.

An added possible problem is a loose backing plate. The backing plate (A) is fastened to the spindle or the axle housing with four bolts (B). It can come loose, and the result is erratic or "grabby" brake operation. Loose or worn wheel bearings can also result in pulling or grabbing.

NOISY BRAKES

Almost any portion of the interior of the brake drum and backing plate can cause noise. Look for loose springs, brackets, nuts, etc. Squealing of brakes when stopping is usually caused by a buildup of brake dust inside the brake area. This dust is finely powdered brake lining which collects in the bottom of the backing plate lip and the inside of the drum. Grease on the brake linings will also cause a squeal, as will brake fluid, but this will normally be accompanied by grabbing of the affected wheel.

TROUBLESHOOTING DISC BRAKES

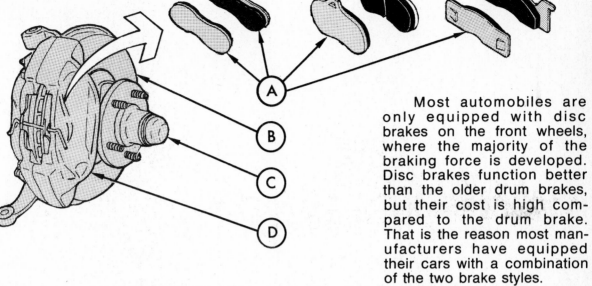

Most automobiles are only equipped with disc brakes on the front wheels, where the majority of the braking force is developed. Disc brakes function better than the older drum brakes, but their cost is high compared to the drum brake. That is the reason most manufacturers have equipped their cars with a combination of the two brake styles.

Disc brakes use the caliper (D) to perform the same task as the wheel cylinder in drum brakes, but the caliper also acts as a holder for the brake lining (A), which is in the form of pads rather than curved shoes. The reader is advised that the caliper should not be taken apart. This is a job for a trained mechanic equipped with special tools and knowledge of disc brakes.

The rotor (B) is a steel disc attached to the wheel hub (C). It is machined perfectly flat on both sides. The caliper (D) rides over it in such a manner that when the brakes are applied, the pads grip the disc between themselves, creating tremendous pressure. The basic troubleshooting steps for disc brakes are the same as for the drum brakes. Careful examination of the master cylinder, lines and the calipers for leakage of fluid is the place to start. Some calipers are designed so that the amount of brake lining left on the pads can be visually checked and measured without disassembling the calipers. See the shop manual for information. The following is a list of the troubles which apply specifically to disc brakes:

EXCESSIVE PEDAL TRAVEL

This can be due to an air leak or fluid leak somewhere in the system, or fluid level can be low in the master cylinder. If the brake pads are not correctly positioned or seated in the calipers, they can cause this trouble. If the rear drum brakes are considerably out of adjustment, they can cause the problem. Wheel bearings that are set too loose can also produce this symptom.

BRAKE OR PEDAL CHATTER

Chatter, or a pulsating vibration felt when the brakes are engaged, is usually caused by a bad rotor (A). The rotor can become warped, bent or worn so that it no longer has flat surfaces for the brake pads to grip. Another problem could be that the front wheel bearings are worn excessively, allowing the rotor to wobble. (The rotor is attached to the hub which is supported by the wheel bearing on the spindle. If the hub wobbles, the sides of the rotor will not be flat to the surface of the brake pads at all times.)

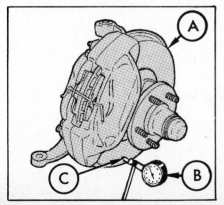

A rotor that you suspect is not true can be checked with a special tool known as a dial indicator (B). This indicator has a sensitive gauge movement which measures movements of the measuring tip (C) in thousandths of an inch. This indicator is set up on a stand so that the tip of the gauge is against the surface to be measured—in this case, the braking surface of the rotor (A). When the rotor is turned, the gauge will show any variations in the surface. This is known as measuring lateral runout. Another measurement can be taken on the rotor, namely measuring the thickness of the rotor to see if it has high and low spots in its thickness, which will produce the same symptoms as a warped rotor. If you do not have access to a dial indicator, have the rotors checked by your local mechanic.

BRAKE PULLS TO ONE SIDE

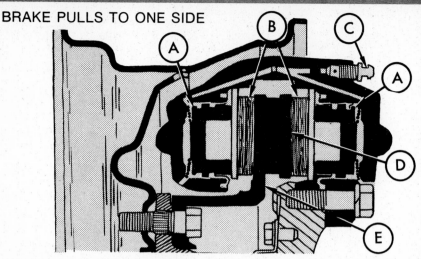

This can be caused by the pistons (A) behind the brake pads (B) becoming frozen by corrosion or dirt. This freezing prevents the pads on one caliper from touching the surface of the rotor (E) and providing braking action. Note that if one brake is not working, it will cause the car to pull toward the *opposite* side. Other possible causes are grease or fluid on the disc linings or rotor or a caliper that is loose or not in good alignment (D) with the rotor.

EXCESSIVE BRAKE PEDAL EFFORT

If the brake pedal feels hard, it could mean that the pistons (A) on both calipers are sticking due to corrosion, but it is unlikely that this will happen on both brakes at once. Brake fluid or grease can cause this problem. Brake pads worn beyond their limits can also be a cause. On Ford cars, the proportioning valve which adjusts braking pressure between front disc brakes and rear drum brakes could be malfunctioning. Since most disc brake systems require some form of power assist to get the high fluid pressures required to make disc brakes work effectively, high pedal pressures coupled with a reduction in braking ability could mean that the power portion of the braking system is bad. (See the section of this chapter on power brakes.)

BRAKE GROAN

Squeaking or groaning disc brakes can be irritating, but the noise is not an indication of a brake problem. It is caused under certain pedal pressure conditions by the rotor slipping between the brake pads. There are commercial liquids on the market that are supposed to reduce the noise, but their effectiveness in questionable.

BRAKE RATTLE

This is a problem that can be corrected. The most likely source of the difficulty is a missing anti-rattle clip on one caliper. This clip holds the pads under a slight spring tension to prevent noise when they are not in contact with the rotor. Another possibility is that brake pads have been installed that are undersized for the holes in the caliper.

NO BRAKING EFFECT WHEN PEDAL IS DEPRESSED

This has much the same cause as with drum brakes. Complete loss of braking effect is usually a sign of a ruptured line or faulty master cylinder or caliper piston (wheel cylinder). Check the level of the fluid in the master cylinder and then examine all of the lines and both calipers (or all four if installed) to see if there is evidence of fluid leaking. Check also the bleeder screws (C) on both calipers to be sure one of these has not come open. Loss of the power braking portion of the system will not result in complete loss of braking under most circumstances. One possible cause which may not be a part of the disc portion of the braking system is that the drum brakes on the rear wheels could go completely out of adjustment.

BRAKES HEAT UP AND FAIL TO RELEASE

This may be caused by caliper pistons that have seized due to overheating, usually after heavy braking while descending a hill. One other cause of this problem is a driver who rides the brake pedal with his foot while driving.

UNEVEN BRAKING ACTION

This is due to roughly the same set of reasons as pulling to one side. Seized pistons, fluid or grease on pads, proportioning valve malfunction or caliper misalignment can all cause this problem.

TROUBLESHOOTING POWER BRAKES

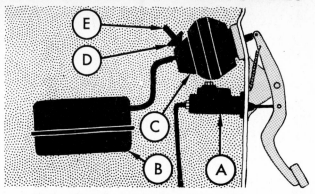

A power brake-equipped car has all the normal brake equipment of a non-power brake car, plus the power booster which steps up the braking force supplied by the driver. This is done by utilizing engine vacuum in much the same way it is used to run windshield wipers and regulate ignition advance. The master cylinder (A) is internally the same as non-power master cylinders. The power components are the vacuum reservoir (B), which provides boost as long as the engine is running, and the control valve (C).

The system works like this. The control valve senses the pressure of the driver's foot on the pedal, then triggers the vacuum boost in proportion to the brake pedal pressure and travel. The vacuum reservoir "stores" sufficient vacuum force to permit several safe stops with the engine off, preventing loss of effective braking in case of engine failure. In case of vacuum failure, the braking system does not fail completely, but pedal pressures required to stop become quite high.

To troubleshoot the power brake system, first road test the car to make sure that the rest of the brake system is working. Stop the car at about 20 mph and note whether the car stops smoothly and in a straight line. If the pedal has a spongy feel, the hydraulic portion has air in the system.

With the engine shut off, place the transmission in neutral. Depress the brake pedal several times to bleed off any vacuum stores in the system. Hold a light pressure on the brake pedal and start the engine. If the vacuum system is working and building a vacuum, the pedal will move up under your foot, and less pressure will be required to hold the pedal in the applied position. If no pushing action on your foot is felt, the system is not working. Stop the engine and press on the pedal several times to deplete any remaining vacuum, then hold the pedal firmly down. If the pedal moves away (toward the floorboard) under your foot, the hydraulic portion of the brakes is leaking or the master cylinder is allowing fluid to seep around the seals inside.

Start the engine again. Leaving your foot off the brake, run the engine rpm to a medium speed and turn off the ignition. At the same time remove your foot quickly from the throttle pedal. This preserves the buildup of engine vacuum. Wait about a minute, then try the brake action again. If there is not sufficient brake vacuum for three or more applications of the brakes, the vacuum check valve (D) between the vacuum storage unit and the engine is faulty and is leaking vacuum back to the engine.

HARD PEDAL

High pedal pressures indicate failure of the system to maintain vacuum for brake boost. Make a check of the external surfaces of the vacuum control valve (C) and examine the vacuum line running from the engine to the storage reservoir for cracks or leaks. (Consult the shop manual for location of all components, as they vary widely from one car to another.) All other problems are internal to the unit and should be checked by a qualified mechanic.

PEDAL GOES TO FLOORBOARD

This could be caused by either the basic brake system or the power portion of the brakes. Again, check the master cylinder fluid level and go over all external portions of the brakes, checking for fluid leaks. (See also the section on non-power brake troubleshooting dealing with this problem.)

BRAKES WILL NOT RELEASE

This means that the check valve in the power brake system is jammed or some other part of the power booster unit has locked up and is keeping braking power on the system. It is sometimes possible to disconnect the vacuum line from the engine (E) to the brake system. Then carefully drive the car to a mechanic.

CAUTION: BE CAREFUL WHEN DRIVING WITH THE BRAKE VACUUM LINE DISCONNECTED, AS BRAKE EFFECTIVENESS IS REDUCED.

TROUBLESHOOTING THE EXHAUST SYSTEM

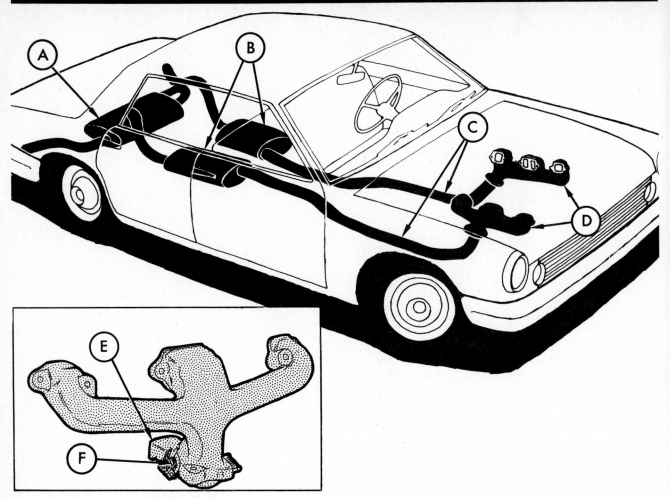

The exhaust system carries gases left over from combustion away from the engine and to the back of the car to be released in the air. The exhaust system begins with the exhaust manifold (D), a cast iron duct which connects each of the exhaust ports in the cylinder head to the exhaust pipe (C). At some point along the pipe, there is a large canister called the muffler (B), which reduces the noise level of the engine's exhaust output. On some cars, a further reduction of the noise level is handled by a resonator (A), another type of muffler usually located near the end of the pipe. Many engines use a small valve called a manifold heat valve (E). When the engine is first started, this device routes some of the hot gases through a duct to the intake manifold to warm the manifold and insure better vaporization of the fuel. The manifold heat valve is operated by a thermostatic spring (F) in much the same way as the carburetor choke. As the engine warms up, the spring slowly closes off the opening to the intake manifold.

The most serious problem that can be created by the exhaust system is the introduction of exhaust gases, primarily carbon monoxide, into the inside of the car through a leaky pipe, muffler or connection. Carbon monoxide gas is odorless, tasteless and highly toxic. Small doses cause sleepiness or nausea; larger doses are fatal.

WARNING: NEVER RUN AN AUTOMOBILE ENGINE IN A CONFINED SPACE SUCH AS A GARAGE. WHENEVER A LEAK IN AN EXHAUST SYSTEM IS SUSPECTED, MAKE ALL CHECKS AND TESTS OUTDOORS.

The exhaust system must do its job well in order for the engine to get good performance and gas mileage. A restriction, such as a large dent in a pipe, can cause problems which may seem to be symptoms of other problems, such as carburetion or internal engine troubles. Broken or loose exhaust pipe clamps and hangers can cause noises which can also be mistaken for something else.

CHECKING THE EXHAUST MANIFOLD AND HEAT VALVE

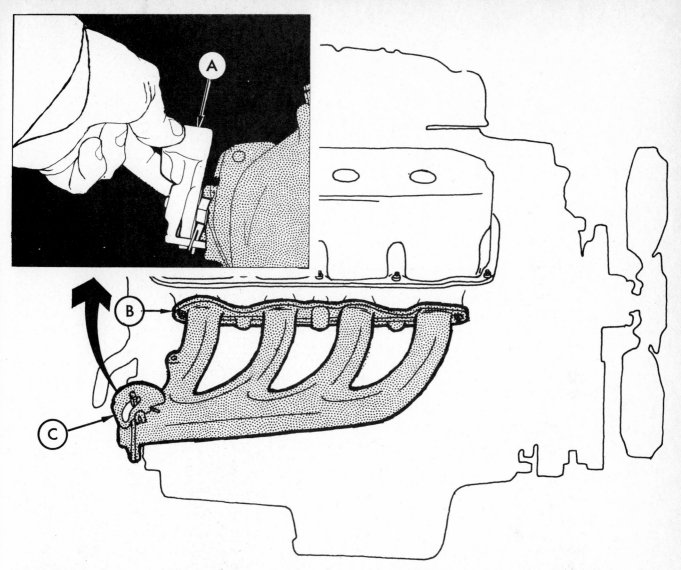

The exhaust manifold seldom causes any problems, but exhaust leaks can occur at the point where the manifold is bolted to the cylinder head or block of the engine. Leaks can usually be found by a visual check of the gasket between the manifold and head (B). Signs of leaking are carbon streaks or discoloration of the metal or the gasket. On V-8 engine cars, be sure to check both manifolds (left and right). Look for cracks in the cast iron around the bolts which hold the manifolds to the heads. Also check the bolts to see if they are tight. Small leaks can show up if manifold bolts loosen due to vibration.

The manifold heat valve (C) can be checked by grasping the balance arm (A) and moving the valve through its range. It should move freely and without undue force being applied. For a further check, note the balance arm's position when the engine is cold, then start and run the engine until it reaches normal operating temperature and recheck the position of the balance arm.

WARNING: BE CAREFUL WHILE WORKING ON THE MANIFOLD HEAT VALVE. EXHAUST MANIFOLDS AND PIPES CAN BECOME EXTREMELY HOT WHEN THE ENGINE IS RUNNING. IF THE ENGINE HAS BEEN RUN, GLOVES AND A LONG-SLEEVED SHIRT MAY BE NECESSARY TO AVOID BURNS.

If the manifold heat valve is stuck, it can often be freed by the use of a hammer. Just tap it lightly until it moves freely. A high-temperature silicone grease will help. This grease can usually be purchased at any auto parts store, or you can obtain it from your dealership's parts department. Do not use normal oils or grease, because they will smoke or catch fire when the engine is hot.

TROUBLESHOOTING THE EXHAUST SYSTEM

CHECKING EXHAUST PIPES AND MUFFLERS

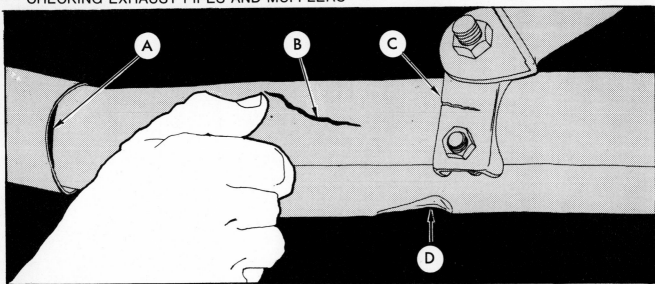

A detailed check of the entire length of the exhaust(s) should be made. Look for dents (D), holes (B), broken brackets (C) and loose connections (A). Be especially careful to check out any areas which look rusty or corroded. These are the first signs of a hole developing in the pipe. Use a screwdriver to lightly probe all suspected spots. If the problem is serious, the screwdriver will break through the pipe and the pipe should then be replaced. Because of their internal design, which slows exhaust gases down, mufflers are especially prone to rusting and corrosion. Check them carefully. Grab the exhaust pipe at various parts and shake it. It should move on the rubber suspension hangers, but should not come in contact with any other part of the chassis.

WARNING: DO NOT CRAWL UNDER ANY AUTOMOBILE UNLESS IT IS ON GOOD AXLE STANDS, RAMPS OR A HYDRAULIC HOIST. SERIOUS OR FATAL INJURY COULD RESULT IF THE CAR FALLS.

When examining the exhaust system (or any other part of the underside of the car), make sure that it is safely raised. Good axle stands or ramps (A) should be used. Don't use a bumper jack to lift the car. Get a good quality hydraulic floor jack from a tool rental outfit or put the car on a hydraulic lift at a service station. Also, be careful when handling the mufflers and exhaust pipes. If the car has been run, they can be very hot and serious burns can result. Wear gloves.

TROUBLESHOOTING CLUTCHES

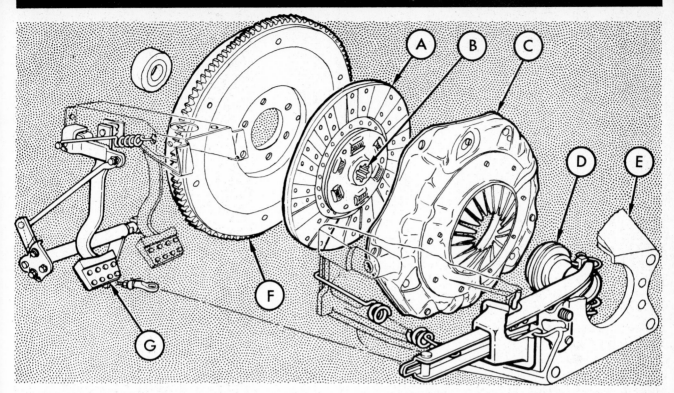

The clutch is a mechanical connection between the engine and transmission. It consists of the clutch disc (A), the pressure plate (C), throwout bearing (D) and clutch linkage and pedal (G). This assembly, except for the external linkage and pedal, is contained in a steel shell called the bellhousing (E).

The clutch uses friction and spring pressure to make a solid mechanical connection between the engine and transmission. The clutch disc is connected to the transmission. Its center has teeth (B) which fit over splines on the input shaft in the front of the transmission. The clutch disc can move forward and back on the shaft but cannot rotate without rotating the shaft. The clutch disc is contained inside the pressure plate, which is bolted to the flywheel (F). When the clutch pedal is depressed, it is no longer forced into contact with the clutch disc by its heavy springs. This takes the pressure off the disc, and the flywheel can rotate without causing the disc to turn. When the pedal is released, the heavy springs of the pressure plate force the disc against the flywheel, causing it to "lock up" and turn with the flywheel. This in turn causes the input shaft to turn, transmitting the power of the engine to the transmission, through the driveshaft and on to the rear wheels to make the car move.

The clutch disc is designed to slip slightly when it is engaged, to make a gradual engagement instead of a sudden one. In this manner, the car can start forward or backward smoothly, without jerking. The force of the pedal is transferred to the pressure plate through a bearing called the throwout bearing. One part of the bearing contacts the rotating pressure plate; the other rests against the stationary clutch arm, which is part of the linkage.

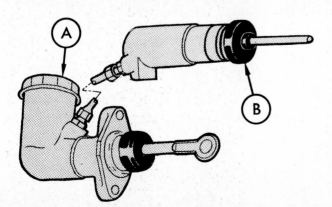

Some manufacturers do not use a mechanical linkage between the clutch pedal and the clutch arm. They substitute a hydraulic system similar to that used on brakes. In the hydraulic system are a master cylinder (A), a slave cylinder (B) and a hydraulic line connecting the two. When the clutch pedal is depressed, the master cylinder sends a high-pressure movement of hydraulic fluid through the line to the slave cylinder. The slave cylinder matches the pedal movement to operate the clutch arm in exactly the same manner as the conventional clutch linkage would.

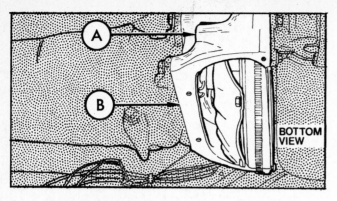

Wear, misadjustment or oil contamination are the most common causes of clutch malfunction. The clutch can be visually examined by removing an inspection plate (B) on the underside of the bellhousing (A). Without expert knowledge of what to look for, the chances of seeing any damage other than oil leaking onto the clutch are slim. Most methods of troubleshooting the clutch can be accomplished without visually examining the clutch itself.

CLUTCH SLIPS

If the clutch slips (does not make a good connection between the flywheel and the pressure plate), it usually shows up as a slight bucking of the car and increases in engine rpm while the car is in motion. To check, set the emergency brake tightly. Press down on the gas pedal until the engine is running at about the same rpm it would be at 30 mph. Depress the clutch and put the transmission in third or fourth gear. Let the clutch pedal out. If the clutch is not slipping excessively, the engine will stall.

The causes of a slipping clutch are: worn clutch lining, weak pressure plate springs, sticking clutch release levers on the pressure plate, clutch linkage out of adjustment. For all but the clutch linkage, corrective action requires that the clutch be removed. For clutch linkage adjustment, see your shop manual.

CLUTCH CHATTERS

Clutch "chattering" occurs when the clutch slips in short, jerky movements when being engaged (let out). The most common causes of the problem are: oil or grease on the clutch lining (caused by a leak in the rear main oil seal around the crankshaft), a glazed clutch lining from overheating, a warped pressure plate or clutch disc, loose or broken engine mounts or loose universal joints or transmission mountings. All require removal of the clutch to correct (see your local mechanic or shop manual).

CLUTCH NOISE

Clutch noises are often confused with other engine noises, but are generally heard only when the clutch is disengaged (pedal pushed in).

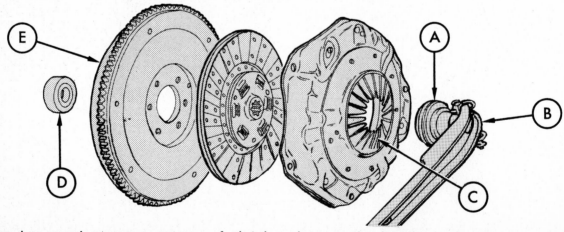

The two most common causes of clutch noise are the bearings: the throwout bearings (A), which ride between the clutch arm (B) and the fingers on the pressure plate (C); and the pilot bearing (D) or bushing. The pilot bearing is fitted in the center of the flywheel (E). It supports the tip of the transmission input shaft and maintains precise alignment of the shaft with the centerline of the crankshaft. Both bearings can cause a clattering sound if worn, and the clutch assembly must be disassembled to remove them. (See your shop manual or your local mechanic for instructions.)

TROUBLESHOOTING STANDARD TRANSMISSIONS

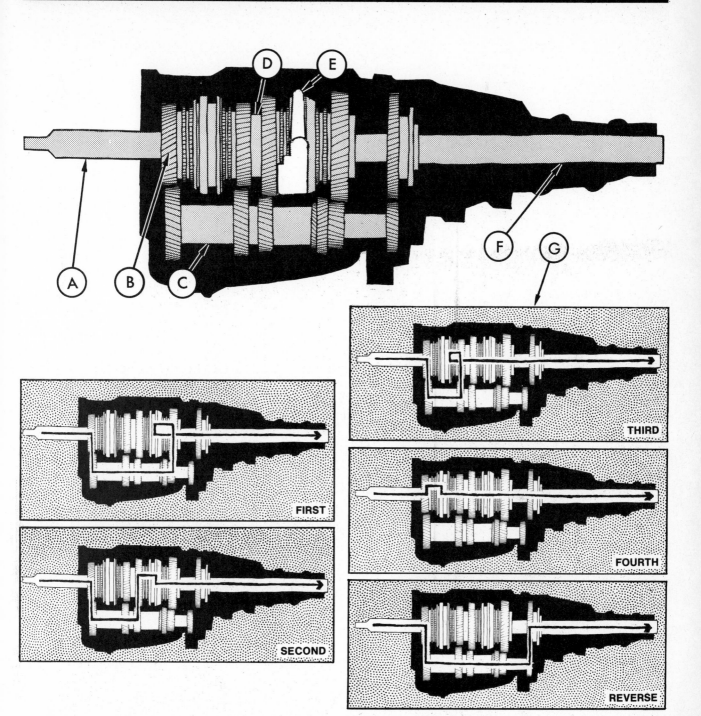

FIRST

SECOND

THIRD

FOURTH

REVERSE

The automobile transmission is a mechanical torque multiplier. The gasoline engine develops its least amount of motive force (torque) at low rpm, and the transmission must multiply that force at low rpm to move the vehicle. In this respect, both automatic and standard transmissions are alike.

Rotational force from the engine is transferred into the transmission mainshaft (D) through the input shaft (A). The main drive gear (B) is rotated by the input shaft, and it rotates other gears on a countershaft (C). These other gears (when selected) rotate gears on the mainshaft (D), transferring drive force to the rear wheels. Inside the transmission are a series of shifting forks (E) which contact sliding gears. By movements of the shifting lever, the driver can select which gear positions (G) he desires. The gear positions (G) show how engine torque is transmitted through a typical four-speed (four forward speeds plus reverse) transmission. Once the specific gears have been selected and moved into position, the torque is transmitted to the rear wheels by the output shaft (F).

TRANSMISSION NOISY WHEN CAR IS IN MOTION

WARNING: BE SURE YOU ARE ON AN OPEN STRETCH OF ROAD WITH NO TRAFFIC WHEN ATTEMPTING TO CHECK FOR TRANSMISSION NOISES. THIS TEST SHOULD NOT BE PERFORMED IN ANY TRAFFIC SITUATION.

Transmission noises can include whining, clicking or rattling sounds which are often difficult to identify when driving. Transmission noises can be heard much better by turning the engine off and coasting. By moving the shift lever from neutral into the various gear positions, different gears can be selected for testing purposes.

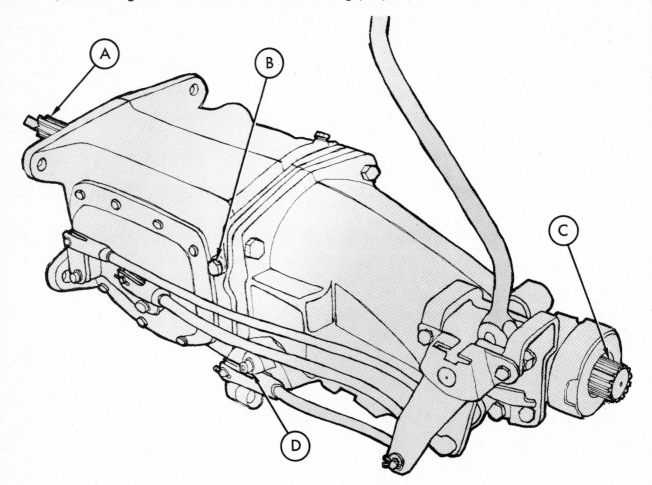

The first item to check if the transmission is making noises is the level of oil in the transmission. Most transmissions have a filler hole on the side (B). Remove the plug and stick your finger into the hole to determine the level of the oil (see your shop manual or owner's manual for specific oil levels). If the level is down, refill the transmission with the manufacturer's recommended oil and retest. Examine the outside of the transmission for evidence of leaks, particularly around the input shaft (C), the output shaft (A) and the speedometer drive (D) on the side of the transmission. Other things that can cause transmission noise are the internal bearings and moving gears, but these are beyond the repair capability of the average car owner. See your shop manual or local mechanic for repair. A noise associated with a particular gear (first, second, third or reverse) indicates a worn or chipped tooth on that cluster gear.

TRANSMISSION NOISY IN NEUTRAL

If the transmission makes noise in neutral with the engine running but when the car is not in motion, check the oil level. Noise may also indicate a worn clutch gear, clutch gear bearing, countershaft drive gear or countershaft drive bearings.

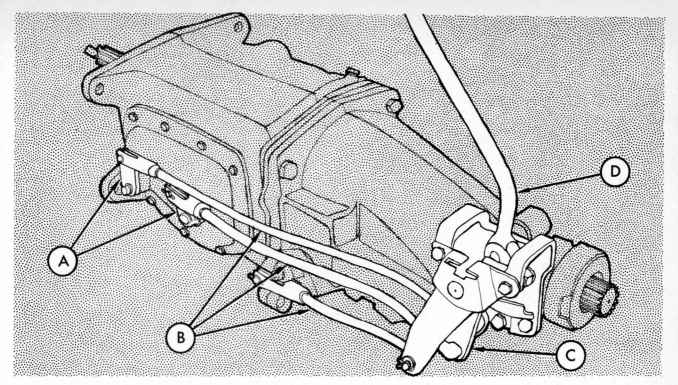

TRANSMISSION SLIPS OUT OF GEAR

If the transmission suddenly slips out of gear into neutral while the car is in motion, the obvious problem and the easiest one to check is misadjustment of the shift linkage. The shift linkage contains the shift lever (D), the connecting linkage (B) and the transmission shift arms (A). Most shifting mechanisms use a spring-loaded detent (C) to correctly position the shifting forks inside the transmission. Refer to your shop manual or local mechanic for specific information on setting the shift linkage on your transmission. Other problems are internal and will require removal and repair of the transmission.

TRANSMISSION DIFFICULT TO SHIFT

If the transmission is hard to shift from one gear to another, the clutch or the shifting linkage may be out of adjustment. Also, severe damage may have occurred inside the transmission, such as a broken gear, chipped gear tooth or a broken synchro. If the clutch does not release all the way when the pedal is depressed, it places a restriction on the transmission and makes shifting difficult. Check and adjust the clutch linkage.

The final possible problem is a shift linkage that's out of adjustment. Check and adjust the shift linkage. If the transmission will not shift at all but the shift lever moves easily, the problem is most likely that the shift linkage has become disconnected at some point. Inspect and repair. If the shift lever will not move and the transmission cannot be shifted even with considerable force applied to the lever, there is serious damage inside the transmission. See your local mechanic.

GEARS CLASH WHEN SHIFTING

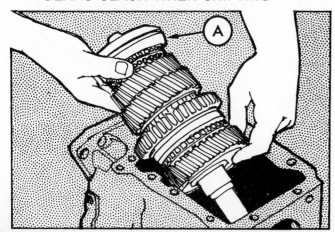

Gear clash or "grinding" can be caused by one of several problems. The most likely is that the synchronizing units (A) are worn. These devices match the rotational speed of different gear clusters so they can mesh smoothly. Worn synchronizers must be replaced. Another possibility is shift linkage misadjustment or slight dragging of the clutch. Dragging of the clutch takes place when the clutch does not completely release when the clutch pedal is depressed. This can be due to faulty linkage adjustment or a worn clutch pressure plate assembly.

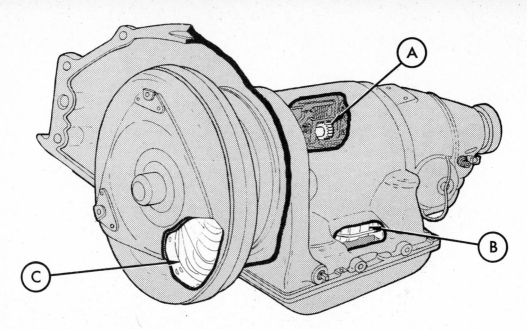

The automatic transmission is much more complicated than the standard (manual) transmission. All the operations carried out by the driver in cars equipped with a standard transmission are handled by automatic features on the newer transmissions. In essence, all automatic transmissions have the same features. There are one or more sets of planetary gears (A), a fluid coupling or torque converter (C) and a valve body (B), which has control valves to direct hydraulic fluid inside the transmission to operate different parts of the equipment.

The control systems of various manufacturer's transmissions may vary considerably. This is because the automatic transmission can be controlled hydraulically by throttle movements, by engine vacuum, speed-sensitive governors or by some electrical device. Any or all of these types of controls can be included on any one manufacturer's transmission.

The biggest difference between the automatic transmission and the standard transmission is the manner in which they transfer the engine torque to the transmission. The standard transmission uses a clutch to disconnect the engine from the transmission when shifting gears or when the car is stopped with the engine running and the transmission in gear.

The automatic transmission uses a fluid coupling known as a torque converter. This hydraulic connection has finned wheels, something like turbine blades. One of these is attached to the engine, the other to the transmission. Both are sealed in a housing inside the converter cover. Automatic transmission fluid is pumped into the housing. When engine speed is low, the engine-driven turbine wheel simply slides through the fluid without imparting much torque to the transmission. But as rpm go up, the pressure of the fluid against the driven wheel increases until at normal engine speeds it is like a solid physical connection between the engine and transmission. This yields the same effect as the clutch in a manual transmission-equipped car.

Also included inside the housing is a set of fixed blades called stators, which direct the fluid against the driven wheel in such a manner that the torque output of the engine is multiplied several times at low speeds. This helps to get the heavy weight of the car moving.

Power from the torque converter is transferred by a shaft to a clutch or drum assembly inside the transmission housing. This assembly is similar in operation to the clutch used on the front of a standard transmission, because it engages and disengages using pressure and friction to operate parts of the transmission as it changes gears. These gears are connected to the clutch or drum assembly and intermesh like the gears in a standard transmission to produce the final drive ratio of the transmission. The entire operation of the clutch or drums and gears is controlled by hydraulic pressure, provided by a pump which is part of the transmission. Actual repair of the automatic transmission or internal troubleshooting requires specialized knowledge beyond the scope of this book, but some troubleshooting can be done externally.

AUTOMATIC TRANSMISSION FLUID

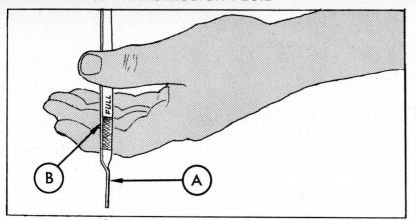

The hydraulic fluid which the transmission uses is a special fluid. It can be checked by removing a dipstick (A) just like that used to check engine oil level. The transmission fluid level must be checked with the engine running and the transmission shift selector lever in the park ("P") position to get a correct reading. Make sure the engine has reached operating temperature before checking the fluid level. The dipstick is marked (B) like the engine oil filler dipstick.

CAUTION: CARE MUST BE TAKEN WHEN ADDING FLUID TO THE TRANSMISSION. THE MARKS (B) ON THE DIPSTICK ARE OFTEN QUITE CLOSE TOGETHER, AND IT IS EASY TO ADD TOO MUCH FLUID. TOO MUCH FLUID CAN DAMAGE THE TRANSMISSION.

Fluid is added directly into the dipstick tube (C), using a funnel with a long, flexible tube (D). Fresh automatic transmission fluid is light pink, almost clear in color. If the color of the fluid on the dipstick is amber or brown, it should be changed. Dark brown fluid which smells burnt indicates transmission damage and the need for transmission servicing. This includes changing the transmission fluid, cleaning the transmission, changing all filters inside the transmission and inspecting and adjusting the bands. Continued driving risks incurring an expensive repair bill.

NOTE: EACH AUTO MANUFACTURER HAS A RECOMMENDED TRANSMISSION FLUID FOR HIS AUTOMATIC TRANSMISSION. NEVER SUBSTITUTE TRANSMISSION FLUID WITHOUT FIRST MAKING SURE THAT IT IS THE CORRECT TYPE FOR YOUR CAR. THE SALESMAN AT YOUR AUTO PARTS STORE OR THE DEALER'S PARTS DEPARTMENT CAN GIVE YOU THE INFORMATION YOU NEED. ALSO SEE YOUR OWNER'S MANUAL.

TROUBLESHOOTING AUTOMATIC TRANSMISSIONS

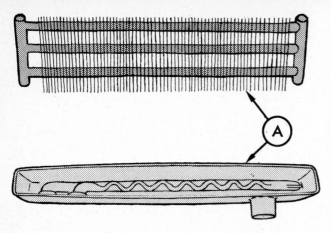

Burnt fluid or other signs of transmission overheating may indicate a problem with the transmission cooler (A). This device is usually a part of the lower reservoir tank of the radiator, although on some cars it may be an added piece of equipment not attached to the radiator. Fluid from the transmission is circulated through the cooler by a pump in the transmission and is cooled. Leaks in the lines or blockage of the lines or the tubing in the cooler can cause the transmission to overheat, especially when subjected to heavy loads such as trailer towing or long uphill climbs.

TYPICAL AUTOMATIC TRANSMISSION PROBLEMS

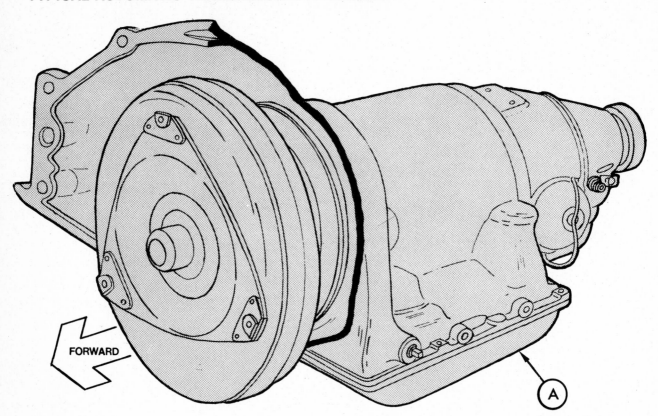

Because of the complexity of the automatic transmission (A), there is very little that the troubleshooter can do to remedy a problem without special tools and knowledge. The various shifting operations are controlled by so many different methods inside the transmission that the troubleshooter must have access to the shop manual to determine how his transmission is controlled and operated. Any malfunction of the automatic transmission should be examined by a transmission mechanic.

Some symptoms of automatic transmission trouble are similar to those of clutch problems in cars equipped with standard transmissions. One of the most common problems in transmissions is transmission slipping, in which the effect is much like that of a slipping clutch. This is an indication of future major transmission problems. Other trouble areas are: sticking in one gear or drive range, loss of transmission kickdown capability (passing gear), slipping in one gear but not another. All of these symptoms could lead to a major problem. Sometimes these symptoms can be eliminated by a simple transmission linkage adjustment. For more information on automatic transmissions, see your shop manual, Petersen's BASIC CLUTCHES AND TRANSMISSIONS, THE BIG BOOK OF AUTO REPAIR or your local mechanic.

TROUBLESHOOTING DRIVELINE/REAR AXLE

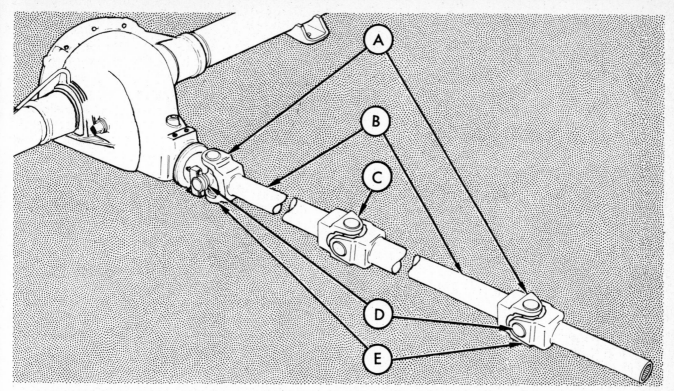

Engine torque from the transmission is routed to the rear axle by the driveshaft (B). This is a hollow metal tube connected at each end by universal joints (A), called U-joints. The U-joints are designed to allow the rear axle to move on its springs without binding or stopping the driveshaft rotation. The U-joint consists of a cross-shaped casting (D) suspended between two C-shaped holders (E). The holders (E) are set at right angles to each other and the ends of the casting are held in bearings. This allows the joint to swivel 360° without interference. On some cars, due to their construction (four-wheel drive and some longer vehicles), there may be an additional U-joint (C) in the middle of the driveshaft, making in reality two driveshafts.

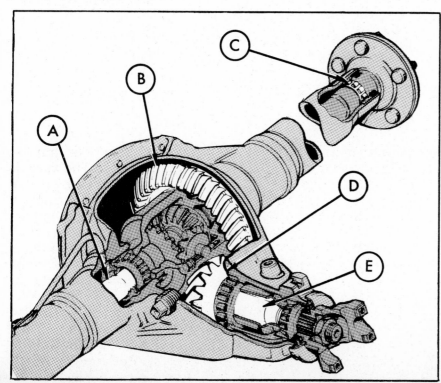

The rear of the driveshaft connects to a pinion shaft (E) on the rear end. Inside the rear end housing is a set of gears which convert the rotary motion of the driveshaft to drive the rear wheels. On the end of the pinion shaft is the pinion gear (D). The pinion gear meshes with a larger gear called the ring gear (B). Rotation of the driveshaft by the engine and transmission causes the pinion gear to drive the ring gear, rotating the axles (A). The outer ends of the axles are supported by axle bearings (C), which have grease seals to contain the lubricant for the bearings inside the axle housing. Bolted to the ends of the axles are flanges to support the drums and wheels.

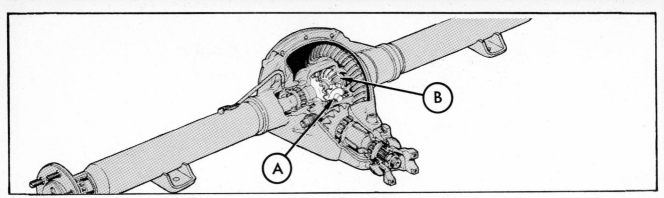

The gear set (B) in the middle of the rear end housing is much more complicated than a simple ring and pinion gear. There are small sets of gears called spider gears (A). These provide the differential action which allows the car to change direction without damaging the tires. When the car is going straight, the spider gears do not rotate on their shaft. They are only turning two side gears with an equal torque from the main pinion gear. When the car turns a corner, the inside wheel follows a shorter line than the outside wheel. This causes the inside axle to want to make *fewer* revolutions than the outside axle. The spider gears take care of this by rotating in such a manner that the inside axle can slow down without damage. Once the car has turned through the corner and has straightened out again, the spider gears cease to function and again both axles drive at the same speed.

A variation of this, the locking differential, uses a system of clutch plates and discs to perform the same process but still applies engine torque to both wheels for better driving capability in mud or sand. This feature is known under various trade names such as *Posi-Traction, Sure-Grip, No-Spin,* etc.

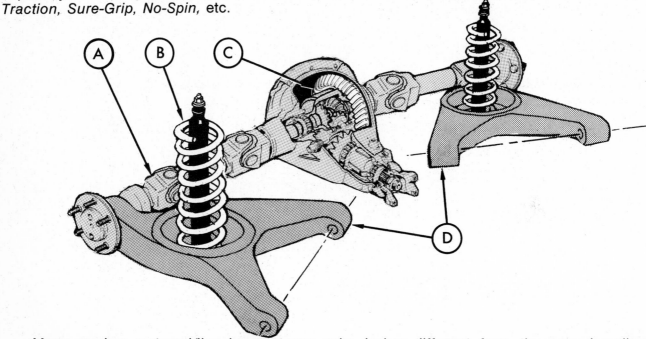

Many modern automobiles have a rear axle design different from the one described above and known as independent suspension. This design allows each rear wheel to move freely, independent of the other. The axles used in these rear ends are really short drive-shafts which may have either U-joints (A) or constant-velocity joints (basically like the U-joint described earlier) at both ends to handle the changing angles between the ring gear (C) and the wheel as the suspension works up and down. The suspension is still a combination of springs (B), either coil or leaf, and shock absorbers, but the rear end is usually fastened directly to the frame and the outer members which contain the brakes and wheels. The rear axle, with brakes and wheels, is held by control arms (D), which are the large, stamped steel parts that support the entire assembly and keep it from moving, except for the up and down motion required.

TROUBLESHOOTING THE DRIVESHAFT

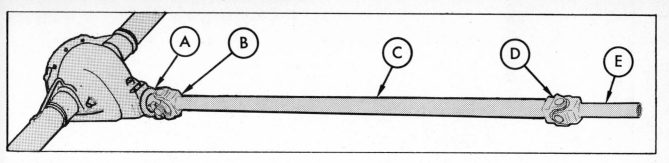

Because the driveshaft (C) is such a simple device, it is easy to check out. Most driveshaft problems will be associated with the U-joints. At the front of the driveshaft, the forward U-joint (D) attaches to a slip yoke (E), a hollow, splined tube which slides over the splines on the transmission output shaft. At the other end, the U-joint (B) may connect directly to a shaft or to a companion flange (A). This flange is a method of attachment which allows the driveshaft to be unbolted from the rear end and removed without disassembling the U-joint itself.

Because the driveshaft rotates very fast when the car is moving at highway speeds, its most common problem is vibration. Vibration is most often noticed at certain speed ranges and can be confused with rear end, suspension and tire problems. Tire noise can be detected by driving the car on a variety of surfaces. Changes in the vibration or noise level indicate the problem is with the tires rather than the driveshaft or rear end. Engine noise or exhaust noise can be distinguished from driveshaft noises by running the engine at various speeds with the transmission in neutral and the car motionless. If the vibration or noise occurs while the car is standing still, it cannot be coming from the driveline.

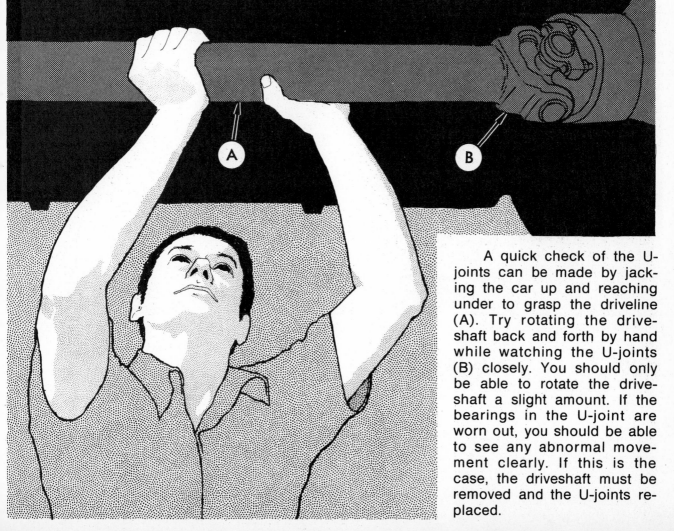

A quick check of the U-joints can be made by jacking the car up and reaching under to grasp the driveline (A). Try rotating the driveshaft back and forth by hand while watching the U-joints (B) closely. You should only be able to rotate the driveshaft a slight amount. If the bearings in the U-joint are worn out, you should be able to see any abnormal movement clearly. If this is the case, the driveshaft must be removed and the U-joints replaced.

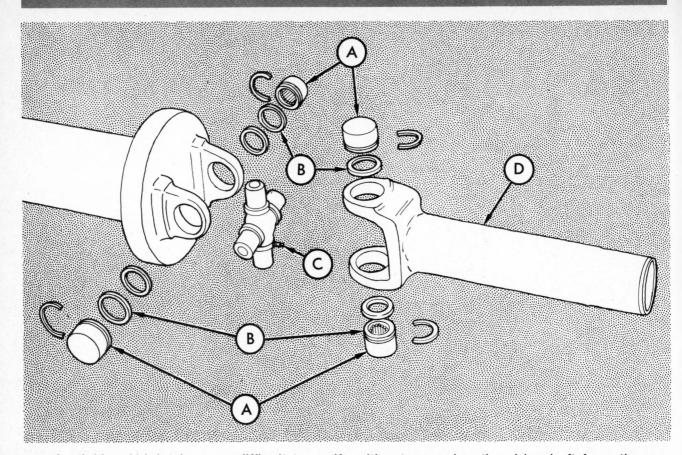

A sticking U-joint is more difficult to verify without removing the driveshaft from the car. With the driveshaft removed (see the shop manual for instruction on removal), you should be able to move the yokes (D) at each end of the driveshaft without too much effort. If the U-joints are hard to move, look for signs of overheating or corrosion around the bearing caps (A). This is an indication of bearing failure due to lack of lubrication. Your U-joints may have fittings (C) called zerks to lubricate the bearings. If so, you might try forcing fresh lubrication into the bearings to see if rust and dirt come out around the grease seals (B) on each bearing. In any event, the U-joints are not expensive and should be replaced if they are suspected.

Another common problem with the driveshaft is an out-of-balance or bent shaft. Both are hard to check without special tools, and if the U-joints do not seem to be the problem, see your local mechanic and have him check the shaft properly.

TROUBLESHOOTING THE REAR END ASSEMBLY

WARNING: BE SURE YOU HAVE OPEN STRETCHES OF ROAD WITH NO TRAFFIC WHEN ATTEMPTING TO CHECK FOR REAR END ASSEMBLY NOISE. THIS TEST SHOULD NOT BE PERFORMED IN ANY TRAFFIC SITUATION.

Just as with the driveshaft, most problems inside the rear end can be diagnosed by listening to the sounds the rear end makes while the car is being driven. Rear end noises are often confused with driveshaft, tire, clutch, transmission and exhaust system noises. Coasting the car with the engine turned off is one way of checking out the rear end without being bothered by engine and exhaust sounds.

WARNING: COASTING CAN BE DANGEROUS. DO NOT COAST DOWN STEEP HILLS OR AT EXCESSIVE SPEEDS. SELECT AN OPEN AREA SUCH AS AN EMPTY PARKING LOT AND COAST ONLY FOR SHORT DISTANCES AT LOW SPEEDS.

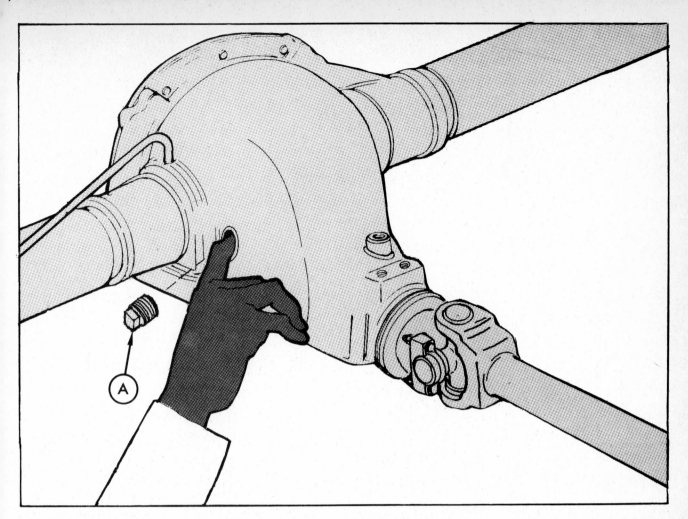

Lubrication level is checked by removing the filler plug (A). The lubricant should be within finger distance of the opening and should be clean and fresh. Lubrication for rear end gears is specially designed for the type of installation by the manufacturer. Always use the recommended lubricant listed in the owner's manual or shop manual.

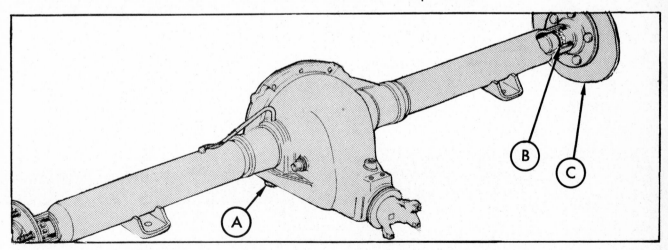

If you suspect a problem in the rear end, the first step is to check the level of lubricant in the housing. Look for leaks around the drain plug (A) or at the axle seals (B) on the ends of the axle housings. Lubrication loss at the axle seals can usually be seen on the inside of the wheels or tires.

NOTE: LEAKING BRAKE FLUID CAN BE CONFUSED WITH REAR END LUBRICATION. IF THERE IS CONSIDERABLE FLUID ON THE WHEEL BACKING PLATES (C) OR INNER SURFACES OF THE TIRES, CHECK THE BRAKE SYSTEM.

TROUBLESHOOTING DRIVELINE/REAR AXLE

The car can be tested for rear axle and driveline noise by operating it under four driving conditions:

DRIVE

Operate the car on a straight and level road. Use just enough throttle to keep speed gradually increasing. This should help determine what noises are constant under load conditions. A steady whining or humming sound could be due to a loss of lubrication, the use of an improper lubricant or incorrect mesh (adjustment) of gears. It may also indicate worn or dry (require lubrication) wheel bearings.

NOTE: TIRE NOISE CAN CAUSE SIMILAR SOUNDS. TRY DRIVING ON BOTH BLACK-TOP AND CONCRETE ROAD SURFACES TO SEE IF SOUND CHANGES. IF IT CHANGES OR DISAPPEARS, THE SOUND IS PROBABLY COMING FROM THE TIRES.

CRUISE

Operate the car at a constant speed. If the problem is caused by things other than the rear end or driveline, it should show up using this method. Engine noise, exhaust noise and tire noise can all make sounds which might be mistaken for driveline sounds. In the cruise test, they will be easier to hear and eliminate.

COASTING

Operate the car at a constant speed. Release the throttle (take your foot off the gas pedal) and let speed decrease. This takes the torque load off the drive train and puts the vehicle weight on the back side of the ring gear in the rear end. Steady noise when coasting indicates bad gear teeth or improper adjustment of bearings in the rear end assembly.

ALTERNATING SPEEDS

This is a combination of the methods already described. Starting with the car at a steady speed, accelerate slightly. (Low road speeds are best here; speed should not exceed 10 mph.) Then take your foot off the gas pedal suddenly. This will cause sudden torque transfer in the driveline and rear end. Worn bearings inside the rear end assembly or in the wheel bearings or excessive clearance (wear) between gears will produce a sharp "clunking" noise. Worn U-joints can also produce this sound, but if you are troubleshooting step by step, you should already have inspected the driveshaft.

Other noises that indicate problems in the rear end and driveline are a sharp metallic click when shifting from a forward gear to reverse and clicking when turning a corner. These sounds indicate loose nuts or chipped teeth in ring and pinion gears or spider gears in the rear end. If you don't hear noise until you are turning a corner, the problem is probably in the spider gears of the rear end.

ENGINE STALLS

Engine "stalling" (stopping at idle or when the car is first put in motion) can result from several conditions. Often troubleshooting the problem as an engine idle problem will correct the stalling situation. The list below contains the standard situations you are likely to run into.

IDLE SPEED TOO LOW: When a running automobile engine is suddenly required to put the entire weight of the automobile into motion, a tremendous load is placed on the engine. If the engine speed is not high enough, it may be more than the engine can handle and it will stall.

To remedy the problem of low idle speed—idle speed should be approximately 400 to 750 rpm (revolutions per minute) or higher for some car models—locate the idle adjustment screw on the carburetor (refer to the shop manual or the owner's manual for exact location). Using a screwdriver, adjust the idle speed to the desired rpm.

Idle speed can be set by ear, or if you want to establish the exact idle speed, a tachometer (engine speed indicator) can be used.

IGNITION POINTS: Worn, burned or badly adjusted ignition points can cause idle problems. See Petersen's BASIC IGNITION AND ELECTRICAL SYSTEMS.

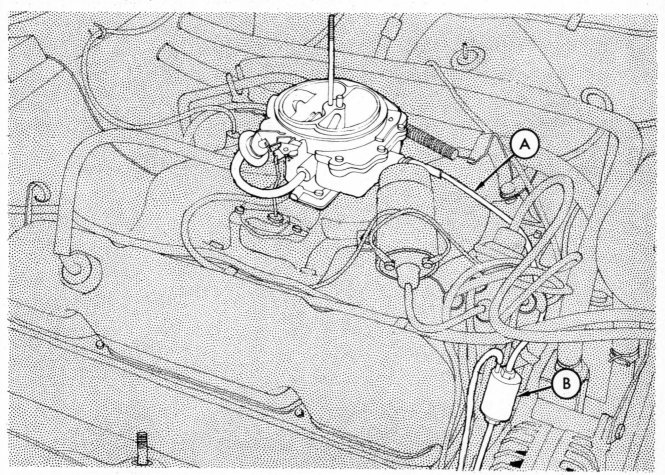

VAPOR LOCK: This is an engine stall condition brought on by the overheating of the fuel lines and carburetor. If the temperature goes too high in the engine compartment, the fuel will change from a liquid to a vapor. This can form a vapor bubble in the line (A) between the fuel pump and the carburetor, shutting off the flow of fuel into the carburetor float bowl.

NOTE: MANY LATE MODEL CARS, ESPECIALLY THOSE WITH AIR CONDITIONING, ARE EQUIPPED WITH A DEVICE CALLED A VAPOR BYPASS SYSTEM. THIS IS A SPECIAL FUEL FILTER (B) WHICH HAS A METERED VENT IN THE TOP. ANY VAPOR THAT FORMS IS BLED OFF TO THE OUTSIDE AIR, REMOVING THE RESTRICTION IN THE FUEL LINES. IF YOUR CAR VAPOR LOCKS AND IT IS EQUIPPED WITH THIS FILTER, EXAMINE IT TO MAKE SURE THAT THE VENT IS NOT PLUGGED.

ENGINE STALLS

Vapor lock is most common on hot days and when the engine is being worked hard, as in climbing a steep grade, towing a trailer or other heavy loads or crawling along in heavy traffic for long periods of time. Usually the onset of vapor lock will cause engine surging (engine power increases and decreases at odd intervals). If things get bad enough, the engine will stall. The symptoms are exactly like running out of gas, which is actually the case. The carburetor *is* out of gas; the lines are blocked with a vapor bubble.

Correcting a vapor lock is simple. Just let the temperature under the hood fall below the point at which it vaporizes gasoline and the vapor lock will disappear. You can speed this process by opening the hood and applying a small amount of cool water to the fuel lines, fuel pump and outside the carburetor (do not get water in the carburetor opening).

If you have a car that is plagued by vapor lock problems in hot weather, the addition of some form of heat-sink or insulation (such as aluminum foil and clothespins or asbestos cloth) around the fuel lines inside the engine compartment can correct the problem to some degree.

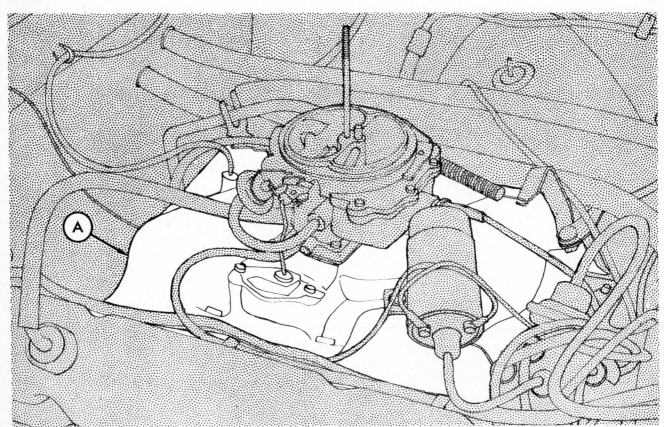

VACUUM LEAK: A vacuum leak in the engine intake manifold (A) can cause irregular idle and stalling. A good example of this would be a windshield wiper hose or vacuum ignition advance line that has become disconnected or broken. A close visual check can often determine the source of the trouble. If not, there are several procedures for finding a vacuum leak, but they require some shop tools and a shop manual to remedy the problem.

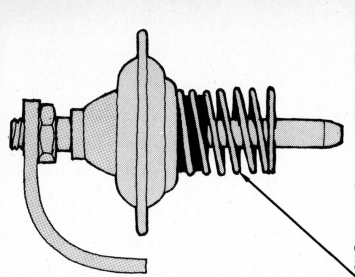

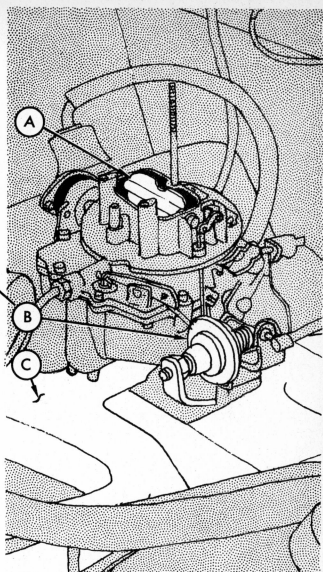

DASHPOT: The dashpot, or throttle stop modulator (B), is a device used on many cars from 1969 to the present and on some pre-1969 cars with automatic transmissions. It is an electrically operated solenoid connected to the throttle linkage. The dashpot maintains a normal idle speed as long as the ignition switch is on and the engine is running. It decreases the idle speed setting (with throttle in completely closed position) several hundred rpm when the ignition is turned off to prevent the engine from dieseling (continuing to run after the engine has been stopped).

If the dashpot is not working, it can lower the idle speed below that required for normal operation and the engine will stall.

To check for proper dashpot operation, start the engine and hold the idle speed high enough so that the engine runs normally. You can do this either by having someone press on the gas pedal while you watch the dashpot or by operating the throttle linkage near the carburetor by hand. Turn the ignition off while watching the dashpot. If it is working, you should be able to see the throttle stop retract suddenly as the ignition is turned off.

If the dashpot is not working, replace it. Adjustment of the dashpot is covered in the chapter on fuel systems.

FLOODING: This is too much fuel inside the intake manifold (C). Flooding destroys the proper ratio of air to fuel and prevents the engine from working correctly.

The normal causes of flooding are: a defective float or needle and seat in the float bowl; overchoking, in which case the engine is not getting enough air; or percolation, in which the heat from the engine boils the gas in the carburetor after the engine is turned off.

NOTE: PERCOLATION IS A FORM OF VAPOR LOCK.

These problems can be checked for in two ways. First, remove the air cleaner and look into the carburetor venturi (A) to detect the presence of raw (liquid) fuel inside the carburetor or down inside the intake manifold. Next, remove one or more spark plugs and examine them to see if they are wet. If the plug is coated with raw fuel, the engine is flooded.

Flooding can sometimes be overcome by pressing the gas pedal all the way to the floorboard and holding it there while operating the starter. Under no circumstances should the gas pedal be pumped. The pumping action will simply add more raw fuel to the intake manifold. Another method of overcoming flooding is to remove the air cleaner and blow into the carburetor venturi (A). This will help remove excess fuel that has built up in the carburetor and intake manifold.

ENGINE NOISES

ENGINE TROUBLESHOOTING

This section deals with internal engine problems that may not be reflected in the three logic trees on starting, ignition and fuel systems. Many of the components of an engine are checked by professional mechanics with sophisticated test equipment and special tools. This book will limit its coverage of troubleshooting methods to those that can reasonably be expected to be done with simple tools by the home mechanic or student mechanic. In cases where the use of more specialized tools is required, we direct the reader to other sources, such as manufacturer's shop manuals, for more complete information concerning the use of these tools.

The modern internal combustion engine is highly reliable as long as it is kept in decent operating condition through preventive maintenance. With proper cooling, required lubrication, good fuel and tune-ups and adjustments at the required intervals, the engine will usually last for many years without major problems. Many of the faults discussed in this chapter apply to engines that have been in service over long periods of time rather than problems of a minor nature that can occur at any time.

When troubleshooting an engine, *check the obvious first!* Look for signs of mechanical problems such as loose or broken components, oil, water or fuel leaks in the engine or on the ground beneath the engine. The first section of this chapter on engine troubleshooting deals with just such a method of troubleshooting: using your ears to detect engine malfunctions.

ENGINE NOISES

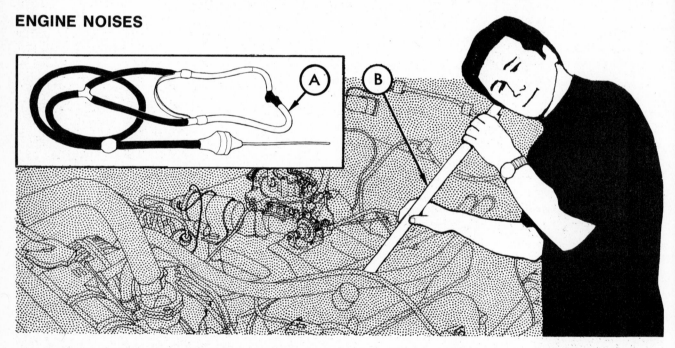

Engine noises are a good indicator of problem areas. Often a malfunction inside the engine will reveal itself first as a strange sound, before the effects of the problem become apparent in any other manner. There is, however, a drawback to using engine noises to troubleshoot. Unless you have some experience in listening to the various sounds that an engine can make, sometimes it's hard to determine just what you are listening to and exactly where it is coming from.

One simple tool which will aid the troubleshooter attempting to find a problem is a sounding stick (B) or mechanic's stethoscope (A). A sounding stick may be a piece of broom handle or a hollow tube. The sounding stick works by slightly dampening the sound around it while permitting the troubleshooter to hear a particular sound easily. The stick should be placed on the engine in the desired location, then the ear or the side of the head should be touched to the stick to listen to the sounds coming from inside the engine. Moving the stick from place to place on the engine will help to isolate the location of the sound that you are interested in. The mechanic's stethoscope works on exactly the same principle, but is capable of giving clearer results.

MAIN BEARING NOISE

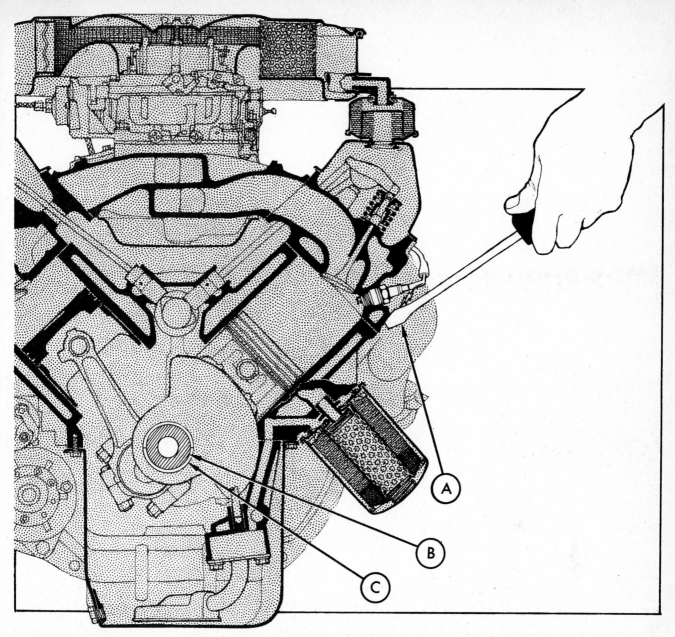

The engine main bearings (C) are bearings which fasten around the crankshaft (B) to support it inside the engine block. A problem in this area is accompanied by a strong, dull knocking or thudding sound, especially when the engine is under a load (going uphill). If more than one of the bearings is developing a problem, the sound will be a steady clatter.

The cause of main bearing noise is either a lack of lubrication or a bearing that has been worn to such a degree that insufficient lubrication is reaching the bearing surfaces.

This problem should not be allowed to persist. Main bearing failure can result in severe engine damage, so the engine should not be run any longer than it takes to confirm the source of the noise.

Main bearing noise or "knock" can be narrowed down to an individual bearing by shorting out spark plugs on cylinders adjacent to the bearing. Unless your ignition system wiring has a full rubber cover insulating the entire tip of the spark plug, it is fairly easy to short out the plug with a long-bladed screwdriver (A).

When the cylinder closest to the main bearing that is making the noise is shorted, it kills the power stroke and reduces the driving force transmitted to the crankshaft. This lessens the load being put on the faulty bearing, and the noise decreases or disappears.

Once it has been determined that the main bearing(s) are knocking, repairing them requires complete disassembly of the engine for an overhaul. Consult the manufacturer's shop manual for engine disassembly instructions. (Also see Petersen's BASIC AUTO REPAIR MANUAL and Petersen's BIG BOOK OF AUTO REPAIR.)

ROD BEARING NOISE

Rod bearing noise is much like main bearing noise and comes from the same basic troubles. If a rod bearing problem is allowed to persist, it can cause considerable damage to an engine.

The sound is much like a main bearing, but is slightly more metallic and may be pitched slightly higher.

The procedure for isolating a rod bearing knock is exactly the same as for the main bearings. Shorting the spark plugs adjacent to the bad bearing will cause the sound to be greatly reduced or eliminated.

PISTON PIN NOISE

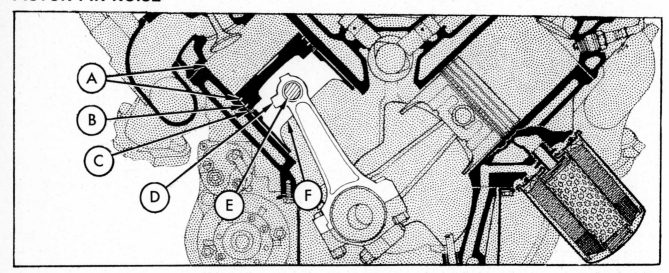

The piston pin (E), which connects the piston (F) to the top of the rod, makes a metallic knocking sound which is sometimes difficult to distinguish from the sound of a rod knock. The sound is a sharp double knock or clicking sound. The sound is most commonly heard when the engine is idling, but it can also be heard clearly on some engines when traveling at approximately 25 to 35 mph.

The problem is caused by a broken pin retainer (D), which allows the pin to move back and forth and come in contact with the side of the cylinder wall.

The procedure for determining piston pin noise is the same as for rod and main bearing noise, but the result is exactly the opposite. When the spark plug for the affected cylinder is shorted, the sound will increase instead of decrease. This is a good way to tell the difference between piston pin noise and that of rod or main bearing noises. In the case of multiple piston pin noise, it may be difficult to tell the difference between this and several other internal noises.

Some other piston-associated noises are:

1. Broken piston (E).

2. Broken piston ring (C).

3. Top piston ring strikes ridge at top of cylinder (A).

4. Piston slap (too much clearance between piston and cylinder wall). This is most common when the engine is cold.

5. Excessive side clearance of the ring in the piston lands (B). Lands are the retaining grooves machined in the sides of the pistons to hold the piston rings.

6. Carbon deposit on top of the piston, which will strike the cylinder head at the top of the piston's stroke.

7. Out-of-round or tapered cylinder bore. (This is due to wear that causes the material of the cylinder to be ground away.)

Any or all of these additional sources of noise may account for piston noises, but all mean the same thing. An engine which is making considerable noise is probably in need of an overhaul or replacement of parts such as bearings, rings, etc.

One additional check to isolate piston noises to a single cylinder or determine if the sound you hear is really a piston problem is to remove the spark plug from the suspected cylinder and squirt some heavy oil into the spark plug hole. This will briefly seal bad rings and provide lubrication. After squirting in the oil, crank the engine over a few times with the ignition disabled (coil high-tension lead disconnected), then start the engine. The cylinder that has been oiled should remain quiet for several minutes.

VALVE TRAIN NOISE

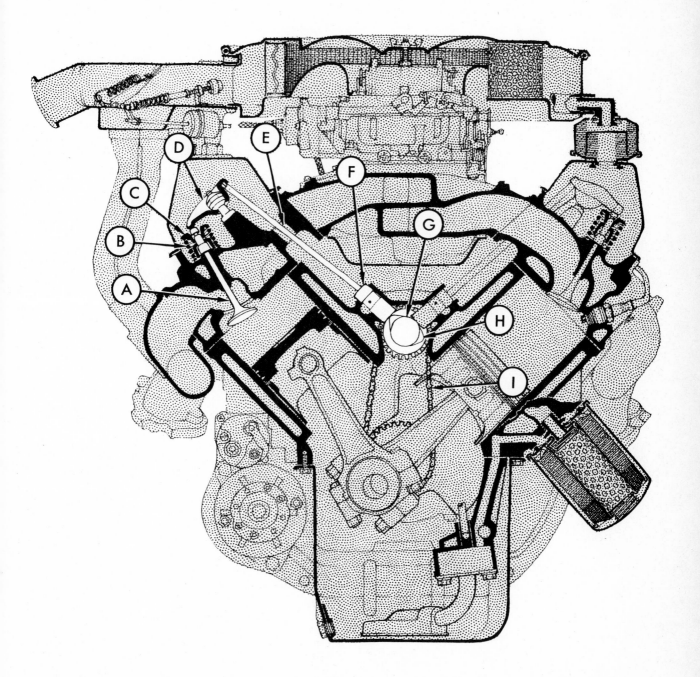

The valve train in the modern automobile engine includes the valves (A), springs (B), retainers (C), rocker arm (D), pushrods (E), tappets (lifters) (F) and the cam (G), which actuates the valve train. The cam is connected to the crankshaft by a chain drive (I) or belt drive in some late-model overhead cam engines. The cam rotates at half the engine speed. As the cam rotates, the eccentric cam lobes (H) push against the tappets, moving them up and down. This up and down action is transmitted through the rest of the valve train (pushrods and rocker arms) to open and close the valves in the correct sequence.

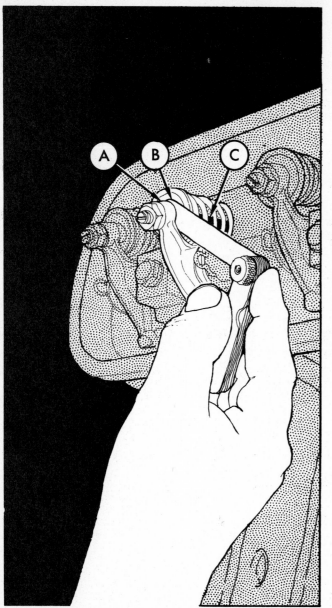

The most common cause of valve train noise is excessive clearance between components. Adjustment to the correct clearance is a job that is usually done during routine tune-ups. It is likely that if your car is making slight noises from the valve area, the valves are out of adjustment.

The sound of out-of-adjustment valves is a regular clicking sound. Since the valves are operated at half the engine speed, the frequency of the clicking noise will generally be less than other noises.

Locating a noisy valve with excessive clearance is easy; the only tool required is a feeler gauge (C). Remove the valve cover from the engine and start the engine.

NOTE: REFER TO A SHOP MANUAL FOR INFORMATION ON VALVE COVER REMOVAL AND THE REMOVAL OF ACCESSORIES BEFORE THE VALVE COVER CAN BE REMOVED. ALSO CHECK YOUR OWNER'S MANUAL OR SHOP MANUAL FOR THE CORRECT VALVE CLEARANCE SPECIFICATION FOR YOUR CAR.

With the engine running, select the correct size feeler gauge blade and insert it between the valve stem (B) and rocker arm (A).

If the problem is excessive clearance, the insertion of the feeler gauge will quiet the sound of the valve train for that valve.

To adjust the valve, refer to the shop manual or your owner's manual. (Also see Petersen's HOW TO TUNE YOUR CAR and Petersen's BASIC AUTO REPAIR MANUAL.)

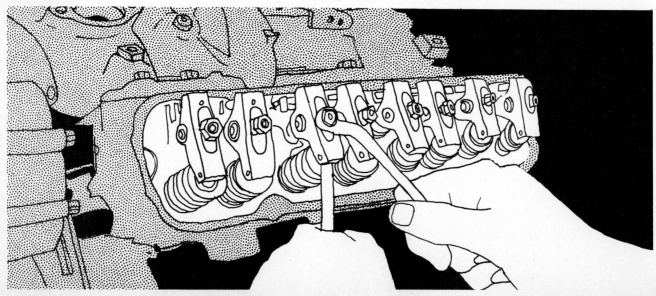

HYDRAULIC LIFTER NOISE

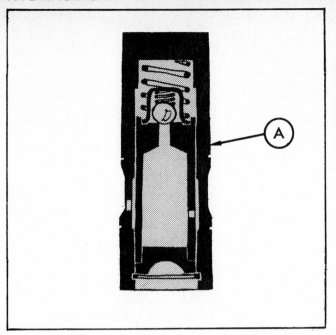

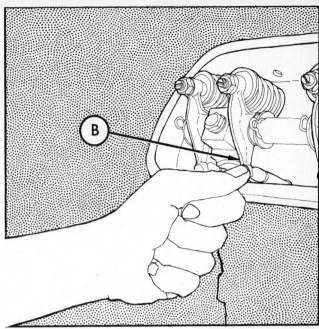

The hydraulic lifter (tappet) (A) is designed to cushion the opening and closing of the valve and reduce the shock to the valve train by the use of oil as a self-adjusting device. These hydraulic lifters frequently become noisy. The most common cause is either lack of oil or dirt plugging the oil holes in the body of the lifter, preventing it from working properly.

1. To locate a suspected noisy hydraulic lifter, remove the valve cover and start the engine.

2. Place a finger on each rocker arm (B) in turn (with the engine idling).

3. If the hydraulic lifter is not functioning properly, you will feel a sharp and distinct shock (not an electrical shock) as the valve returns to its seat.

4. To adjust the hydraulic lifter. refer to the shop manual or your owner's manual for instructions.

STICKING VALVE NOISE

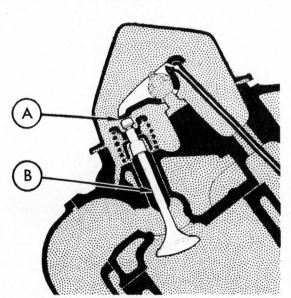

A valve which is sticking during its travel will make a noise very similar to that of a badly-adjusted valve (B).

To check for suspected sticky valves, drive the car at high speed, then quickly stop and allow the car to idle.

If there is a sticky valve, the clicking sound will be quite loud, but will gradually grow quieter and in some cases disappear completely as the engine cools down.

> **NOTE:** THE NOISE MAY ALSO BE ACCOMPANIED BY A JERKY OR ERRATIC ENGINE IDLE. WHEN RUNNING THE TEST JUST DESCRIBED, THE ERRATIC IDLE SHOULD DISAPPEAR ALONG WITH THE NOISE.

Some other valve-train-associated noises are caused by:

1. Insufficient oil reaching the valve components.

2. Worn or scored parts anywhere in the valve train.

3. Weak or broken valve springs.

4. Lower end of the tappet becoming rough, chipped, worn or broken.

5. Excessive valve stem to valve guide clearance (A).

ENGINE NOISES

LOOSE FLYWHEEL NOISE

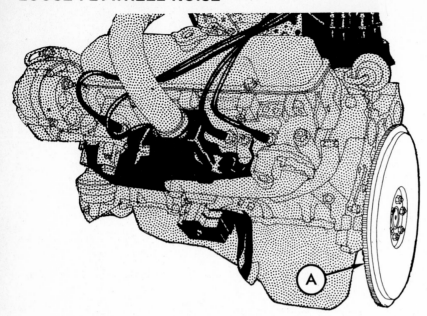

The heavy flywheel (A) attached to the back of the crankshaft on standard transmission-equipped cars can cause a strong clicking sound if it becomes loose. The sound is usually intermittent. To check for a loose flywheel, start the engine with the transmission in neutral and run the engine up to approximately 20 mph (simulated).

Turn off the ignition switch, and when the engine has just about stopped, turn the switch on again. This process should be repeated several times. If the flywheel is loose, you should hear the clicking sound each time the switch is turned on.

EXCESSIVE CRANKSHAFT ENDPLAY NOISE

Excessive crankshaft endplay (fore and aft movement) will cause a sharp click or rap which is quite easy to hear.

To check this, run the engine at idle speeds with transmission in neutral. Engage and disengage the clutch several times. The sharp click or rap should be heard during engagement of the clutch.

PRE-IGNITION NOISE

Pre-ignition noise, commonly called "ping," is a ringing metallic sound usually heard when the engine accelerates strongly (quick takeoff or climbing a hill) or is hot. One cause is an incandescent (glowing with intense heat) particle of carbon or metal in the combustion chamber which ignites the air/fuel mixture before it is fired by the spark. Because this happens while the piston is still moving up and compressing the air/fuel mixture, very high pressures are built up in the cylinder.

Other causes of pre-ignition are:

1. Ignition timing that's advanced too far.
2. Using gas with too low an octane rating for your engine.
3. Transmission in wrong gear, causing the engine to lug down.

The method of correcting pre-ignition ping where carbon is suspected is to partly disassemble the engine (remove the cylinder heads) and remove the built-up carbon from the tops of the pistons and the insides of the combustion chambers. (For more complete information, refer to a shop manual or Petersen's BASIC AUTO REPAIR MANUAL.)

EXTERNAL ENGINE EQUIPMENT NOISES

All of the accessory equipment associated with the engine can cause strange noises that worry the driver. Generators, alternators, air conditioning pumps, water pumps, power steering and brake equipment—each can make a number of noises, all of which may sound basically the same to the person trying to troubleshoot the source of a strange noise under the hood of his car.

Each of these individual parts can be isolated by disconnecting it from the engine. For example: A squeaky sound which seems to be coming from the auto's air conditioning pump can be checked by loosening the drive belt so that the pump does not operate when the engine is running. If the sound goes away, chances are that you have found the general area of the problem. You can then refer to the specific part of this book or other references for more information on fixing the problem part.

ENGINE OIL PRESSURE PROBLEMS

Among the most critical elements inside an automobile engine are the oil supply and the components which deliver the oil to areas in the engine where it will be used. No engine could run more than a few minutes without oil to lubricate moving parts and reduce friction. Without a lubricant, moving parts that come in contact with each other would start to fail.

ENGINE LUBRICATION SYSTEM

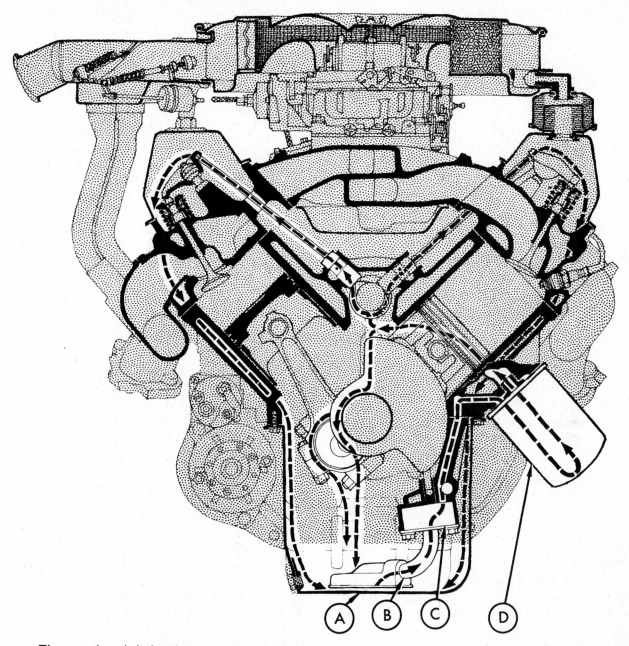

The engine lubrication system consists of a sump (A), the oil pan at the bottom of the engine that holds a supply of oil; a pickup tube (B) inside the sump; an oil pump (C) that forces oil through the engine; and a filter (D) which cleans the oil and removes metal particles, carbon and other foreign materials from the oil.

Oil is picked up from the sump by the pickup tube. It passes through the pump, through the filter and into the engine oil galleries (galleries are holes or passageways inside the engine block and heads which route the oil to the various parts of the engine). The oil is in constant circulation while the engine is running.

One good indicator of engine condition is the amount of oil pressure being delivered by the oil pump. Without oil, moving metal surfaces will rapidly wear or heat up due to friction. If the heating problem becomes severe enough, the moving parts of the engine can actually melt or weld themselves together. Below is a list of things that can cause a low oil pressure reading.

OIL PRESSURE GAUGE

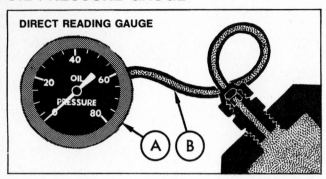

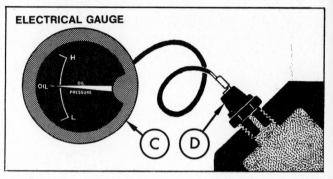

Remember to *check the obvious first!* The gauge or warning light mounted in the dashboard of your car may be the problem. These gauges and lights are designed to give a warning of low or no oil pressure, but they can fail even if there is no real problem in the oil system.

There are two basic types of oil pressure warning systems. One uses direct oil pressure through a length of tubing (B) which carries oil directly to a dashboard-mounted gauge (A). The other, much more common system is electrical. It uses a sensor (D) in the oil system which converts oil pressure into an electrical signal and sends it to the gauge (C) by wiring. Both do the same job, and checking them is about the same. Look for broken or pinched tubing or wiring to the gauge, leaking oil around the sensing unit or any other unusual conditions. Also, direct-reading gauges which use tubing should be checked to be sure that the tubing is not clogged with debris. Electrical gauges can be checked with a test meter (see detailed checks of automobile electrical accessories). Those electrical systems which use a warning light can be checked in the same manner.

CAUTION: IF THE OIL PRESSURE GAUGE OR WARNING LIGHT INDICATE A LACK OF PRESSURE, STOP THE ENGINE IMMEDIATELY AND DETERMINE WHAT THE PROBLEM IS. IF THE PROBLEM IS NOT IN THE GAUGE OR SENDING UNIT, RUNNING THE ENGINE WITH NO OIL PRESSURE WILL CAUSE SEVERE ENGINE DAMAGE.

LACK OF OIL

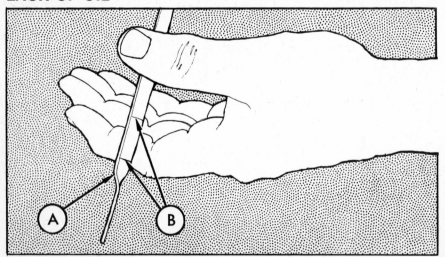

Low engine oil pressure can occur if the amount of oil available to the engine is reduced. If the oil level becomes low enough, engine damage can result. Checking oil is done by removing the dipstick (A), a metal shaft which reaches into the oil pan to show oil level. The dipstick is marked with lines (B) to show the proper oil level. If a check of the dipstick shows a low oil level, you may need to refer to the sections on oil leaks and excessive oil consumption.

CAUTION: DO NOT RUN THE ENGINE WITH LITTLE OR NO OIL. SEVERE ENGINE DAMAGE WILL RESULT.

OIL TOO THIN

Low engine oil pressure can sometimes be the fault of oil that has been thinned out by water or gasoline. If examination of the dipstick shows tiny bubbles of water or the oil smells strongly of gasoline, something is wrong. The engine should be torn down to check for blown gaskets or other possible problems, such as a crack in the head or block.

Low oil pressure can also occur if the oil is the wrong weight.

NOTE: OIL WEIGHT DESCRIBES ITS VISCOSITY OR THICKNESS. FOR EXAMPLE, A LIGHTWEIGHT OIL IS A 10 WEIGHT, WHILE THE STANDARD WEIGHT OF MOST AUTOMOTIVE OILS IS 30 WEIGHT. IF THERE IS ANY DOUBT THAT THE WEIGHT OF THE OIL IN THE ENGINE IS CORRECT, DRAIN IT AND FILL THE CRANKCASE OR SUMP WITH THE MANUFACTURER'S SUGGESTED WEIGHT OIL.

OIL PUMP WORN

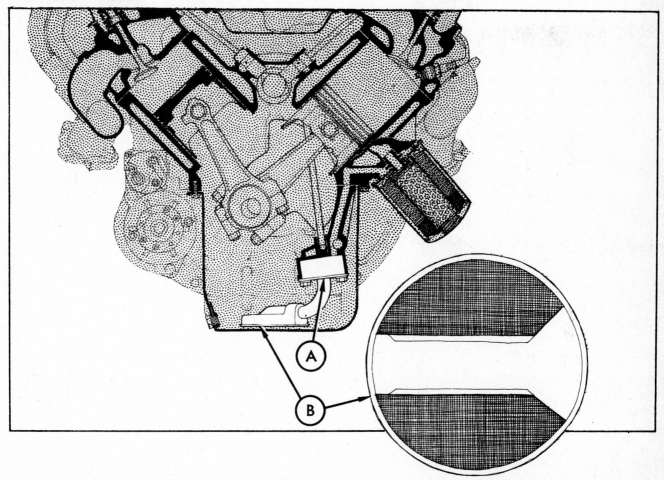

The oil pump (A) used to circulate the oil inside the engine is a gear-driven type. Several kinds of wear on moving parts or the failure of a gasket in the pump can reduce the pump's ability to pump oil. These are not problems easily found and repaired by the home mechanic, as they require removal of the oil pan to get at the pump.

NOTE: SOME PUMPS ARE MOUNTED OUTSIDE THE OIL PAN WITH THE PICKUP INSIDE.

OIL INTAKE SCREEN CLOGGED

The oil pickup (B), which rests in the bottom of the oil pan, sucks up oil, which is then passed through the pump and on to the rest of the lubrication system. The pickup is usually fitted with a filter in the form of a mesh screen. This mesh screen can become clogged with debris if the oil is not changed regularly. The oil pressure in the engine will drop if the pump cannot pick up enough oil.

ENGINE OIL PRESSURE PROBLEMS

OIL PRESSURE RELIEF VALVE

Incorporated inside the oil pump is a spring-loaded relief valve which maintains engine oil pressure within certain limits. As the engine rpm increase, so does the speed of the oil pump. It often pumps oil faster and at a higher pressure than is necessary to lubricate the engine. At a certain limit, the excess pressure opens the relief valve and allows some of the oil to go directly back to the pan without going to the rest of the engine. This lowers both the oil volume and pressure. If the relief valve sticks or becomes weak, however, it will not allow the oil pressure to come up to normal limits.

OIL FILTERS

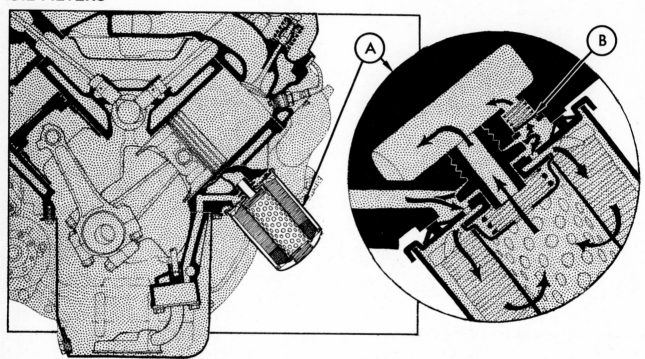

After the oil is passed through the pump, it goes through a filter (A) to remove particles and other matter which might damage bearings and other parts inside the engine. There are two basic filter types: *full flow* and *partial flow*. In the full-flow design, all the oil that passes through the pump goes through the filter to be cleaned, except when the oil is cold or the filter is plugged with dirt. When this happens, a bypass valve (B) opens, bypassing the filter to provide oil to the engine. The other system, the partial-flow filter, only receives and filters a part of the engine oil at any one time. Normally the oil filter will not cause a low or no oil pressure reading unless (in the case of the full-flow system) the filter becomes so clogged with dirt and debris that it also plugs the bypass valve.

AIR LEAK IN PICKUP TUBE

If the oil level is very low in the pan, the upper part of the screen at the pickup tube end may be exposed to air. The oil pump will then be pumping air instead of oil (this is called pump cavitation). Also, it is not uncommon for the pickup tube to come loose from the pump housing or to develop a crack which permits air to enter the pump.

WORN BEARINGS

As main, rod and camshaft bearings wear during their normal service life, the clearance between their surfaces becomes larger. Since a larger volume of oil is then required for lubrication, lower pressure results.

NOTE: IF WORN BEARINGS ARE BAD ENOUGH TO CAUSE A SERIOUS DROP IN OIL PRESSURE, CHANCES ARE GOOD THAT YOU WILL HEAR SOME OF THE ENGINE NOISES ALREADY DESCRIBED IN THIS CHAPTER.

NO OIL PRESSURE

CAUTION: IF THE OIL PRESSURE GAUGE OR WARNING LIGHT INDICATE A LACK OF PRESSURE, STOP THE ENGINE IMMEDIATELY AND DETERMINE WHAT THE PROBLEM IS. IF THE PROBLEM IS NOT IN THE GAUGE OR SENDING UNIT, RUNNING THE ENGINE WITH NO OIL PRESSURE WILL CAUSE SEVERE ENGINE DAMAGE.

If the reading on the oil pressure gauge is zero or if the oil warning light comes on and stays on, the problem areas are exactly the same as those already outlined in the section on low oil pressure. CHECK THE OBVIOUS FIRST. If a check of the gauge or warning light system fails to turn up the problem, you must assume that something major is wrong with the engine lubrication system. (For more information, see the shop manual or Petersen's BASIC AUTO REPAIR MANUAL.)

HIGH OIL PRESSURE

If oil pressure reads much higher than normal, several things could be wrong. (You will not get an indication of high oil pressure with the light system.) First, check the gauge to make sure that it is working (not physically broken and the wiring to the gauge not damaged). Then determine that the oil used is the correct type and weight for the engine. Too heavy an oil weight will cause a high-pressure reading. Other things that could cause this are: The oil pressure relief valve adjustment could be set too high, or the valve could be stuck shut by sludge. It is also quite possible that the main oil passages on the pressure side of the pump are clogged with sludge.

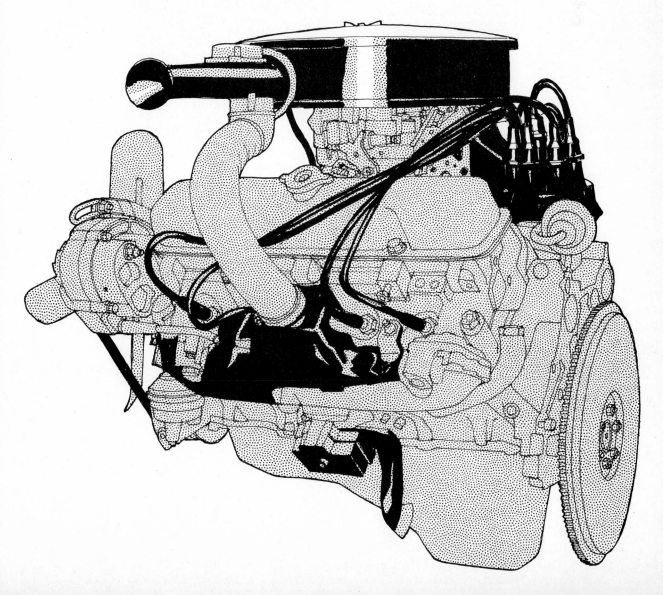

EXCESSIVE OIL CONSUMPTION

EXTERNAL OIL LEAKS

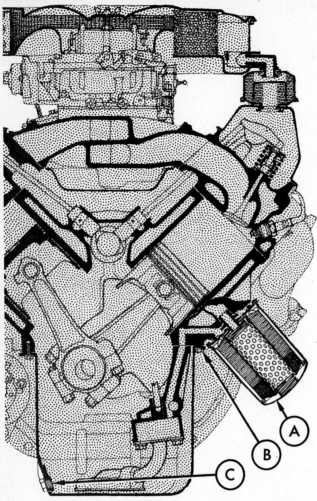

Excessive oil consumption can result from engine oil simply leaking out through openings in a gasket or at points where two parts of the engine are joined (valve cover to heads). Other spots where oil leakage can be expected are around oil seals and around moving parts that leave the inside of the engine, such as the crankshaft seals around the fore and aft ends of the crank, where the crankshaft exits from the engine.

The most common points of oil leakage are around the oil filter (A) and around the edges of the pan (B) and the pan drain plug (C). A small loss of oil will occur at these points when the oil is changed, but large amounts of oil on the underside of the engine or on the inner fender areas indicate a major oil leak.

Fresh oil coming from the inside of the engine will be cleaner than oil that has been outside the engine long enough to attract dirt. If the oil leak is really severe and has coated a large area, it may be necessary to steam clean the engine compartment before checking the location of the leak. Once the leak has been found, it can often be cured simply by tightening the part that is leaking. For example, engine valve covers often develop small leaks, because the screws holding them down vibrate loose. In the case of gaskets that leak even when the part is tightly bolted, the gasket should be replaced. Refer to the shop manual for correct procedures.

External oil leaks are often caused by blowby, a problem created when piston rings become so worn that they allow combustion chamber pressure to force its way past them and pressurize the oil pan area. This forces oil out around the pan gasket and other areas that don't leak under normal oil pan pressures.

Blowby usually happens when the crankcase ventilating system is plugged up and unable to relieve the pressure

CRANKCASE VENTILATION SYSTEM

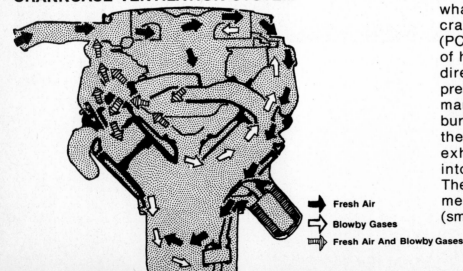

Fresh Air
Blowby Gases
Fresh Air And Blowby Gases

Modern automobiles have what is known as a positive crankcase ventilation system (PCV). This is an arrangement of hoses and a check-valve that directs crankcase vapor and pressures back into the intake manifold so they can be reburned. Older cars did not have the PCV system; they merely exhausted crankcase vapors into the outside atmosphere. The old system was modified to meet new emissions control (smog) requirements.

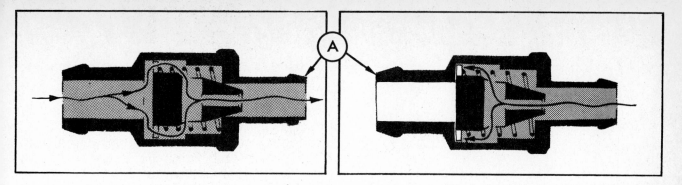

The check valve (A) used in most forms of PCV systems is a simple one-way valve used to prevent the reverse flow of air through the system. The valve can become plugged with dirt and sludge. If this happens, the system cannot relieve the pressure inside the crankcase and oil can be forced out, resulting in leaks.

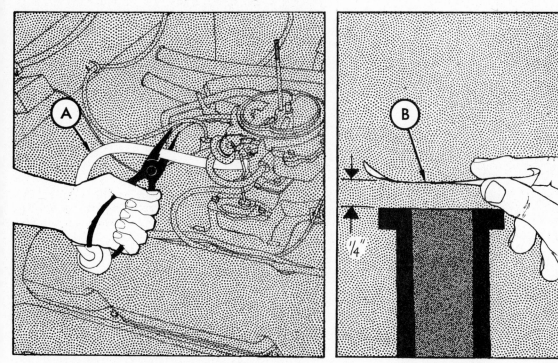

To check the PCV valve, first locate the hose leading from the valve cover or the side of the crankcase to the base of the carburetor. At some point in this line you will find the PCV valve. Start the engine and let it run until it reaches normal operating temperature. Pinch the hose (A) shut with a pair of pliers.

CAUTION: BE SURE PLIERS HAVE SMOOTH JAWS OR YOU'LL DAMAGE THE HOSE.

If the PCV system is working, the engine's idle rpm will drop between 60 and 100 rpm (an audible drop). If the rpm do not drop, there is a good chance that the PCV valve is plugged.

A second method of checking the operation of the PCV system is to remove the oil filler cap and hold a small card or light piece of paper (B) approximately ¼-inch from the opening. With the engine running, suction in the crankcase should pull the paper to the opening.

Some PCV valves can be taken apart and cleaned in solvent, while others are simply thrown away and a new one installed. It's a good idea to replace PCV valves at each tune-up.

NOTE: IF THE PCV VALVE WAS BADLY CLOGGED, THE HOSE MAY ALSO NEED TO BE INSPECTED AND CLEANED BEFORE IT IS REINSTALLED ON THE ENGINE.

EXCESSIVE OIL CONSUMPTION

VACUUM BOOSTER PUMP

On cars equipped with a vacuum booster pump (A) to operate vacuum windshield wipers, excessive oil consumption can occur if the diaphragm (flexible disc inside the vacuum pump) tears or becomes porous. When this happens, the vacuum sucks oil vapor from the crankcase and sends it to the intake manifold area.

To check the vacuum booster pump, turn the windshield wipers on (with the engine idling).

CAUTION: BE SURE TO WET THE WINDSHIELD TO PREVENT DAMAGING THE WIPER BLADES OR SCRATCHING THE GLASS.

If the windshield wipers stop when you accelerate the engine, the booster pump is probably bad.

To confirm this, disconnect the line running from the pump to the intake manifold (B). If there is any oil film present inside the line, the pump is bad. Refer to the shop manual for instructions on how to repair or replace the pump.

INTERNAL OIL CONSUMPTION

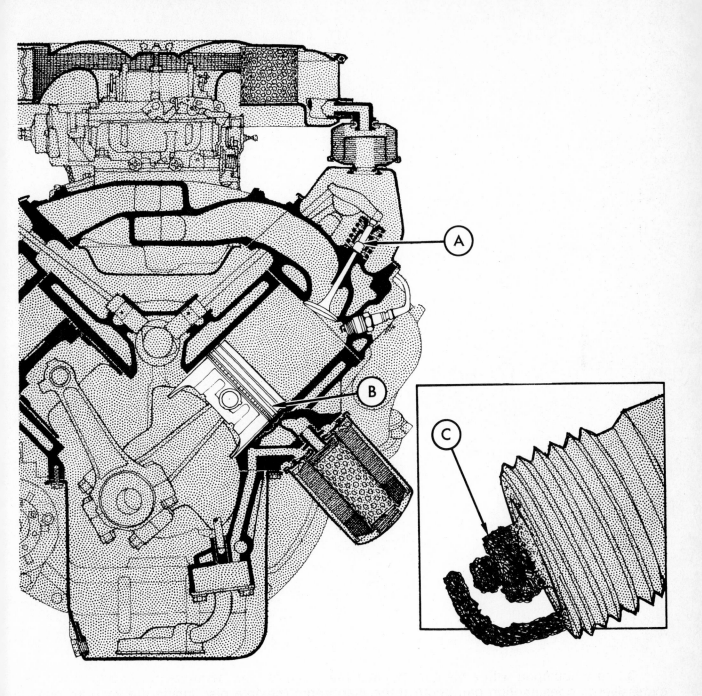

Internal oil consumption means oil is being burned along with the fuel inside the combustion chambers of the engine. A sign of this is a blue, smoky exhaust, especially after the engine has been idling for a few minutes and then accelerates. Another symptom is fouled spark plugs (C), where a black, gummy substance is on the plugs. The positive crankcase ventilation system and the vacuum booster pump (already discussed) can show much the same symptoms, but the effect is much more pronounced in the case of bad engine wear.

The two primary places where oil can get into the combustion chambers are the valve guides (A) and the piston rings (B). The rings and the valve guides act as oil seals. As wear occurs, they begin letting some oil slip by into the combustion chamber, where it burns.

If internal oil consumption becomes severe enough, the engine will require a teardown and overhaul to replace and repair the valve guides and piston rings. Other possible problems are extreme bore wear along with the rings. If you suspect internal oil consumption, refer to the shop manual for overhaul instructions. (Also see Petersen's BASIC AUTO REPAIR MANUAL.)

TROUBLESHOOTING WITH A VACUUM GAUGE

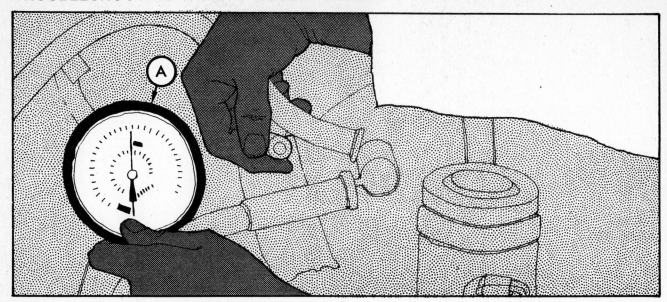

One of the most practical methods of determining the internal condition of an engine is through the use of a vacuum gauge (A). The internal vacuum of the engine varies with each separate operation of its parts. The gauge itself is not expensive, and the information gained from it is very valuable in troubleshooting.

The vacuum gauge reads the level of vacuum built up in the intake manifold while the engine is running. Several parts of the automobile operate off this vacuum, such as windshield wipers (in some models), power brakes and distributor vacuum advance. By means of a hose and fitting, the vacuum gauge connects to the intake manifold or between the manifold and one of the accessories that uses its vacuum to function. Instructions packed with the vacuum gauge or in the shop manual for the car you are working on will give the exact hookup procedure.

The vacuum gauge reads internal engine vacuum in inches of mercury. Inches-of-mercury is abbreviated "ins. Hg", and that's how we will write it in this section. Ins. Hg is a measurement developed by placing liquid mercury in a glass tube and marking the tube off in divisions. A vacuum applied to one end of the tube causes the mercury to rise or fall in the tube a specific distance, a measurement that can be used to rate the strength of any vacuum or change in pressure. A barometer works on this same principle. You don't have to worry about the principles involved; the meter or dial of the vacuum is clearly marked and easy to read. This inexpensive tool is very valuable for both professional and home mechanics.

VACUUM GAUGE TROUBLESHOOTING LIST

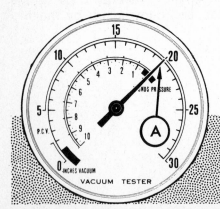

NORMAL ENGINE READING: A normal engine will produce a gauge reading (A) of approximately 18 to 22 ins. Hg with the pointer remaining quite steady.

Eight-cylinder engines will read toward the high end of the scale, while six-cylinder engines will read toward the low end of the scale.

NOTE: SOME LATE MODEL CARS WITH OVERLAPPING VALVE TIMING MAY SHOW A CERTAIN AMOUNT OF NEEDLE MOVEMENT.

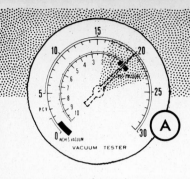

LEAKING VALVE READING: If a valve is leaking, the pointer on indicator (A) will fluctuate from 1 to 7 ins. Hg at regular intervals each time the leaking valve attempts to close (engine at idle).

NOTE: MANY OF THE INDICATIONS SHOWN HERE ARE SIMILAR. THE CORRECT WAY TO PERFORM THIS CHECK IS TO REPEAT THE TEST SEVERAL TIMES TO MAKE SURE OF THE READINGS YOU ARE GETTING. ALTHOUGH SOME OF THESE READINGS MAY BE THE SAME OR NEARLY THE SAME, THEY ALL MEAN THAT THERE IS SOMETHING WRONG INSIDE THE ENGINE AND THAT DISASSEMBLY AND OVERHAUL MAY BE NEEDED.

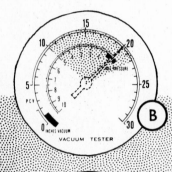

BROKEN OR WEAK VALVE SPRING READING: The pointer on indicator (B) will move rapidly between 10 and 22 ins. Hg with the engine running at 2,000 rpm. If the valve spring is weak, the movement of the pointer will increase as the engine rpm increase. If the valve spring is broken, the pointer will move rapidly each time the valve attempts to close.

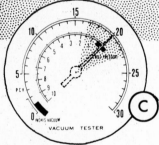

WORN VALVE GUIDES READING: Valve guides (portions of the cylinder head through which the stems of the intake and exhaust valves pass) will give a reading on indicator (C) lower than normal, with slow fluctuations of approximately 3 ins. Hg above and below normal when the engine is at idle.

PISTON RING DEFECTS READING: Bring the engine speed to approximately 2,000 rpm, then release the throttle quickly. The pointer on indicator (D) should jump from approximately 2 ins. Hg to 5 ins. Hg above the normal reading if the rings are good. A lower reading should be followed up by making a compression check.

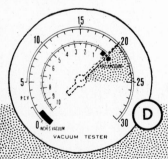

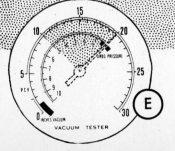

BLOWN CYLINDER HEAD GASKET READING: If some portion of the gasket between the cylinder head and the block has failed and is letting the engine compression leak from one or more cylinders, the pointer on indicator (E) will drop sharply to approximately 10 ins. Hg each time the affected cylinder(s) fire(s).

TROUBLESHOOTING WITH A VACUUM GAUGE

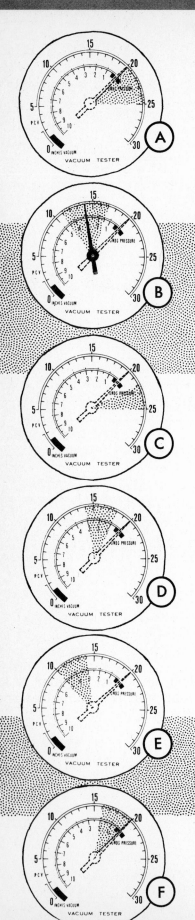

INCORRECT IDLE AIR/FUEL MIXTURE READING: If the needle on indicator (A) drifts slowly back and forth above the normal reading when the engine is idling, the fuel mixture is too rich (too much gas for the amount of air entering the engine). A lean mixture (too little fuel) will cause the pointer to drop slightly at irregular intervals.

INTAKE MANIFOLD AIR LEAKS READING: If there is any air leaking between the intake manifold and the cylinder heads, the pointer on indicator (B) will drop from 3 ins. Hg to 9 ins. Hg below the normal engine reading (engine at idle) and will remain quite steady.

EXHAUST SYSTEM RESTRICTION READING: If there is something causing a restriction (back pressure) in the exhaust system, it can seriously affect engine performance. To check this, open the throttle until the engine reaches approximately 2,000 rpm. Then release the throttle quickly. If there is no restriction, the pointer on indicator (C) will drop to not less than 2 ins. Hg or more above the normal engine reading. If the gauge does not show 5 ins. Hg or more above the normal reading and the pointer seems to stop for a moment as it returns, the exhaust system is partially restricted. Check for bent or dented exhaust pipes or a core shift inside the muffler.

LATE IGNITION TIMING READING: A low, steady reading on indicator (D) at idle indicates late ignition timing (retarded) or that the valve clearances are too tight.

LATE VALVE TIMING READING: A steady but very low reading on indicator (E) is generally caused by late ignition timing. But if advancing the ignition timing does not increase the reading, the valve timing is out of adjustment.

STICKING VALVE READING: A sticking valve is indicated on gauge (F) by a rapid, intermittent pointer drop every time the valve is supposed to close while the engine is at idle. A sticking valve condition can be pinpointed by applying a small amount of penetrating oil or lacquer thinner to each valve guide in turn. When you reach the sticky valve, the problem will clear up for a few minutes.

TROUBLESHOOTING WITH COMPRESSION GAUGE

TROUBLESHOOTING WITH A COMPRESSION GAUGE

The compression gauge (A) is used to check the ability of each cylinder to compress the air/fuel mixture for burning. It is an important tool for troubleshooting. Along with the vacuum gauge, it can tell the mechanic about a number of important internal engine parts and how they are working.

USING THE GAUGE: To use a compression gauge to check engine cylinder compression, remove all the spark plugs. Insert the tip of the compression gauge into the spark plug hole.

NOTE: SOME COMPRESSION GAUGES HAVE A RUBBER TIP WHICH MUST BE HELD IN PLACE, WHILE OTHERS USE A THREADED TIP WHICH SCREWS INTO THE SPARK PLUG HOLE.

CAUTION: BE SURE TO DISCONNECT THE COIL HIGH-TENSION LEAD BEFORE CRANKING THE ENGINE.

With the throttle held wide open, crank the engine over for a long enough period of time to record several complete revolutions of the engine. Most good compression gauges are equipped with a device that traps the air inside the gauge so that the highest reading obtained will stay on the face of the indicator (by the use of a dual pointer) until you release it. Note the reading on the indicator (write it down), then go to another cylinder and repeat until you have checked all the cylinders.

CHECKING THE RESULTS: Because all engines are not identical, it is best to refer to the shop manual for the engine you are working on for the correct readings. The gauge readings should be within 10 pounds above or below ($\pm$ 10 pounds) the reading specified by the manufacturer.

Readings *below* the listed specifications indicate that the rings, valves or pistons require maintenance. You can further check this by squirting some medium-weight oil into each spark plug opening. Work the oil down into the rings by cranking the engine over for a few seconds, then repeat the checks with the compression gauge. If the readings come up normal, the problem is the rings, pistons or cylinder.

If there is no increase in the readings as the oil attempts to seal the rings, it indicates that the valves are in poor condition.

BLOWN HEAD GASKETS: A serious drop in pressure in one or more cylinders can mean several things, from broken rings to a hole burned in a piston, but the most likely cause is a blown head gasket. Another strong sign of a blown head gasket is two side-by-side cylinders that show approximately the same low compression reading while other cylinders check as good. This indicates that the head gasket is blown (torn or broken) between the cylinders.

TROUBLESHOOTING AIR CONDITIONERS

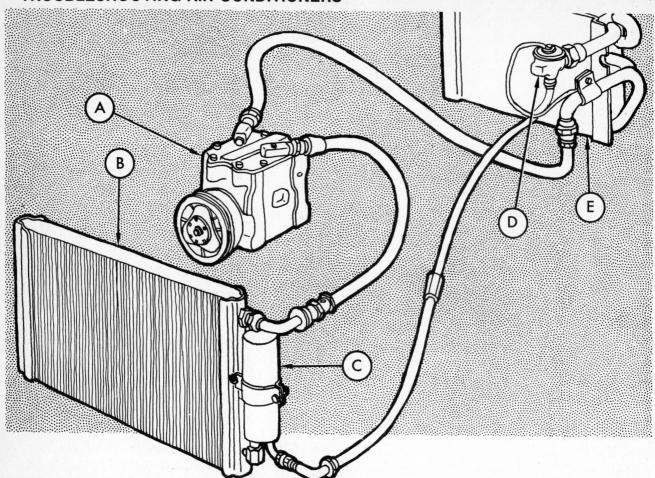

The typical automotive air conditioner is composed of the following pieces of equipment: the compressor (A), the condenser (B), the receiver (C), the expansion valve (D), the evaporator unit (E) and the connecting hoses. An air conditioning unit works on the simple physical principle that when a liquid is converted to a gas, it absorbs heat from its surroundings. When it is reconverted from a gaseous state back to a liquid, it gives up this heat.

The air conditioning unit in your car works this way. It circulates a liquid called Refrigerant 12 (Freon) through a system that causes it to turn into a gas while passing through the evaporator (E) inside the driver's compartment. The gas draws heat from the air inside the car, then is pumped back into the engine compartment through lines to a condenser (B), where it is reconverted into a liquid and stored in the receiver (C). As the gas turns back into a liquid, it exhausts or gives up the heat removed from inside the car.

The compressor (A) is nothing more than a pump driven by a belt, like the power steering unit or the generator. This pump picks up the gas coming from the evaporator (E) inside the car (which closely resembles a radiator) and compresses it. The high-pressure gas then flows into the condenser (B), which is a small radiator usually fitted in front or to the side of the radiator for the engine. Inside the condenser the high-pressure gas is cooled by the flow of cool air through the radiator and changes from a gas back to a liquid (still under high pressure). It then flows out of the condenser into the receiver (C), which is a holding tank for the liquid being supplied to the evaporator. The liquid coolant then flows through a hose to a device known as an expansion valve (D). This valve is the controlling factor for the flow of coolant through the evaporator. It senses the temperature of the gas leaving the evaporator and balances the incoming flow of liquid so the system works properly. If the expansion valve were not present, the coolant would flow through the evaporator so quickly that it could not draw enough heat from the inside of the car and would still be a liquid when it left the evaporator. This would not remove heat from the car. The compressor cannot compress a liquid. If liquid were to get back to the compressor, it would be damaged.

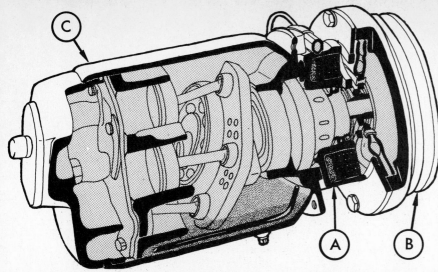

The compressor is connected to the drive pulley on most cars by a magnetic clutch (A). This device disconnects the compressor from the drive pulley and belt if the temperature drops below the temperature selected by the driver. This stops the compressor from working even though the belt is still turning the pulley. When the temperature inside the car again rises enough to require cooling, the clutch automatically engages and starts the compressor working.

Inside the driver's compartment are the evaporator and the controls for the air conditioning. There is an electric motor and fan incorporated with the evaporator to direct air over the evaporator and out through adjustable vents to cool the inside of the car.

WARNING: THE REFRIGERANT USED IN AIR CONDITIONING SYSTEMS IS HAZARDOUS. IT IS AN ODORLESS, TASTELESS GAS OR LIQUID AND CANNOT BE READILY DETECTED. DO NOT ATTEMPT TO DISASSEMBLE ANY PORTION OF THE SYSTEM. TAKE THE CAR TO A QUALIFIED AIR CONDITIONING MECHANIC. THE REFRIGERANT BOILS AT 21 DEGREES FARENHEIT AND CAN SEVERELY INJURE SKIN BY FREEZING.

SYSTEM DOES NOT COOL

Check the drive belt for signs of glazing or fraying. Examine it to see if it is tight enough to prevent slipping when the air conditioning is turned on. If the belt shows signs of wear, replace it. Using two people, check out the operation of the clutch (A) between the pulley (B) and the compressor (C). Have one person sit in the car and start the engine. Have him turn the air conditioning on and off several times while you watch the clutch. You should be able to see the clutch operate and hear a sound each time the clutch engages. If the clutch does not operate, the trouble could be in either the clutch or the sensing device which operates it.

Visually check all of the hoses and connections for obvious signs of worn or ruptured areas. Look at the condenser to see if it is clogged with dirt, leaves or bugs. Materials that clog up the fins of the condenser can result in a loss of cooling efficiency. If there are any obvious spots of ice or frost on the outside of the condenser after the air conditioning has been operating for a while, it can mean that there is some internal destruction in the condenser core.

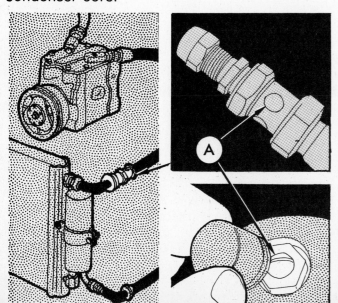

If the compressor and condenser appear to be working, examine the sight glass (A). This gives you a look at the condition of the coolant itself. There may be bubbles in the sight glass for a few moments just after the system is turned on, but they should soon disappear. If the liquid is cloudy or foamy, there is something wrong, probably moisture contamination. If the bubbles persist more than a few moments you are probably low on Freon coolant. Take the car to your local air conditioning mechanic for further checking.

The presence of the bubbles in the sight glass may indicate that the filter element in the receiver unit is used up. Most receiver units have a combination filter/dehydrator to remove moisture and small dirt particles. The receiver can be replaced as a unit, but it is not recommended that the reader do it.

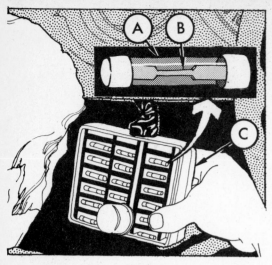

The next step is to check the electrical operation of the system. If turning on the air conditioner does not produce a flow of air from the outlets in the dashboard (some units may have a separate switch for different blower speeds), the blower motor is not operating. The first thing to check is the fuse block (C) for the electrical accessories. The different fuses are marked with writing to denote their function. Find the one marked A/C or AIR. (If in doubt, see the shop manual or owner's manual for the location of the fuse block and markings for your model car.) Check the fuse to see if it has blown. The fuse (A) may be clear glass, permitting visual inspection of the wire (B) inside, or it may need to be checked with a meter as you would check continuity of a wire. (See the chapter on electrical accessories.)

If the fuse checks out as good, examine the wiring and the switch. You may wish to check the switch with a meter as you did when checking out the starter and ignition systems. If both switch and fuse are good, the problem is most likely in the blower motor itself.

SYSTEM COOLS PARTIALLY

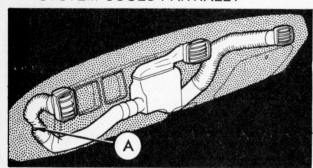

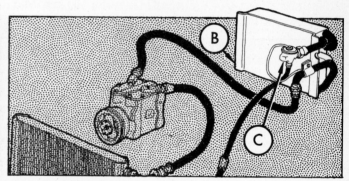

If the air conditioner works but will not deliver sufficient cooling air, the problem may be a slipping clutch mechanism or a loss of coolant from the system. It is also possible that something other than the air conditioner is at fault. Check the fresh air vents to see if one is stuck partially open, allowing hot outside air to enter the car. Also look at the ducting for the air conditioner which runs from the evaporator housing to the outlets. One of these may be collapsed or loose (A). If so, replace the ducting. A torn or detached duct can be repaired with tape.

The evaporator unit (B) itself can be the problem. In normal operation it should be cold and "sweating" (condensed moisture on the outside), but it should not have any frost or ice on it. If there is frost or ice on the surface of the evaporator, the problem is most likely the expansion valve (C) or the temperature sensor element. The evaporator is equipped with a drainage system to remove the water that condenses on the surface. This should be checked to make sure it is working properly. If it is clogged with dirt, it can cause water to drip on the floor carpet.

Air conditioners that work but do not cool completely are usually suffering from coolant loss. This can be repaired by having an air conditioning mechanic recharge the system with a fresh load of coolant. Some coolant loss is normal, but if efficiency falls off within three months or so after being recharged, the leakage rate is too high for normal use and the system should be checked.

For best results and long operating life, air conditioners should be operated every few days even in cold weather. It is not necessary to run the system for more than two or three minutes, but it should be done at least twice a month.

We do not recommend that you attempt to troubleshoot the internal workings of the air conditioner or recharge the system. It requires special tools and knowledge which are beyond the scope of basic troubleshooting. Take the car to a qualified air conditioning mechanic for detailed troubleshooting and repair.

TROUBLESHOOTING HEATERS

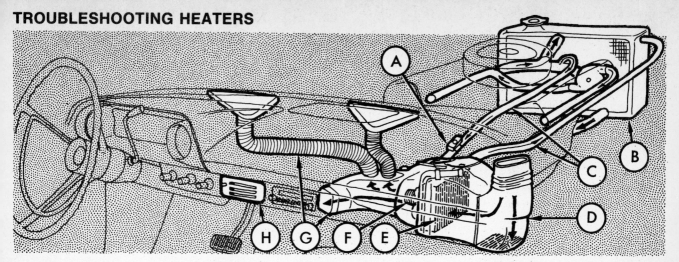

The heater is nothing more than a small radiator (E) through which circulates the engine coolant. It is connected to the engine by hoses (C). A small amount of the heated coolant leaving the engine passes through the heater before going to the engine radiator (B) for cooling. Once the engine is up to normal operating temperature, the coolant is hot enough to warm the air directed over the heater core (E).

The heater is equipped with an electric motor and fan (F), usually with several speeds and a system of ducting (G) to direct the heated air either under the dash toward the floorboards or to the inside of the windshield for defrosting. These ducts have doors in them operated by cable controls (H) mounted on the dash.

> **NOTE:** SOME LARGE AND MORE EXPENSIVE AUTOMOBILES USE VACUUM TO CONTROL DUCT DOORS RATHER THAN CABLES. CHECK THE MANUAL FOR YOUR CAR.

The driver can manually adjust the position of these doors to direct the air flow from the heater as he desires it.

Heat level is controlled in two different ways. One type of heater allows the heated coolant to flow through it at all times. It simply blocks the heat off when not required—by closing doors which prevent air from passing around the core (E). The other type of heater has a valve (A) in the incoming line from the engine to shut off the flow of heated coolant when it is not wanted.

There is very little that can go wrong with a heater. If the fan motor will turn on and run at its full range of speeds, the electrical portion is good.

Basic heater problems fall into three categories: not enough heat, heat all the time or no heat. If there is no heat, it is possible that the coolant is not reaching the heater core (E). This means a collapsed or plugged hose or a frozen valve (A). (In heaters where the coolant flows through the core all the time, the problem will be that one of the doors is not operating correctly to allow air to flow over the core.) If there is heat all the time, the control valve or door is stuck wide open. Not enough heat can mean the valve or door is stuck in a partially open position or the coolant coming from the engine is not hot enough. If the coolant is not hot enough, it could mean the thermostat in the cooling system is stuck open, allowing coolant to pass through the engine so rapidly that it does not get hot quickly enough. If your car is equipped with a temperature gauge instead of a warning light, watch to see if engine temperature rises to normal operating ranges after it has been driven for a reasonable distance.

To reach the heater and the control cables, you will have to get under the dashboard. This can mean the simple removal of some cardboard covers or, in the case of air-conditioned cars, it can mean a day-long task. Check to see that all controls operate smoothly and that doors to ducts open easily and close completely. Usually it is easy to spot a binding door or valve, because the control on the dashboard becomes hard to move or turn.

One other item worth checking out if you have a problem of not enough heat is the fresh air ducting system (D). It can cause problems if one of the doors is sticking partly open, allowing cold air to enter the car. Once in a while, a heater core will spring a leak just like the radiator. It is usually not practical to repair the core, but a good core obtained from a wrecking yard is easy to install on most cars.

TROUBLESHOOTING ELECTRICAL ACCESSORIES

In this chapter we will again be using the multimeter as an electrical tester, as in the chapters on ignition and starters. Electrical equipment differs widely among the various types of automobiles, and it would be impossible to provide detailed electrical troubleshooting for each manufacturer's automobiles. We will give *generalized* instructions only for a variety of electrical equipment and rely on common sense troubleshooting techniques to allow the reader to find and fix his own electrical troubles. We will also show only a few *simple* electrical schematics. Schematics are hard to read for the average user and are very specialized for each individual automobile.

WIRING CIRCUITS AND DIAGRAMS

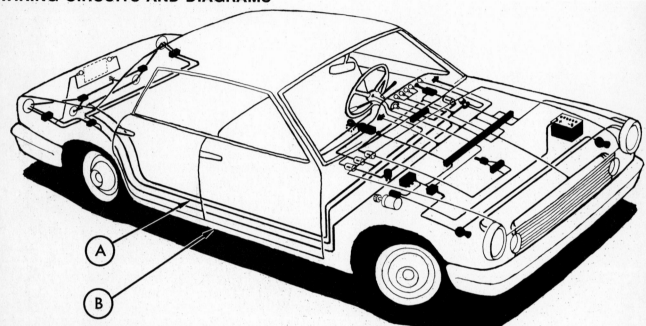

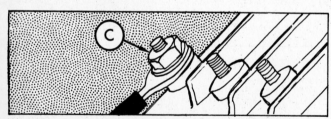

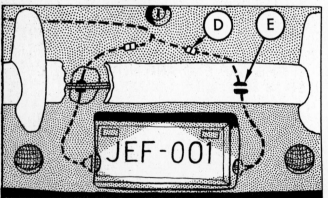

All of the electrical devices in the automobile are tied together in a wiring circuit or harness. The wiring between the power supply (battery and generator) and equipment is gathered together in a harness (A) of several wires which run in and through the interior of the automobile's structure (B). These wires are marked by a color to denote different wires and functions. Unless you are familar with the part that you are troubleshooting, it is a good idea to have the shop manual handy for reference to the wiring diagram. Where bundles of wires pass through panels or bulkheads from one compartment to another, they pass through rubber grommets (E) and usually split to terminate in a plug (D), which connects to another plug. If the wires do not go to a plug, they are terminated (connected) to terminal strip posts (C) with nuts.

These plugs, especially where the plug is exposed to the weather or moisture, are often a source of trouble. Corrosion and dirt can ruin the electrical connection at these points, resulting in equipment failure or intermittent problems. A good point about interconnecting plug connectors is that they provide an easy method of breaking a circuit down into sections for troubleshooting purposes. Also, if a component in the engine compartment or under the dash has to be removed, it is much easier to disconnect an electrical plug than individual wires.

As an example, suppose you are troubleshooting a headlight problem. Using the meter, you discover that when the switch is turned on, there is power to the headlight switch but not to the headlights themselves. A check of the headlights and their sockets turns up no visible problem. Your next step would be to see if the wiring from the switch to the lights passes through a plug connector. In fact, this switch usually does pass through a plug connector in the firewall. By disconnecting the plug connector you can then check for the presence of power at the plug connector. If there is power present, it means the trouble is between the plug connector and the headlights. If not, the trouble is between the plug connector and the switch. You have simplified the problem by checking for power at a halfway point in the wiring harness.

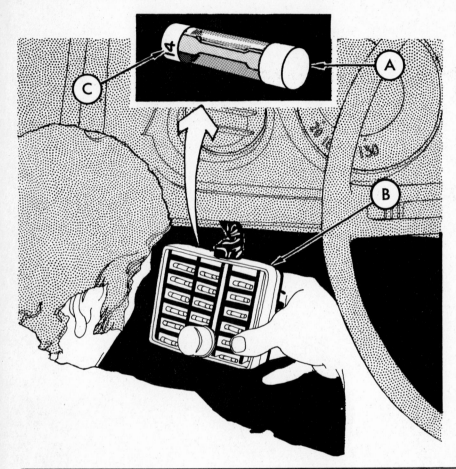

The heart of the electrical system is the fusebox or fuse panel (B). This is usually found under the dashboard, sometimes mounted on the inside of the firewall. The fuses for the various circuits are clipped into compartments, which are lettered to provide identification.

The fuse (A) is a protective device which consists of a small glass tube capped at each end with a metal tip. Inside the glass is a fine wire or metal strip connected to the metal tips. This fine wire or metal strip is designed to allow the amount of current required for the circuit to flow through it without a hitch, but it will rapidly overheat and melt in two if the current goes above its recommended value. Some fuses do not have a clear glass tube, and these must be checked with a meter to determine if they are good.

NOTE: IT IS BETTER TO CHECK ALL FUSES WITH A METER RATHER THAN RELY ON VISUAL MEANS. SOME FUSES WILL MELT AT THE CAP END AND NOT IN THE CENTER. THE TINY FUSE WIRE ON SOME FUSES IS DIFFICULT TO SEE, EVEN UNDER THE BEST CONDITIONS.

Fuses come in a wide variety of sizes and shapes, and each has a series of numbers and letters (C) printed on the metal cap. This gives the size and electrical rating of the fuse.

NOTE: DO NOT INSTALL A FUSE OF A HIGHER THAN SPECIFIED RATING IN ANY CIRCUIT. THIS COULD CAUSE DAMAGE OR EVEN FIRE IF THE CIRCUIT BECOMES OVERLOADED.

If examination of a circuit shows that the fuse protecting the circuit has blown, there is probably some trouble in the circuit. Momentary overloads can cause the fuse to blow, and they can also fail because of age or vibration. However, until you have checked the circuit and know it is good, a blown fuse should be considered as a warning of electrical trouble.

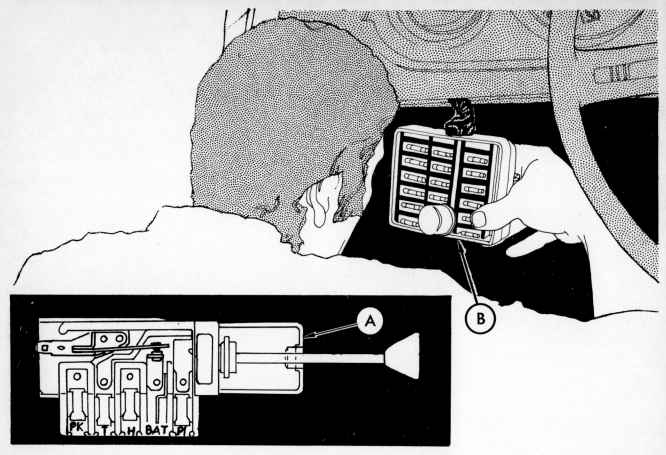

A newer device for protecting circuits is the circuit breaker (A). This small device is designed to break the contact like a fuse, but it will return to normal operation if the overload was momentary. The circuit breaker is often a sealed unit and cannot be serviced or repaired. If a circuit breaker fails completely, it must be replaced like a fuse. Circuit breakers may be located throughout the system, sometimes attached directly to the electrical part. They are usually a separate unit rather than grouped together on a block like fuses. The electrical portion of the shop manual will give the locations of the circuit breakers in your car, if it is so equipped.

Armed with the wiring diagram from the shop manual and an ohmmeter, it becomes easy to trace and locate troubles in the wiring system. The fuse block (B) is the ideal place to start, since all the major electrical systems have a fuse in its system. Voltage measurements can be taken directly from the fuse contacts while the system is operating, and resistance measurements can be taken with the power removed to check continuity of circuit wiring.

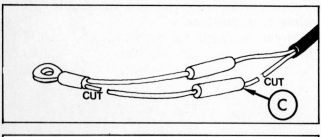

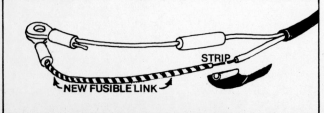

Certain circuits in late-model cars are protected by a device called a fusible link (C). This is a short section of wire inserted into the regular wiring that functions like a fuse if current flow becomes too high. Fusible links are usually marked with a special color or lettered tab, and they can burn out without showing any external change. It is wise to examine one closely before declaring it good while troubleshooting. If a burned fusible link is discovered, it can be replaced by cutting the old link out of the circuit and installing the new link with the aid of a soldering iron. The new link should be installed in the same place and should be cut to the same approximate length as the original.

TROUBLESHOOTING LIGHTING CIRCUITS

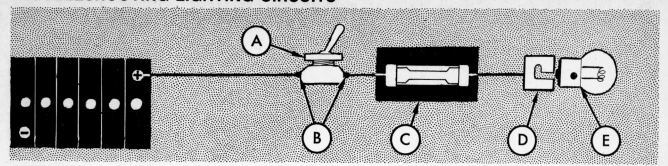

Troubleshooting any lighting circuit is a relatively simple task. The procedure for checking any light is simple and straightforward. First, remove and examine the bulb (E) itself and the socket (D) it fits into. If the light and socket are good (no burned-out filaments or corrosion and dirt in the socket), go to the fuse panel. Check the fuse (C) for that circuit. If the fuse is blown, try replacing the fuse and checking again. If the fuse blows again, start checking the wiring in that circuit for possible short circuits or burned wires. If the fuse is good, check the circuit at that point for power. (Use the multimeter, set for voltage.) If there is power at that point, the wiring from the battery to the fuse panel is good.

Next check the switch (A) that controls the light. Check for power at the switch terminals (B). Remove power from the circuit and test the switch for continuity as explained in the chapters on troubleshooting ignitions and starters. If the bulb, fuse and switch are good and power is present at all points except the light socket when the switch is on, the problem is a broken or shorted wire at some point in the harness. See the shop manual and trace all wires in that circuit. Remember to closely examine any connectors in the wiring.

HEADLIGHT TROUBLESHOOTING

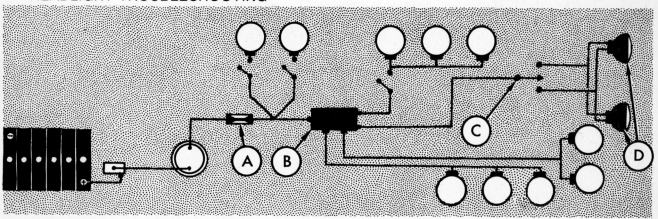

The headlight circuit consists of the headlight switch (B), the protecting fuse or circuit breaker (A), the dimmer switch (C) and the headlights (D). If the lights fail to switch from bright to dim or if they go out entirely when the dimmer switch is pressed, the problem is in the dimmer switch. This switch is mounted on the floorboard, with the underside of the switch and its wiring exposed to weather, road grime and moisture.

The headlight sockets themselves are frequently exposed to moisture and corrosion behind the grille. Check them carefully. The switch that turns the headlights on and off also controls the taillights, parking lights and license plate light. If the headlights will not operate at all and the fuse checks as good, one or more of these other circuits may be out also.

NOTE: IN MANY CARS, THE POWER FOR THE LIGHTING CIRCUITS COMES FROM THE BATTERY TERMINAL OF THE IGNITION SWITCH (BATT). THE POWER DOES NOT GO THROUGH THE SWITCH; IT IS SIMPLY A CONVENIENT PLACE TO CONNECT THE WIRING. IF TAILLIGHTS AND HEADLIGHTS ARE OUT, CHECK THIS CONNECTION.

If the headlight is out on one side, it could be the fault of the light itself or of the wiring between the headlights. On many cars, the wiring is arranged so that it runs down the inside of one fender to the light, then across the grille to the opposite light.

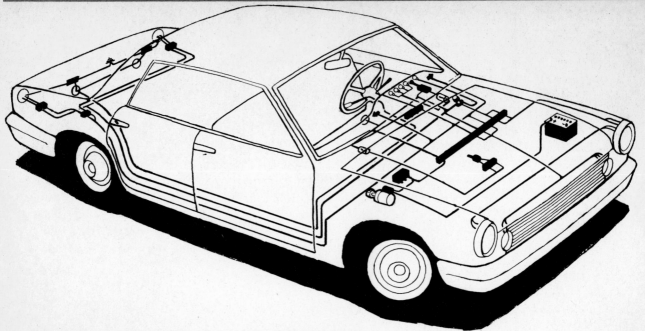

TAIL- AND BRAKE LIGHT TROUBLESHOOTING

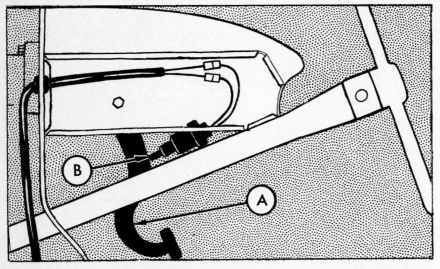

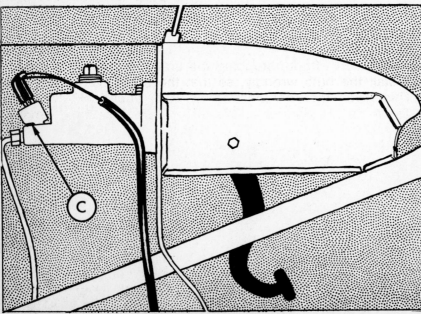

On older cars, the brake and taillights are combined units which use a bulb with two filaments. One is for taillights, the other for brake lights. New cars have separate brake and taillight bulbs. The taillights on all models are controlled by the light switch that turns on the headlights. The brake lights are controlled by the brake switch, which functions when the brake pedal is depressed.

There are two different types of brake light switch. One is a simple mechanical switch, which is usually mounted on a bracket near the brake pedal arm (A).

When the brake pedal is depressed, the switch button (B) is released and completes the circuit to turn the brake lights on.

The other type of brake switch is a hydraulic switch (C). This is mounted in the brake line, usually on or near the master cylinder. This switch senses an increase in hydraulic pressure as the brakes are applied and completes the circuit to turn the brake lights on.

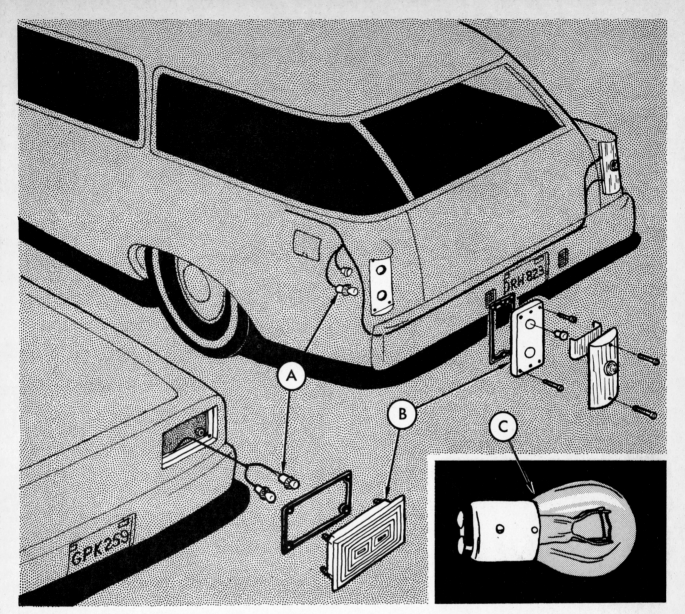

On most cars, the rear of the brake light housings (B) is easily reached from the inside of the trunk. The bulb holders (A) are usually clipped in place and are easily removed to get at the bulbs. The most common wiring problem for taillights is a loose light bulb socket which is not establishing a good ground path for the return of the current. (In other words, the metal end of the bulb is not making good contact with the metal in the bulb socket.) Taillights are also subject to corrosion and moisture and should be examined carefully.

Taillights with dual-filament bulbs (C) can lose one filament without harming the other one. This will eliminate the taillight function without stopping the brake light or vice versa. It is also possible in some cars to install the bulb wrongly, so that the brake filament is lit by taillight power and vice versa. This gives the rear lighting an unbalanced effect, as the brightness of the tail and brake filaments are different. This error simply requires removing the bulb and reinstalling it in the correct position.

If the rear lights do not light at all (the license plate light will also be out), the problem is an interruption of power. Check all connectors in the wiring leading to the taillights and check the fuses for these circuits. If only the brake lights are out and the taillights are on, the problem is the brake switch, the brake fuse or wiring from the light switch which operates the lights. On models with the switch on the brake pedal arm, it may be that the switch is simply out of adjustment. See your shop manual for adjustment instructions.

Another problem which might occur is brake lights that remain on even though the brake pedal is not depressed. This can be caused by an out-of-adjustment switch as above, or in the case of the hydraulic pressure switch, it may mean that there is debris clogging the line coming out of the master cylinder, leaving some residual pressure to keep the switch closed.

TROUBLESHOOTING TURN SIGNALS

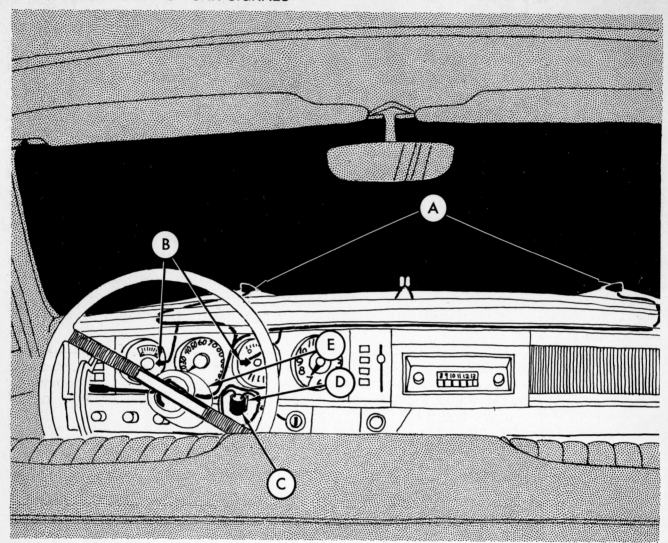

The turn indicator system uses the parking lights and brake lights to indicate the direction the driver intends to turn. (On some late-model cars, the turn signal lights in the rear may be separate from the brake and taillights.) The parts of the system include: the lights (A); the switch, mounted in the steering column (E); and the flasher unit (C), which produces the blinking of the lights by intermittently completing and breaking the electrical circuit (thus the clicking sound heard). Turn indicator lights are self-canceling in most cars. This means that they shut themselves off automatically when the steering wheel is returned to a position in which the wheels of the car are straight. The driver is informed of the operation of the turn signals by two small indicator lights (B) which are mounted in the dashboard (usually in or near the speedometer).

The turn signals have a built-in failsafe design. *All* bulbs on one side of the car must be working or the signal will not flash in that direction. If the indicator light burns steadily when you try to signal a turn, check the bulbs for that side of the car. If all bulbs check out as good, the problem is in the wiring or the flasher unit itself. If the indicator light does not light when you turn on the turn switch, check the flasher (C) and the bulb behind the green indicator arrows behind the dashboard. If you can hear the flasher clicking, it is probably okay. If the flasher is not clicking, a light tap with your finger will usually start it working. Flashers are usually located near the bottom of the steering post (E) or mounted in a clip (D). under the dashboard (middle or right-hand side).

If the turn signals continue after the turn is completed and the steering wheel straightened, the problem is in the self-canceling mechanism of the switch in the steering column. See your shop manual for information on checking or replacing the switch.

WINDSHIELD WIPER/WASHER TROUBLESHOOTING

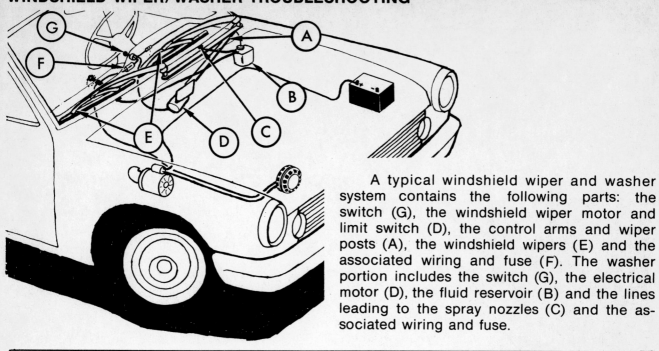

A typical windshield wiper and washer system contains the following parts: the switch (G), the windshield wiper motor and limit switch (D), the control arms and wiper posts (A), the windshield wipers (E) and the associated wiring and fuse (F). The washer portion includes the switch (G), the electrical motor (D), the fluid reservoir (B) and the lines leading to the spray nozzles (C) and the associated wiring and fuse.

> **NOTE:** WINDSHIELD WASHERS AND WIPERS MAY BE LINKED TOGETHER TO FORM ONE UNIT.

Windshield wipers are easy to troubleshoot but difficult to adjust if the automatic cycle is disturbed. We do not recommend that the reader take the wiper motor or the limit switches apart and try to repair or adjust them. If you are convinced that you have a problem in this area, take the car to a qualified mechanic for repairs.

If the windshield wipers will not operate at any speed, check the fuse (F) first. If the fuse and the wiring leading to the switch and motor look good, the wiper switch should be checked by bypassing it with a jumper wire. If the wipers work normally with the switch bypassed, the switch is bad and should be replaced. Non-electrical problems can also make the wipers fail to operate. Check the linkage and wipers to see if they are in a bind.

> **NOTE:** GETTING AT THE LINKAGE UNDER THE DASH IS HARD ON ALL CARS, AND THOSE EQUIPPED WITH AIR CONDITIONING ARE ALMOST IMPOSSIBLE TO SERVICE AND TROUBLESHOOT.

Check your shop manual for information on how to gain access to the wiper linkage and motor.

Most windshield wipers are multi-speed. Some have a special intermittent operation as well as high- and low-speed continuous operation. If the wipers will not operate in one particular switch position but will work in all the others, the switch is bad or the wiring for that switch contact is bad. Replace the switch and recheck the system. If the wipers will only work slowly even though the switch is placed in the fast position, the problem could be binding linkage or low power to the motor. Check the linkage and wipers and examine the wiring to the motor for signs of broken or frayed wiring. See your shop manual for information on how the motor is grounded and check for a good ground.

Windshield wiper blades that do not return to the stowed (out-of-the-way) position at the base of the windshield when they are turned off but instead simply stop wherever they are have a motor switch problem. The motor has a special switch section inside which sets the limits of wiper movement. This switch also returns the wipers to the stowed position when the power is removed by turning off the main wiper switch. It is not recommended that the reader attempt to adjust this switch. Take the car to a qualified mechanic for repair or adjustment.

Wipers that will not shut off unless the ignition switch is off may have a failure in either the motor switch or the system on/off switch. Each will have to be replaced in turn to find the problem.

TROUBLESHOOTING ELECTRICAL ACCESSORIES

TROUBLESHOOTING BACKUP LIGHTS

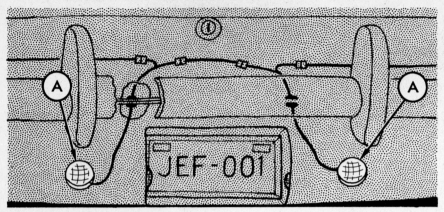

At the rear of the automobile, along with the brake, tail and license plate lights, there are two lights used to enable the driver to see behind him at night while backing out of a driveway. The lights (A) are controlled by a switch on the gear shift lever mechanism or on the transmission, which turns the lights on whenever reverse gear is selected.

If the lights do not operate, first check the bulbs, then the switch. You may try moving the shift lever in and out of reverse gear several times while a friend watches the lights. This switch can go out of adjustment easily, and sometimes wiggling the shift lever or moving it in and out of gear will cause the lights to come on briefly.

If the lights cannot be made to work in this manner, the switch (if accessible) should be bypassed with a jumper wire to see if the lights will come on. If the backup lights work with the switch bypassed, the switch is bad.

Faulty wiring is often the cause of backup light failure. The transmission area is usually dirty and oily. This can lead to corrosion or a bad ground. Check wiring carefully.

You can troubleshoot several other small accessories, such as the clock, cigarette lighter, glove compartment lights, etc., by using the same methods described above.

TROUBLESHOOTING DOME AND COURTESY LIGHTS

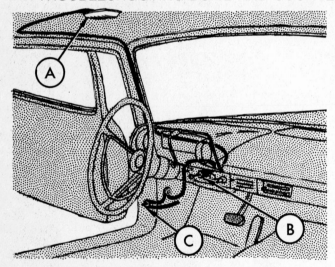

The interior of all cars is equipped with one or more lights which come on when the car doors are opened. On older cars they are usually mounted in the roof. Newer cars have smaller lights in the doors and at the base of the back seat. There is also a hand switch for turning the light on when the car is moving and the doors are closed. Usually turning the headlight switch (B) fully clockwise or counter-clockwise activates this switch. The door switch (C) is a simple, spring-loaded switch mounted in the door opening. It is operated by the opening and closing of the door. If the light does not come on when the door is opened, try the headlight switch or the dome light switch (A).

NOTE: MANY DOME LIGHTS ARE PART OF THE MAIN HEADLIGHT SWITCH. IF EITHER SWITCH WILL TURN ON THE LIGHT, THE BULB, FUSE OR WIRING IS BAD.

If the light comes on when the doors open but not when the manual switch (dome or headlight) is used, then the switch is bad. If the manual switch works but the lights will not come on when the doors open, the door switches could be bad.

NOTE: ON MOST CARS, THERE IS A SWITCH FOR EACH DOOR. YOU CAN CHECK THEIR OPERATION BY OPENING ONE DOOR AT A TIME WHILE WATCHING THE LIGHT OR BY OPENING THE DOORS ONE AT A TIME AND OPERATING THE SWITCH BY HAND.
